MAKING
NEWS

MAKING NEWS

A Study in
the Construction of Reality

Gaye Tuchman

THE FREE PRESS
A Division of Macmillan Publishing Co., Inc.
NEW YORK

Collier Macmillan Publishers
LONDON

The Free Press
A Division of Macmillan Publishing Co., Inc.
866 Third Avenue, New York, N.Y. 10022

Collier Macmillan Canada, Ltd.

First Free Press Paperback Edition 1980

Library of Congress Catalog Card Number: 78-53075

Printed in the United States of America

Hardcover printing number

2 3 4 5 6 7 8 9 10

Paperback printing number

5 6 7 8 9 10

Library of Congress Cataloging in Publication Data
Tuchman, Gaye.
    Making news.

    Bibliography: p.
    Includes index.
    1. Journalism--Objectivity. 2. Journalism--
Social aspects. 3. Journalism--Psychological
aspects. I. Title.
PN4756.T8 1978   070.4'3   78-53075
ISBN 978-0-02-932960-3

The author wishes to thank the publishers of the following of her previously published works for permission to revise copyrighted material:

"Making News by Doing Work: Routinizing the Unexpected." *American Journal of Sociology* 78 (July 1973): 110-31. Copyright © 1973 by the University of Chicago.

"The Newspaper as a Social Movement's Resource." Pp. 186-215 in *Hearth and Home: Images of Women in the Mass Media*, edited by Gaye Tuchman, Arlene Kaplan Daniels, and James Benét. New York: Oxford University Press, 1978. Copyright © 1978 by Oxford University Press, Inc.

"Objectivity as Strategic Ritual: An Examination of Newsmen's Notions of Objectivity." *American Journal of Sociology* 77 (January 1972): 660-79. Copyright © 1972 by the University of Chicago.

"TV News: The Control of Work and Construction of Reality." *Politics* (The Australasian Political Studies Journal) 10:2 (1975): 149-54.

Freedom of the press is guaranteed only to those who own one.
                                        —A. J. Liebling

For better or worse, editing is what editors are for and editing is the choice and selection of material.
                                        —Chief Justice Warren E. Burger

The headline of the *Daily News* today reads BRUNETTE STABBED TO DEATH. Underneath in lower case letters "6000 Killed in Iranian Earthquake" . . . I wonder what color hair they had.
                                        —Abbie Hoffman

CONTENTS

PREFACE

In 1954 the Army–McCarthy hearings flickered across the nation's television sets, displacing soap operas, game shows, and daytime movies. I was one of the many children who came home from school to watch that new form of daytime serial. Later I heard the adults discuss the issues at family gatherings. In 1966, partially recalling those experiences and prompted by concern about the Vietnam war, I began to study news. I reasoned that the news media set the frame in which citizens discuss public events and that the quality of civic debate necessarily depends on the information available. Accordingly, I wanted to find out how newsworkers decide what news is, why they cover some items but not others, and how they decide what I and others want to know. In short, I sought to uncover what sociologists now call the latent structure of news.

This book is the product of my attempt, over the past eleven years, to learn about news as the social construction of reality. It is a study of the constraints of newswork and of the resources available to newsworkers. It is a study of newsworkers as professionals and of newspapers and television newsrooms as complex organizations. And it is a study of methods of inquiry—how newsworkers determine facts and frame events and debates pertinent to our shared civic life.

I cannot prove my early supposition that the news media set the context in which citizens discuss public issues, but I continue to believe that they do so. Nor can I prove an early hunch, prompted by my participant observation, that news has an even greater impact upon policy makers and politicians, although I continue to suspect that news is an interchange among politicians and policy makers, newsworkers, and their organizational superiors, and that the rest of us are eavesdroppers on that ongoing conversation. Other researchers, more skilled in the study of the media's effects than I am, may choose to present those aspects of news in other volumes. I hope that I have offered enough material to facilitate their task.

As well as presenting concrete descriptions, examples, and analyses of newswork, this book addresses a theoretical debate about the role of consciousness in the construction of social meanings and the organization of experience. With one exception, a brief review of interpretative theories appearing on pages 185-92, the debate is readily accessible to nonsociologists. Readers who are not concerned with the technical issues may skip those few pages and still follow the thrust of my argument.

I was a graduate student at Brandeis University when I began this study. I am grateful for the National Institute of Mental Health Field Training Fellowship that enabled me to conduct the initial participant observation on which this book partially draws. As administrator of that program, Samuel Wallace read my field notes regularly. Everett C. Hughes, Maurice Stein, and Kurt H. Wolff served on my dissertation committee. Robert Weiss and student-fellows Natalie Allon, Barbara Carter, Robert Emerson, Robert Laufer, Nancy Stoller Shaw, Jerold Starr, and Barrie Thorne provided encouragement and criticism that I still recall.

Since the completion of that early work, I have been fortunate in having other friends and colleagues who offered prompt critical comments when I needed them. Among those who read drafts of articles partially incorporated in this book are: Howard Becker, James Benét, Rue Bucher, Lewis A. Coser, Rose Laub Coser, Howard Epstein, Robert Emerson, Carolyn Etheridge, Kenneth A. Feldman, Mark Fishman, Eliot Freidson, Todd Gitlin, Fred Goldner, Erich Goode, Robert Kapsis, Melvin Kohn, Marilyn Lester, Harvey Molotch, Charles Perrow, Dorothy E. Smith, David Street, Barrie Thorne, and Roland Wulbert. Arlene Kaplan Daniels has been my most constant reader and editorial advisor, steering me from the passive voice and the horrors of sociologese. Aaron Cicourel, Nina Kressner Cobb, Mark Fishman, Milton Mankoff, and Joann Vanek each read a draft of a problematic chapter. Lewis A. Coser, Mark Fishman, and Rolf Meyersohn criticized the final manuscript with care; Mark Fishman offered particularly detailed comments.

Others helped too. In 1976 the Russell Sage Foundation, through Walter Wallace and Tony Cline, funded an exploratory grant to analyze data on reporters covering the women's movement and to gather comparative data on the press room of New York's City Hall. Gladys Topkis asked me to write a book like this one in 1971. In 1977, when I announced I was prepared to try, she was very supportive. Gerald Barrett provided unerringly astute comments as he typed chapters. My weekday luncheon companions at the Graduate Center of the City University of New York and my weekend tennis partners at our shared house near Woodstock helped to transform an arduous summer of writing into an almost pleasant experience.

I could never have completed this work without the tolerance and friendship of the newsworkers whom I interviewed and observed. At this moment, I regret that I promised them anonymity and so cannot thank them more personally.

I recall with fondness my father, Jack Tuchman, writing the first sentences of assigned grammar school essays for a child made anxious by the very word "essay." My mother, Evelyn Tuchman, has always encouraged me. My sister, Phyllis Tuchman, has taken pride in my accomplishments, as I do in hers. Henry Edelheit and my close friends in Sociologists for Women in Society helped me to feel that I could and would write what I think, as did the very existence of SWS.

I thank them all.

CHAPTER ONE
News as Frame

News is a window on the world. Through its frame, Americans learn of themselves and others, of their own institutions, leaders, and life styles, and those of other nations and their peoples. The urbanized and urbanizing nation's replacement for the town crier ("Ten o'clock and Mrs. Smith had a baby daughter"), the news aims to tell us what we want to know, need to know, and should know.

But, like any frame that delineates a world, the news frame may be considered problematic. The view through a window depends upon whether the window is large or small, has many panes or few, whether the glass is opaque or clear, whether the window faces a street or a backyard. The unfolding scene also depends upon where one stands, far or near, craning one's neck to the side, or gazing straight ahead, eyes parallel to the wall in which the window is encased.

This book looks at news as a frame, examining how that frame is constituted—how the organizations of newswork and of newsworkers are put together. It concentrates upon newspapers and television stations as complex organizations subject to certain inevitable processes, and upon newsworkers as professionals with professional concerns. It does not consider newsworkers as individuals with per-

1

sonal concerns and biases, topics better left to the psychologist and social psychologist. Rather, it emphasizes the ways in which professionalism and decisions flowing from professionalism are a result of organizational needs. It explores the processes by which news is socially constructed, how occurrences in the everyday world are rendered into stories occupying time and space in the world called news. This theoretical tack makes this book not only an empirical study in the sociologies of mass communication, organizations, and occupations and professions, but also an applied study in the sociology of knowledge.

By seeking to disseminate information that people want, need, and should know, news organizations both circulate and shape knowledge. As studies (e.g., McCombs and Shaw, 1972) have indicated, the news media play an important role in the news consumers' setting of a political agenda. Those topics given the most coverage by the news media are likely to be the topics audiences identify as the most pressing issues of the day. This research on agenda setting tentatively indicates that the priorities in the media's ranked attention to topics may prompt the rankings given those same topics by news consumers.[1] Additionally, the news media have the power to shape news consumers' opinions on topics about which they are ignorant. For example, when a rash of pockmarks in automobile windshields occurred mysteriously in Seattle, possible explanations offered by the media were grasped as an exhaustive list of "causes" by Seattle residents.[2] Studies (e.g., Halloran, Elliott, and Murdock, 1970) have also indicated that the news' explanations of events may serve as the context in which news consumers debate the meaning of events, even if participants in the event have diametrically opposed understandings of the same occurrence. Today, discussions of the antiwar movement still reflect the media's language. For instance, young men who refused to serve in Vietnam are commonly referred to as draft "evaders" (the media's term), rather than draft "resisters," as they prefer to be called. The words "evaders" and "resisters" imply different political orientations to these men and their relationship to their country and the war.

[1] This research has not established a causal connection.

[2] Larsen (1964) provides a report of this study. For a somewhat contradictory account of reactions to explanations of the unknown, see Shibutani's (1966) description of Japanese reactions to explanations of the destruction at Hiroshima and Nagasaki.

By stressing news as knowledge, I do not mean to suggest that news reports are the only mass medium shaping understanding of the everyday world, particularly interpretations of novel phenomena. Communications researchers (see Klapper, 1960) have established that news may be of limited force in swaying public opinions and attitudes. Equally well accepted is that mass entertainment, particularly television, influences political and social attitudes. The spate of TV programs whose plots incorporated hippies in the mid-1960s and feminists in the late 1960s and early 1970s may have had as much or even more impact upon viewers who had never met a hippie or a feminist than news had. Studies of white youngsters (e.g., Greenberg, 1972) indicate that their view of blacks is drawn from television more than from their parents. TV entertainment has also been shown to lower the educational and occupational aspirations of adolescent girls if they are heavy viewers and the children of college-educated parents (Gross and Jeffries-Fox, 1978). After controlling (experimentally or statistically) for social class and education, researchers (Robinson and Zukin, 1976) also find that heavy TV viewers are more politically conservative than light viewers. Their findings suggest that television is the probable cause. The popular situation comedy "All in the Family" is known to reinforce the conservative political views of those most likely to watch it (see Vidmar and Rokeach, 1974).[3] Entertainment appears to have an awesome impact upon viewers' attitudes and beliefs.

What I mean to suggest is that news imparts to occurrences their *public character* as it transforms mere happenings into publicly discussable events. Robert Park (in Park and Burgess, 1967) had just this characteristic of news in mind when he referred to news as the modern replacement of the town crier. Park argued that a fire is a big event in a village or small town; the town crier's report of a fire or a birth or death enabled townspeople to keep track of their neighbors and to offer help or initiate criticism as appropriate. News disseminated by the town crier was gossip as a form of knowledge. But, Park continued, increased urbanization decreased the ability of a

---

[3]Vidmar and Rokeach (1974) explain that both selective exposure and selective perception are operating here. Conservatives are more likely than liberals to watch "All in the Family." Conservatives prefer the character Archie; liberals, son-in-law Mike. Each group also tends to believe that its preferred character has won exchanges with his antagonist.

city's residents to keep track of one another. For instance, a city has many fires daily. News of every fire is not accessible to every citizen. Nor is every citizen potentially interested in every fire or the happenings of every parish church. Newspapers (and today news magazines, television, and radio) enable geographically dispersed individuals to know something about one another, one another's ethnic and neighborhood groups, and events in group life. To paraphrase Lasswell (1948), news coordinates activities within a complex society by making otherwise inaccessible information available to all. It tells residents of New York that tornado victims in Kansas need assistance. It acquaints residents of Vermillion, South Dakota, with urban problems. It teaches black southerners the living conditions of black northerners. It permits institutions to coordinate their activities. And it enables officials to anticipate reactions to proposals under consideration. For instance, the secretary of state (when identified as a "reliable source") may anonymously float an idea in the mass media in order to gauge the reactions of other cabinet officers, senators, or citizens to a potentially controversial program.

Because news imparts a public character to occurrences, news is first and foremost a social institution. First, news is an institutional method of making information available to consumers. The consumer buys the newspaper because he or she wants to read the comics or the bridge column, learn the weather forecast, find out what movies are playing, or read about floods, fires, or the frenzy of social life. Second, news is an ally of legitimated institutions. The secretary of state can float an idea in the news media. The "average" man or woman does not have such access to the media. Nor does an average citizen have the same power, held by legitimated politicians and bureaucrats, to convert his or her reactions to the news into public policies and programs. Third, news is located, gathered, and disseminated by professionals working in organizations. Thus it is inevitably a product of newsworkers drawing upon institutional processes and conforming to institutional practices.[4] Those practices necessarily include association with institutions whose news is

---

[4]I use the terms "institution" and "organization" as though they were interchangeable. Generally, though, "institution" refers to a routinized pattern of transactions or behavior that fulfills some function. Thus news as an institution enables consumers to learn about the social world. The term "organization" generally refers to complex social establishments. Complex organizations are, though, legitimated social institutions.

routinely reported. Accordingly, news is the product of a social institution, and it is embedded in relationships with other institutions. It is a product of professionalism and it claims the right to interpret everyday occurrences to citizens and other professionals alike.

Saying that newsworkers are professionals in organizations immediately raises a theoretical specter in sociologists' minds. Sociologists generally hold that the interests of professionals and of organizations conflict: Employed professionals and managers or owners are said to battle one another for the right to control work—to define how work will be done. When I began to study newswork, I expected to find the conflicts between reporters and management predicted by sociological theory. I did find some. For instance, reporters and editors resent and, to some extent, resist running stories on the friends of the newspaper's or television station's executives and influential managers. But more generally, I found, news professionalism has developed in conjunction with modern news organizations, and professional practices serve organizational needs. Both, in turn, serve to legitimate the status quo, complementing one another's reinforcement of contemporary social arrangements, even as they occasionally compete for the control of work processes and the right to be identified with freedom of the press and freedom of speech.

My approach to news classifies it with other stories and assumes that stories are the product of cultural resources and active negotiations. Thus, "once upon a time" is the obvious start of a fairy tale. "Egyptian planes bombed and strafed a Libyan air base today, a military spokesman here announced," is the obvious start of a news story. "Once upon a time" announces that what follows is myth and pretense, a flight of cultural fancy. The news lead proclaims that what follows is factual and hard-nosed, a veridical account of events in the world. But, ultimately, both the fairy tale and the news account are stories, to be passed on, commented upon, and recalled as individually appreciated public resources. Both have a public character in that both are available to all, part and parcel of our cultural equipment. Both draw on the culture for their derivation. Asian fairy tales are necessarily different from the Western variety, and American newspapers are inextricably different from the wall posters of contemporary China. Both take social and cultural resources and transform them into public property: Jack Kennedy and

Jack of beanstalk fame are both cultural myths, although one lived and the other did not. Drawing on cultural conventions, members of Western societies impose distinctions between stories about the two men that obscure their shared features of public character and social construction.

One can quickly imagine the social construction of fairy tales by conceiving of the interaction between parent and child as a parent responds to a child's demand for a story. When the child objects to a turn of the plot, the parent alters it. When the child smiles, the parent may elaborate the theme being developed. We claim that the parent tells the story, without admitting how much the child is an active participant in the story's construction.

Similarly, by imagining a conversation, we can see how making news is a negotiated enterprise. Take the following example.[5] Arriving home after a day's work, a professor is asked by her husband, "How was your day?" That day was composed of many details ("particulars"). One answer might be, "When I drove home, I caught each of the three traffic lights on the main road when it was green." Making all three green lights may be a rare occurrence of great interest to the driver who keeps track of such details in her life. But it may not be an acceptable topic of conversational interaction. The questioner may become exasperated that his inquiry was slighted by being given such a picayune response. He may repeat the inquiry to learn what *really* happened that day. He may take the answer as indicative of the tenor of the day: "You mean it was a good day; everything went well." Alternatively, the professor called upon to describe the day may seize upon a particular item of interest to her questioner: "You know that son-of-a-bitch Joe? Just listen to what he said to me in the department meeting today!" This response may be an appropriate way of giving "the news of the day" if both spouses agree that Joe is a son-of-a-bitch whose impingement upon their lives is a topic of mutual interest. Both answers, about the three green lights or Joe's nasty comment, are replies to the question, "How was your day?" However, in the context of this particular marriage, only one answer may qualify as "news." The "newsworthy" answer simultaneously transforms the day into a shared (therefore public) phenomenon. Indeed, at some time in the future

---

[5]This example expands upon an instance described in Molotch (1978).

one spouse may say to the other, "Do you remember that day when Joe said X in the department meeting?" The day has been transformed from any day to "the day Joe said X," much as the story the parent and child negotiated may become the "story about the good little girl" that may be told and retold on other occasions.

Just as it is possible to imagine alternate plots and endings to stories produced for and with children, so, too, we can imagine alternative ways for the professor to organize (frame) the strip of ongoing occurrences that constituted her day as events to be produced as news.[6] In the version produced above, both particulars were directly experienced; they were within her immediate spatial and temporal grasp.[7] But by selecting them, she necessarily excluded other items in the strip of ongoing experience from her tale of the day.

Consider some items the professor may have omitted. She could not have related happenings pertinent to her work but as yet unknown to her. Suppose that two such inaccessible conversations had occurred that day. In one, the university's president and provost had discussed firing younger faculty members in order to meet economic exigencies. In the second, a student hired a friend to write a term paper to fulfill the requirements of the professor's course. Held behind closed doors, neither conversation could be related at that moment as news of the day, although each may eventually be pertinent to her life. She may get fired, or discover and decide to fail the plagiarizing student.

Second, the professor could not have included as news particular items or details in her strip of activity that she did not notice. Drivers do not customarily register characteristics of other cars as facts to remember. Thus she did not state, "Three other cars also made the sequence of lights. One was a blue Volkswagen; one, a red Dodge Dart; and the third, a gray Chevrolet. All three were 1974 models." Nor may she have noticed the placement of the department's chairperson at the head of the seminar table during the de-

[6]According to Goffman (1974: 10-11), a frame is "the principles of organization which govern events—at least social ones—and our subjective involvement in them." Frames organize "strips" of the everyday world, a strip being "an arbitrary slice or cut from the stream of ongoing activity" (Goffman, 1974: 10). Accordingly, I speak of how frames transform *occurrences* and *happenings* (strips of the everyday world) into defined *events*. For an elaboration of these concepts, see pp. 192-95.

[7]For a discussion of the social world as spatially and temporally experienced, see p. 187.

partmental meeting. That item may be taken for granted by her and her spouse as a general characteristic of meetings of small groups and so may fail to warrant inclusion in the news of the day. Nor may the professor have discussed her right and duty to attend departmental meetings. Attendance may be taken for granted as part of her professional milieu. Her understanding of those meetings (like her ability to distinguish between a term paper warranting an A and another deserving an F) may be assumed to be a professional skill.

In sum, items must be judged pertinent to both speaker and listener in order to be judged newsworthy and must somehow present themselves to the speaker in the course of the day. Similarly, other items cannot emerge from the strip of daily occurrences because: they do not present themselves as pertinent (the color of cars); they are taken for granted as appropriate occupational skills (understanding how meetings are conducted); or they are not within the speaker's temporal and spatial reach (the president and provost's conversation and the students' deal concerning the term paper).

If we were to continue our imaginary reconstruction of the professor's day, we could locate situations altering our assessment of unmentioned occurrences. For instance, the gray 1974 Chevrolet might have struck the professor's car as she went through the third green light. Each alteration would change the situation we were describing, making it more or less newsworthy for the purpose of having a conversation with one's spouse. The possibility of changed status as news is interesting theoretically because it reveals that individuals may experience each particular of the day as either idiosyncratic and memorable (my car was struck by a gray 1974 Chevrolet) or as nonnoticeable (other cars were there, too). In relation to an imaginary conversation between husband and wife, these points seem minor. But these same issues may be raised regarding the production of news by professionals in formal organizations:

1. How can particulars embedded in strips of ongoing activity come into the reporter's spatial and temporal purview?
2. Are some items not related because knowledge is embedded in stratification systems? (The professor did not have access to conversations of those with more power, the president and the provost, or those with less power, the students.)
3. Are some items not noticed because they are taken for granted as aspects of the social world?
4. Are some items not noticed because of newsworkers' perspectives

as professionals, their trained incapacity?

5. How can individuals and organizations process information about the social world if each particular is considered as an idiosyncratic phenomenon?

To answer these questions, I draw on data collected at four field sites.

The Field Sites

The data were gathered by participant observation and interviews over a period of ten years.

Site One: During the academic year 1966–1967, I spent at least one day a week observing news processes at NEWS, a pseudonym for a television station in Seabord City, a metropolitan area and a major television market. From June 1967 to January 1969 I continued observations, sometimes on an intermittent basis and sometimes daily.

The television station was owned by a corporation maintaining other media interests but with a license to operate only that one VHF station. The station was affiliated with a network whose evening news it carried nightly. In addition, it produced at least two news shows a day. The early evening newscast lasted a half hour. The other, broadcast after prime-time programming, lasted an hour during the first year of my research. During the 1967–1968 television season the late-night newscast was shortened to a half hour. That same year, the station introduced a half hour midday news program and experimented with an ill-fated early-morning program. All staff contributed to all programs, since a story used on one newscast might be repeated on another, but discrete responsibilities were assigned. The same staff produced documentaries, generally lasting a half hour. As is common, this local television station carried mostly network programming, syndicated movies, and reruns. Aside from news and public affairs, its in-house production included only a children's show and a monthly variety hour.

Although the size of the news staff varied according to the length and number of programs produced, the core group included twenty-six men:[a] seven reporters (including anchormen), six writers,

[a]Throughout this book, the term "he" refers to a specific man. "She" refers to a specific woman. "He or she" is used as an indeterminant reference. Following newspaper practice, I have used the terms "press room" and "press conference." Television personnel prefer "news room" and "news conference."

one editing supervisor, two editing technicians, six cameramen, two managing editors, one assignment editor, and two directors. (I have omitted other technical and executive personnel with whom I did not come into regular contact.) For a few months the station also had a woman reporter, who resigned, claiming sexism.

Site Two: Needless to say, the staff of the newspaper, here called *Seaboard City Daily,* was much larger, as required by the more labor-intensive print technology. Also located in Seaboard City, the newspaper was a family corporation controlled by descendants of its founder, although there were also publicly held shares.

My observations (virtually daily from October 1967 through April 1968, and subsequently supplemented as needed or thought advisable) centered on the editorial staff, the daily reporters, the city desk, and the night-side. Including the editor-in-chief, the editorial staff comprised four writers and a cartoonist. The newspaper employed about twenty general, beat, and bureau reporters and rewrite men (not counting the culture writers, the education editor, the Sunday paper's staff, and the staffs of the sports, financial, and women's pages). All but one were men. Seven men were in the editorial hierarchy: the managing editor, assistant to the managing editor, assistant managing editor, local editor, wire-service editor, make-up editor for the general pages, and a liaison to the publisher. Four manned the city desk; six served as copy editors. About ten photographers and a photography editor rounded out the complement of people I observed covering and processing stories. I also had brief interactions with three compositors and the production manager, whom I encountered in the course of observing editorial work, and with the staff of the Sunday paper. As at the television station, I watched the process of assigning tasks, sat in on editorial discussions, covered stories with reporters, and followed stories through their eventual dissemination. I also observed each part of the news process as though it were independent. Although I preferred watching a story from its assignment to its printing, I found daily research from 8:00 A.M. until 2:00 A.M. much too arduous a task.

Site Three: In the summer of 1975 I entered the field once more to interview New York City newspaper reporters who were covering or had covered the women's movement. Included were personnel from the *News, Post,* and *Times,* with most of my time concentrated on the *Times'* newsworkers. The reporters referred me to one another (ten women in all), and I stopped interviewing when I was not given any new names to contact. Some of the interviews lasted as long as an hour and a half. The reporters' comments upheld those offered by members of *Seaboard City Daily*'s women's page with whom I had chatted sporadically and informally during coverage of election returns. I also spoke with leaders of the New York feminist movement. These were not formal interviews. Rather, I encountered these women in the course of my nonprofessional activities, and the topic of news coverage of the movement inevitably arose. The most extensive conversations were with Betty Friedan, whom I drove from Queens to Manhattan once a week during the 1975 spring semester. My colleague Cynthia Epstein contributed recollections over informal dinners. Ti-Grace Atkinson recalled early news coverage as we discussed discrimination against a female sociologist and sought to set the wheels of Sociologists for Women in Society in motion to render assistance. Other early and still active feminists contributed information about coverage of social movements, as did Barrie Thorne, when she was researching the antiwar movement and I was observing news processing in Seaboard City.

Site Four: The New York City Hall Press Room was the last research site. There I observed the nine-person reportorial staff (including one woman) of a daily newspaper with a much larger circulation than the *Seaboard City Daily*, as well as that newspaper's beat photographers, and other reporters and photographers in the room, representing the city's other two dailies; *Newsday* and the *Long Island Press*; Associated Press; United Press International; some magazines; and assorted radio and television stations. In all, I watched the work of a group that varied daily from twenty to thirty-five people from October 1975 through January 1976—the period when New York's fiscal crisis moved from a city affair to a national issue.

I observed one day a week, more often during my university's Christmas and winter recesses. In contrast to my ready rapport with the newsworkers I encountered on the other three projects, I was barely tolerated in the press room. Inevitably, because of insufficient space and chairs, I was in the way. (Space limitations were so severe that an auxiliary press room had been established in the basement directly below the main press room. Of the nine reporters on whom I was concentrating, five had desks in the basement, as did several re-

porters from a competing newspaper and a television newsworker.) I
was also hampered by the reporters' reticence to discuss and disclose
their sources. Nonetheless, although I am not wholly satisfied with
this set of observations, it does complement my earlier (1969) conclusions about newswork, and so I have drawn upon it to write this
book. Indeed, as is well known among participant observers, the difficulties one encounters provide insights into the activities being
observed.

With the exception of New York City reporters and editors who
covered the women's movement and who gave permission for their
names to be used, all names of newsworkers are fictitious.

Plan of the Book

The theme that the act of making news is the act of constructing
reality itself rather than a picture of reality runs throughout this
book. Newswork transforms occurrences into news events. It draws
on aspects of everyday life to tell stories, and it presents us to ourselves. By accomplishing this second task, it serves as a basis for
social action. But the process of making news is not accomplished in
a void, and so a second theme is that professionalism serves organizational interests by reaffirming the institutional processes in which
newswork is embedded.[9]

Chapters 2 and 3 introduce both themes by looking at the most
basic arrangements of newswork—the dispersion of reporters and
editors in time and space. Chapter 2 examines how news organizations place reporters in order to find occurrences that can be transformed into news stories. It examines the bureaucratic chains of
authority developed to keep track of occurrences, the negotiation of
overlapping responsibilities, and the negotiated selection of the news
of the day. These collective negotiations, I argue, assign the attribute
of "newsworthiness" to everyday occurrences.

Chapter 3 examines newsworkers, news organizations, and the
social arrangement of time. It notes that the dispersion of reporters
to find enough items to fill the news product creates a glut of in-

[9]The titles and specific duties of newsworkers vary from one news organization
to another. For instance, some newspapers have a managing editor and others an
executive editor. Unless otherwise specified, I follow the usage and practice of the
Seaboard City Daily.

formation that must then be winnowed and weeded. Most important, though, to process these items, news organizations have objectified deadlines and created rhythms of work. Using their past experiences with the unfolding of news events, newsworkers have created classifications of newsworthy occurrences. These classifications influence the assignment of newsworthiness to occurrences. They also reduce the idiosyncrasy of occurrences as the raw material of news.

But, chapter 4 notes, the classifications still leave room for a great deal of reportorial flexibility. And, although the stories themselves are edited and so supervised, other aspects of reportorial work are relatively unsupervised. As professionals, reporters negotiate with colleagues in their own news organizations and with those in other organizations about coverage of specific stories and about appropriate news practices. These negotiations include the sharing and hoarding of both information and sources.

Ultimately, chapter 5 argues, news sources and facts are mutually constituting, for the news net identifies some sources and institutions as the appropriate location of facts and dismisses others. Additionally, news practices create quasi-legitimated leaders to serve as sources when legitimated leaders are not available to generate facts. Chapter 5 pays particular attention to reportorial methods of creating a "web of facticity" in order to maintain the credibility of news. And it explains how the web of facticity legitimates the status quo.

Chapter 6 examines the representational style of the web of facticity by closely analyzing news film. It discusses both specific shots and narrative structures. It also examines how those shots and narratives are differentially applied to natural disasters, riots, demonstrations, and legitimated leaders. Additionally, chapter 6 looks at how television presents reporters as impartial and neutral arbiters of social reality. It also explains how professional practices of handling film meet organizational needs.

Many of these themes—professionalism, organizational routines, and ties to legitimated institutions—are drawn together in chapter 7. This is a consideration of coverage of the women's movement, demonstrating the simultaneous institutionalization of that movement and the development of reporting on it. It pays particular attention to the professional blinders and organizational constraints that first dismissed the movement and later transformed its radical issues into a reformist thrust. The chapter stresses how the women's movement was created as a news topic.

Chapter 8 adds a historical dimension by its consideration of news as a legitimating ideology. It argues that the emergence of news, news organizations, and news professionalism are tied to the challenge posed by nineteenth-century capitalism to colonial mercantilism. Subsequent developments link news professionalism and news organizations to the emergence of corporate capitalism. The chapter also considers freedom of the press as a legitimation of owners' and professionals' independent claims to freedom of speech. And finally, it suggests that these claims, like routine news practices, constitute news as an ideology—a means not to know, a means to obfuscate and so to legitimate the intertwining of political and corporate activity.

Chapter 9 reviews the stance toward social actors maintained by interpretive sociologies in order to understand how everyday practices can be a means not to know. After contrasting two approaches to newswork, the traditional and the interpretive, it explicates concepts implicit in the empirical chapters. These include Alfred Schutz' (1962) concept of the "natural attitude"; the ethnomethodologists' notions of "reflexivity" and "indexicality" (Garfinkel, 1967); Goffman's (1974) treatment of "frame" and "strip"; and Berger and Luckmann's (1967) handling of the "social construction of reality."

These theoretical materials, the historical data in chapter 8, and the field observations organized in chapters 2 through 7 are the basis for chapter 10, which offers conclusions and a theoretical discussion of news as knowledge. Chapter 10 compares news to other kinds of knowledge, particularly in the natural and social sciences. It assesses the claims of news to facticity against the backdrop of recent developments in the philosophy of social science. I propose a theoretical formulation of news as a social construction and a social resource. That formulation, I suggest, may also apply to other forms of organizationally and professionally produced knowledge. And I conclude that through its routine practices and the claims of news professionals to arbitrate knowledge and to present factual accounts, news legitimates the status quo.

CHAPTER TWO
Space and the News Net

"Due to circumstances beyond our control, nothing new happened today and so CBS is canceling tonight's Evening News. Walter Cronkite will return tomorrow—if something interesting happens." This hypothetical announcement or one like it might be heard in an imaginary social system that defined news by objective notions of immediacy.[1] To be disseminated in such a system, a news story might have to be measured against statistical indices of importance, significance, and interest. For instance, an editor might use past assessments of events-as-news to develop a regression equation of newsworthiness. The editor might then assign numerical values to an occurrence's importance, significance, and interest, plug these values into the regression equation, and use the resulting numerical value to determine whether the item should be disseminated.

Or this hypothetical cancellation might be plausible under other social and cultural conditions. Journalists, such as Hedrick Smith (1976), have commented extensively on the seemingly alien definition of news in the Soviet Union. There, high-ranking officials receive daily summaries of events akin to our daily newspapers, but reports

---

[1]Roshco (1975) attempts to describe criteria defining immediacy as a key to American journalism.

provided to the general populace omit key items that would receive wide dissemination in the American media. Similarly, Murray Davis (personal communication) recalls listening to the midnight news on a nonprofit counterculture radio station in Berkeley during the early 1960s and one night hearing the announcement that no news had occurred. He reports the shock of meeting implausibility, as though he had bought a newspaper to find only columns of blank space (generally reserved for news) interspersed with lively advertisements.[2]

In the American context, the cancellation of a network news program or the publication of blank columns due to a dearth of news is improbable simply because the news media claim to sell news. They insistently identify news as their primary concern, even though news consumers may find the ads more lively than the stories (McLuhan, 1964), and even though the ads, not the consumers, subsidize the product and account for the profit. Publishers of major American dailies claim to ignore the cost of gathering stories (Sigal, 1973) and decry the recent practice of television stations to search for an entertaining format for presenting news in order to attract advertising dollars by building a larger audience.[3] Yet, all news media must still provide stories, if only to have material to sandwich between money-producing ads. On Saturday, newspapers must have enough information on hand to fill the news columns of ad-crammed Sunday editions. On days when there are fewer ads (especially weekdays between Christmas and February 1), editors may have to discard information that might have been printed on a Sunday. Similarly, television's evening news must fill a prespecified amount of air time day in and day out to justify the time devoted to commercials. The Berkeley radio station could cancel its midnight news precisely because it carried no ads. Nor was it locked into a rigid schedule of programs, as are, for instance, public broadcasting stations. These stations set up their programming schedules in advance and must meet programming obligations to corporate underwriters, among others.

[2]Postal regulations limit the proportion of advertisements a newspaper may carry and still qualify for inexpensive mailing rates. The Federal Communications Commission provides comparable regulation of television.

[3]Nonetheless, one finds the same pattern of providing entertainment to increase readership in the intensely competitive circulation wars of the 1880s. Indeed, a comic-strip character, "The Yellow Kid," prompted the name applied to newspapers of that period, yellow journalism.

The requirement of disseminating news to meet financial agreements is a relatively new phenomenon. The town crier did not have to rattle off information continuously so that he could take a break while a colleague lauded "the pause that refreshes." Nor did the earliest American newsletters print ads, although they did carry information of commerical value. Colonial papers competed fiercely to carry stories of ships' arrivals and to list the goods in the ships' holds. Boys stationed on hills overlooking a harbor would pass the alert to waiting rowboats, which would go out to gather the information (Mott, 1952: 62). Publication was frequently sporadic, depending on the arrival of a ship from England bearing goods and stories of English politics.

Early nineteenth-century newspapers did not carry ads either. Published more regularly, generally as weekly newsletters, these were firmly attached to political parties, purchased by subscription, and circulated among a party's members. Their columns were filled with what we would now call news analyses, including scurrilous attacks on opposition leaders. Designed for the urban elite, newspaper subscriptions were too expensive for laborers and average men.[4]

Another characteristic of these early American papers is of general theoretic interest: their dependence upon central sites. The town crier could pass on news because he gathered items while making his rounds. The earliest newsletters were put out by postmasters, harbor masters, and an occasional proprietor of a general store. The locations of these publishers were social foci for the exchange of information. The importance of central sites to the gathering of news was increased and refined by the introduction of ads to newspapers.

The first newspaper designed for "the common man," the *New York Sun*, appeared in 1833. Drawing on advances in print technology, it sold for a penny and was subsidized by advertisements for patent medicines and the wares of early (proto-) department stores. Geared to a new audience whose attention could be sold to advertisers, the *Sun* redefined news. It retained some political reports, though they were neither as partisan nor as sophisticated as those of the earlier party press, written for the wealthy and educated merchants. It introduced human interest stories and accounts of sensa-

---

[4]Disenfranchised even if they were property owners (Ryan, 1975), women were considered irrelevant to political processes, including party politics and news consumption.

tional and shocking events. The emphasis was upon telling stories.[5] De Fleur reports that the *Sun* carried

news the man in the street found exciting, entertaining or amusing. [The] staff even invented an elaborate hoax, concerning new "scientific discoveries" of life on the moon. When the hoax was discovered by another paper [the *Sun*'s] readers took it with good humor because it had been fun to read about it [1966: 13].

As more popular newspapers joined the *Sun*, competition for items suitable for storytelling increased. Seeking the sensational, reporters left the office to find news in the city. Unlike the postmaster and harbor master, they could not depend upon news coming to them, especially because they published daily, not weekly. But the new reporters did not disperse through the city in either a random or an arbitrary manner. Rather, there were several logical locations where stories might be expected to occur, such as central police stations and courts processing crimes that might titillate the urban masses. There, reporters might hope to learn *systematically* of occurrences that could be shaped to fit and thus to define the emerging conception of popular news.

The importance of systematic location can be traced through the subsequent history of news in the United States. The social impetus of early muckrakers at the turn of the twentieth century was nurtured by stints of reporting the happenings at night court. Equally important, the location of a central source of information facilitates contemporary newswork. Mark Fishman (1977) describes the dilemma of a contemporary small-town reporter trying to ascertain the damage from a California fire. It is impossible to assess the total value of destroyed property by contacting those made homeless. Precisely because they are now homeless, they are difficult to locate. It is time consuming and therefore inefficient to contact every insurance company in the area to ask about claims filed. But the insurance companies must all report their claims to a central agency. Locating the central agency means locating data deemed essential to the production of news in the most expeditious manner.

[5]Schudson (1978) distinguishes between two modes of newspaper writing in the 1880s. One, now exemplified by scandal sheets such as the *Enquirer*, he terms "telling stories." The other, as offered by the *New York Times*, he terms "informational." But, he points out, both modes drew on and institutionalized the same methods of finding and processing news, and so contributed to contemporary news practices.

The Centralization of News Gathering

Increased competition for advertising revenues attained by building circulation led the news media to develop centralized sources of information much like umbilical cords connecting the newsroom to its sources of sustenance. To attract new readers and also to steal readers from one another, the nineteenth-century popular press sought scoops—stories readers would want to know about but as yet unknown to other newspapers. Wealthy newspapers could systematically scatter reporters in state or national capitals, where they might establish a beat, a round of daily activities through which reporters could find news and news brokers could find reporters, to use Fishman's (1977) definition. They could also send reporters to potentially significant events such as Civil War battles to mail or to telegraph their stories to the home office. Stanley's search for Dr. Livingston on behalf of a London newspaper is a famous British example of this phenomenon. Economically marginal papers could not engage in such practices.

Faced with intense competition, limited telegraph service, and high telegraph rates, and fearful that the telegraph company could control their access to information, "ten men, representing the six most important New York newspapers, sat around a table in the office of the *Sun* one day early in May, 1848. . . . They were the autocrats of the city's newspaper world and one room never before had been big enough to hold them" (Gramling, 1940: 19). For their own mutual advantage—to combat the exigencies of the pony express and the power of the telegraph company—they founded the first cooperative news service, the Associated Press. Gradually they introduced the practice of selling dispatches to out-of-town newspapers, like the *Baltimore Sun*, hungry for increased coverage. Gradually they sent reporters to more distant places to gather information for member papers and clients, such as the *Philadelphia Ledger*, subscribing to their dispatch service. Meanwhile, papers that could not buy Associated Press services starved for distant news or used less reliable services founded after the AP. The rapid establishment of other agencies (described by Gramling, 1940) testified to the fierce competition to feed the news columns' hunger.

Some of these agencies were owned by a particular newspaper chain, others were cooperative efforts. Some were based on pooling information among participating newspapers, others on subscription, and still others on a combination of these methods. All, however, testify to the growth of centralization as a method of getting as much information as possible for the minimal investment possible. Together, these wire services eventually formed a worldwide net, capturing occurrences in their mesh. Today they are the primary connectives between the news media and the world they claim to blanket, for the services' bureaus—amalgamized beats—supposedly ferret out news stories.

Two news practices symbolize the key position of the wire services as feeders to the media. The first is a professionally frowned upon practice found in small and financially strapped radio and television stations. Called "rip and read," the practice is to "rip" copy off the United Press International or Associated Press teletype (which spew stories onto a continuous reel of paper) and to "read" it, without changes, on the air. The second is the use of the "Day Books" kept by the Associated Press and United Press International and provided to subscribers and associated media each day. The Day Books list what is supposed to be happening in the city that day so that the media can decide when to cover an occurrence themselves and when to use wire-service accounts. Public-relations firms and individuals strive to get the events they are promoting listed in both Day Books to insure coverage by wire-service subscribers.[6] The *New Yorker* (1976) has noted a high correlation between events listed in the UPI New York Day Book and local media coverage. Of course, it remains to be established whether that metropolitan area's newspapers and television stations base their coverage on the Day Book or learn independently of occurrences and come to similar assessments of their relative importance. However, both "rip and read" and the Day Books point to the role of central locations and agencies in gathering news. Indeed, one may visualize each news-wire service as a spider web, fanning out from a central office to connect with bureaus and beats and also to join diverse news media to a central location. Each associated medium, with its own wire-service sub-

---

[6] For instance, when I asked the Queens College public relations officer how to go about getting publicity for a conference sponsored by Sociologists for Women in Society, he advised, among other steps, that I try to get a listing in the New York AP Day Book.

scriptions, bureaus, and beats, might be seen as a smaller spider's web, spreading outward from a central office. Together, all these webs claim to "blanket the world" to feed the hunger for news.

News Blanket or News Net?

There is a significant difference between the capacity of a blanket and that of a net to gather fodder for daily newspaper columns and television air time. Each arrangement may capture fresh information daily, thus confirming and reinforcing the old adage "old news is no news." (News grows stale like bread and cakes; it is a depletable consumer item.) But a net has holes. Its haul is dependent upon the amount invested in intersecting fiber and the tensile strength of that fiber. The narrower the intersections between the mesh—the more blanketlike the net—the more can be captured. Of course, designing a more expensive narrow mesh presupposes a desire to catch small fish, not a wish to throw them back into the flow of amorphous everday occurrences.

Today's news net is intended for big fish. Consider once more the occurrences the young professor did not tell her husband (in the imagined conversation in chapter 1). The news net is more likely to learn that the university president and provost discussed decreasing the number of faculty at the university than it is to learn of the student's plagiarism. For just as earlier newspapers placed reporters at police stations, where sensational cases might be located, so today's news media place reporters at legitimated institutions where stories supposedly appealing to contemporary news consumers may be expected to be found. In New York, these locations include police headquarters, the Federal Courthouse, and City Hall, where reporters' daily reports bring them into contact with official meetings, press releases, and official documents such as the calendar of the Board of Estimate. The gleanings of reporters stationed at these and similar locations are supplemented by monitoring the police and fire department's radio dispatches, and by assigning other reporters, based in the main office, to follow activities of such legitimated organizations as the Board of Education, the welfare department, and the Metropolitan Transit authority. Significantly, all these organizations maintain files of centralized information, at least partially assembled for reporters' use. Equally significant, placement of reporters at these locations and assignment of these responsibilities reaffirm and reinforce these organizations' public legitimacy. Occurrences are more likely to be defined as news when reporters witness them or can learn of them with little effort.[7]

The news net is refined by attenuating reportorial responsibility and economic reward. The media hire stringers to alert them to occurrences in more specialized organizations, such as local colleges, and in geographic areas of limited but clear circulation value, such as suburbs.[8] The name "stringer" connotes an attenuated relationship to the news net, even as it reaffirms the imagery of the net or web.

Finally, the net is electronically augmented. The wire services link the newsroom to other geographic areas. Telephone cables link television affiliates to a network's newsroom and nightly supplies of fresh stories (called "feeds") that will not be aired on the network's evening news. Telephone cables also link far-flung bureaus to the newsroom, enabling nearly instant transmission of typed and edited copy. (Transmission time is three minutes per page.) The linkages may overlap. For instance, New York dailies maintain Washington bureaus whose work is supplemented by wire-service reports.

This arrangement of intersecting fine mesh (the stringers), tensile strength (the reporters), and steel links (the wire services) supposedly provides a new blanket, insuring that all potential news will be found. But the wire services and the news media substantively duplicate one another's efforts rather than offer substantive alternatives. News media send reporters to occurrences they have learned of

[7]Snyder and Kelley (1977) try to locate objective characteristics of violent events that lead to news coverage. They find that papers in small towns are more likely to cover bar brawls, and that a city that has experienced a riot will be less likely to cover stories of riots in other towns. Unfortunately, like Danzger (1976; cf. Tuchman, 1976), these authors do not come to terms with how news organizations transform occurrences into news events and stories.

[8]At one point the governor of New Jersey threatened to challenge the licenses of New York City television stations because they did not carry a sufficient amount of news about New Jersey. The challenge was to be based on the lack of commercial stations in New Jersey and the large audiences that New Jersey supplies the New York stations. The stations responded by increasing their coverage of New Jersey politics and other sorts of occurrence as well. I use the term "limited value" to describe suburban readers because suburban newspapers are growing while metropolitan papers are declining. In New York, actively competing with *Newsday* for suburban Queens readers, the *Daily News* has a Queens bureau and a complex system of suburban stringers.

through wire-service accounts (Danzger, 1975; Sigal, 1973). They send a reporter to develop the local angle at a national event although there already is wire-service coverage (Altheide, 1976). By complementing the wire services, they reaffirm the sagacity of the wire services' initial identification of the occurrence as a news event. Additionally, they fan their reporters through institutions in the same pattern used by the wire services (*New Yorker*, 1976). And they "borrow" stories from one another. For instance, night editors of morning newspapers receive a copy of their competitor's first edition to learn what stories their own staff missed and to order rewrites from their competitor's columns as deemed necessary. Instead of blanketing the world by their independent efforts, the news media and the news services leave the same sorts of hole in the news net, holes justified by a professionally shared notion of news.[9] Finally, the probability of duplication is enhanced by a common practice of reporters: At bureau, beat, and story site, they commonly share information with colleagues from competing news organizations (Tunstall, 1971; Crouse, 1972). The netlike formation of the dispersion of reporters is of theoretic importance, for it is a key to the constitution of news.[10] The spatial anchoring of the news net at centralized institutional sites is one element of the frame delineating strips of everyday reality as news.[11]

Space and the Constitution of News

The news net imposes order on the social world because it enables news events to occur at some locations but not at others. Obviously, reporters cannot write about occurrences hidden from view by

[9]See chapters 4 and 7 of this volume.

[10]According to Goffman, a key is "the set of conventions by which a given activity, one already meaningful in terms of some primary framework, is transformed into something patterned on this activity but seen by participants to be something quite else. . . . A rough musical analogy is intended [1974: 43,44]."

[11]I mean the term "anchoring" to convey a visual analogy suggestive of the weights attached to the fishers' nets. The weights provide some stability. So, too, the anchoring of the news net at institutional sites lend stability to a fluid search for occurrences qualifying as news and decreases the variability of the occurrences that can be encountered.

their social location, that is, either their geographic location or social class. For instance, the assignment of a salaried reporter to City Hall means that stories generated there may be favored over occurrences at uncovered locations, such as issue-oriented debates among working-class members of an unassigned social movement.

Equally important, the news net is a hierarchical system of information gatherers, and so the status of reporters in the news net may determine whose information is identified as news. Editors prefer stories by salaried reporters to those by stringers, paid less well and on a piecework basis, simply because the news organization has a financial investment in the salaried reporter. For instance, when the education editor of a New York daily sent a stringer from a city college to cover a news conference at City Hall, the daily's City Hall bureau chief fumed because (among other reasons) he had a reporter available to do the story. The bureau chief announced to the education editor, "I have nine reporters down here" for the explicit purpose of writing copy "like this story." Generally, though, avoiding stringers means discarding items regarded as "small fish." And so this practice reinforces the legitimacy of institutions that host beats and bureaus.

Similarly, editors prefer to publish or telecast material prepared by their staff rather than by centralized news services. Rosenblum (1978) reports this pattern in the selection of news photographs. Her participant observation at three major New York City newspapers yielded the finding that their photography editors rarely accept the work of stringers. Faced with a choice of two pictures of the same event, one taken by a staff photographer and the other provided by a wire service, they invariably elected to print their staff member's shot—even if the wire-service's picture was photographically superior.

I observed the same patterns in the newsroom of a television station. Better footage of a story from a centralized service (the news department of the network with which the station was affiliated) was rarely used when one of the station's crews had covered the story. Rather, the superior network footage was used as an opportunity to chastise the crew for inferior work.[12] Similarly, the station hired

[12]The incident involved a national civil rights story. The network hired a local cameraman as part of the crew. As that man had a poor reputation, the scolding was harsher than normal: "If the network could produce better footage using *him* as a cameraman, why couldn't we have done better?"

stringers only in circumstances of dire need. For instance, when a riotlike disturbance unexpectedy occurred in the middle of the night, the editors purchased footage from a stringer, since they had not assigned a crew to the story. But whenever the editors could plan coverage in advance, they avoided hiring a stringer.

Finally, the news net imposes a frame upon occurrences through the cooperation of the complex bureaucracy associated with the dispersion of reporters. Interactions within the bureaucratic hierarchy, reporters and editors jockeying with one another, may determine what is identified as news. Reporters compete with one another for assignments. Editors compete with other editors to get assignments for their reporters and then negotiate to get their reporters' stories in the paper or on the air. As one City Hall bureau chief put it, "My reporters want to see their by-lines in the paper, and I want to see them there." Friendly but fierce competitors, editors wheel and deal with one another as representatives of self-interested fiefdoms, nonetheless sharing a common purpose—to produce news for their organization. To understand the impact of these competitive negotiations upon the constitution of news, one must examine the news net in greater detail.

Originally designed to attracted readers' interest by catching appropriate stories available at centralized locations, the news net incorporates three assumptions about readers' interests:

1. Readers are interested in occurrences at specific localities.
2. They are concerned with the activities of specific organizations.
3. They are interested in specific topics.[13]

Accordingly, the news net is flung through space, focuses upon specific organizations, and highlights topics. Of these three methods of dispersing reporters, geographic territoriality is most important (see Fishman, 1977).

Geographic Territoriality: First, the news media divide the world into areas of territorial responsibility. The actual divisions used by any specific news organization replicate the organization's notion of its news mission—what it believes its particular readers want to know

[13]Readers are also assumed to be interested in specific persons found either at specific localities ("people in the news") or in specific roles (the president and the first lady), and associated with specific topics (as are movie stars and television "personalities").

and what it is financially prepared to bring them.[14] For instance, both the New York *News* and the *Times* have Washington bureaus. Each also has a metropolitan desk whose territorial prerogatives stretch as far as the state capital in Albany. Conceiving itself as a local paper, the *News* has a more extensive system of reporters in boroughs and neighboring states, such as New Jersey, than does the *Times*. Conversely, the *Times*, a self-defined national paper, has an extensive system of national and international bureaus; the *News* does not. At the *News*, local reporters are ultimately responsible to the metropolitan editor; all copy frcm correspondents more than fifty miles from the city and wire-service accounts go to an amalgamated national-international desk. The *Times* has established three coequal desks, metropolitan, national, and foreign, each headed by a senior editor who seeks to place his reporters' stories in a good location in the paper.

Local news programs use a similar system. With the managing editor of the six o'clock news and the local editor of the eleven o'clock news, the assignment editor of NEWS arranged the dispersion of film crews and reporters throughout the city. Selection of national and international stories was jointly handled by the managing editor and the "feed editor" (television's equivalent of a wire-service or telegraph editor) of the eleven o'clock news. Little, if any, national and international news was presented on the six o'clock program since it was directly followed by the network's evening news, a program specializing in national and foreign affairs.

Needless to say, it is not always clear whether an item should be classified as local or national (see Fishman, 1977). For instance, when Henry Cabot Lodge, then chief negotiator at the Paris peace talks concerning the Vietnam war, visited Seaboard City, one member of the station's staff disputed the event's classification. Generally, the eleven o'clock news used a national event as its lead story. Citing the presence of national newsworkers at Seaboard City's airport to cover Lodge's arrival, the program's managing editor designated the station's footage of Lodge as the national lead story. The

[14]Many television stations now base their idea of what readers want to know upon specially gathered survey data. These include tests of stories and of newscasters' potential popularity with viewers. Frequently, when a station hires a new anchorperson or incorporates a new feature, such as consumer news, special consulting firms test-market the proposed innovation through videotapes shown, for instance, in shopping malls.

anchorman countered that Lodge had not said anything significant, that the network had not used its own footage, and that it had placed the item toward the end of its telecast. Accordingly, the anchorman concluded the story was local and that another item should be used as the national lead. Since the classification of a story carries consequences for its handling on the air—in this case, which of two anchormen would read the item—and so becomes part and parcel of the structure of telecast or a newspaper's pages, discussion and negotiation of the coding of a story may be fervent.[15]

Organizational Specialization: A second method of dispersing reporters is to establish beats and bureaus at organizations associated with the generation of news and holding centralized information. For instance, one or more New York dailies have reporters responsible for covering the United Nations, the City Council, the Mayor's office, the police, the Board of Corrections, and the state government. Reporters may be assigned to the building where that organization's activities are centered or keep track of occurrences from desks in the paper's city room. For example, at the *News* some reporters cover politics from the city room, others from the press room at City Hall. The former are directly supervised by the metropolitan editor and assistant city editors; the latter, by the City Hall bureau chief, who is in turn supervised by the metropolitan editor. Still other *News* reporters, located in City Hall's press room, keep tabs on borough politics and are responsible to the City Hall bureau chief and a borough chief located in the main newsroom. Both "chiefs" are under the metropolitan editor.

As is the case with the geographic delineation of responsibility, the coding of stories as "belonging" to one bureau or another is not always clear-cut. The ways in which conflicts are resolved indicate both the priority of territoriality over organizational specialization and how decisions about the delegation of responsibility are embedded in bureaucratic distinctions, as the following field data indicate.

New York Times reporters who do *not* report to specialized topical departments (such as the sports, financial, or family/style department) are ultimately responsible to the metropolitan editor, with

---

[15]One anchorman was responsible for national news, the other for local items. In 1967 the national anchorman earned about $60,000 and the local about $26,000. The former also wrote his own commentaries and had more power in the newsroom.

one exception: the United Nations reporter, who works under the aegis of the national desk. That this man reports to the national desk, not the international desk, reveals the power of bureaucratic solutions. The international desk is responsible for foreign correspondents, maintained by funds provided by that desk's budget. However, whenever the United Nations reporter or any other reporter travels outside the territorial United States, his or her copy is sent to the international desk, since it alone has an international travel budget. Copy is not sent to the editor who routinely supervises that reporter's work. For instance, when a *Times* music critic toured European opera houses, copy was relayed to the international editor.

The primacy of territoriality is also seen when state senate and state assembly committees hold public hearings at Manhattan's World Trade Center. At the *News* the activities of state government fall to the Albany bureau. But the World Trade Center is within walking distance of City Hall, the home of a large *News* bureau claiming responsibility for all activities within lower Manhattan.[16] When a state hearing at the World Trade Center seems politically consequential, both the City Hall and Albany bureaus claim it as their own. When the hearing is expected to be dull, requiring a reporter to spend the day in attendance in order to write a six-paragraph story, each bureau attempts to foist the hearing upon the other. Although the metropolitan editor negotiates each claim on a case-by-case basis, if a City Hall reporter is available, he or she is more likely to draw a a dull hearing than is an Albany reporter, simply because of physical proximity to the story (cf. Fishman, 1977).

Additional evidence from field observation supports the interpretation of the primacy of geographic territoriality. That evidence comes in the form of an internal beat (a round of daily visits and phone calls) developed by one City Hall reporter. When first assigned to his paper's City Hall bureau, Alan Hyde quickly noticed that new bureau reporters were assigned minor items and were expected to dig up (or "enterprise") their own "good stories." Hyde did not wish to compete with the eight other reporters in his bureau and the twenty-five reporters from the other media in the City Hall press room to develop sources of political information by the ortho-

[16]Wall Street is a partial exception to this rule. Generally it has been the domain of the financial section. During the fiscal crisis, though, some Wall Street activity was political news and the responsibility of the City Hall bureau.

dox and arduous method—slow accretion through regular assignments. Rather, Hyde began telephoning a variety of uncovered agencies each morning to ask, "Do you have anything [any news] for me?" Eventually Hyde developed his own beat, including, among others, the water and tax commissions, the special prosecutor's office, and the municipal court, within the City Hall bureau. Yet he remained an official component of the City Hall bureau. On days when he could not enterprise a story within walking distance of City Hall, Hyde was assigned items about city political activities. His development of his own beat had succeeded because it involved routinely extending the physical territory of City Hall to municipal offices within walking distance. Hyde would not have fulfilled his charge of working for the City Hall bureau if he had developed contacts in municipal offices in the midtown area, some two miles away, for that is the official territorial preserve of city room reporters.

Topical Specialization: Formally introduced during the circulation wars of the late nineteenth century, this method is constituted in independent departments with their own budgets. Their editors report directly to a managing or executive editor, bypassing the territorial desks. Topical specialties include finance, sports, and family/style or so-called women's departments, as well as culture and education.[17] Since these departments bypass the territorial desks each day, their editors are told how many columns or pages they are expected to fill, and as in the case of the women's pages and sports department of the *Times*, they may select their own pictures (rather than having them chosen by the photo editor who selects pictures for territorial desks) and determine their own "display" (layout). Finally, when the assistant managing editor maps out ("mocks up") the news product, a culture editor may inform the assistant managing editor of the amount of space needed for cultural copy. For instance, every evening the television editor of the *Seaboard City Daily* emerged from her office, which was set off from the city room (as were the offices of all topical specialists) to tell the assistant managing editor the length of her column.

The television editor's separate office also symbolized her independence from the territorial desks. City rooms tend to be quiet and

[17]Until the early 1960s, the *New York Times'* culture reporters "belonged" to the city desk and the science reporters to the national desk.

cavernous. Because there are no partitions between desks, each reporter can keep track of others' activities. More important, by quickly scanning the room, the metropolitan editor, city editor, and assistant city editors can instantly determine who is available for an assignment. An assistant city editor once confessed to me that he often forgot to assign stories to Bruce Underwood, a young apprentice, because Underwood's desk was hidden by a support column for the traditionally high ceiling. Talese (1966) notes that *Times* reporters jockey for desks from which they can be noticed. But, safe in their partitioned offices, the topical specialists are immune from the possibility of perpetual observation.

Nonetheless, topical specialists are subordinate to territorial editors, as revealed by an error witnessed in the press room of City Hall. The mistake was occasioned by a news conference to announce the formation of a City University basketball league and scheduled for the Blue Room, the traditional site of City Hall news conferences. News releases alerted the education department, sports department, and City Hall bureau of all metropolitan newspapers about the intended event. The education editor from one paper sent a stringer from City College, who wandered into the press room to ask the location of the Blue Room and did not bother to check in with the City Hall bureau chief. (This seeming amenity enables the bureau chief to know which members of his newspaper's staff are theoretically available to him at any moment, or location, in the building.) Additionally, the bureau chief had two of his own young reporters available for the story. Furious, the bureau chief phoned the education editor to inform him of the bureau's rights and abilities. He quickly shepherded one of his own reporters to the Blue Room only to find a sportswriter from his paper also there. Next he telephoned the education editor and sports editor to inform them firmly of the double foul-up and to remind them that their reporters were never again to set foot in City Hall without the bureau chief's foreknowledge.[18]

Needless to say, negotiations concerning overlapping coverage require a great deal of flexibility on the part of reporters and editors. Although a news organization as a complex bureaucracy can generate general rules to cover some situations of overlapping responsibil-

---

[18]The bureau chief explained that the story belonged more to sports than to education since it concerned basketball, not learning. (See chapter 7 for a discussion about identifying the topic of a story.)

ity, it cannot anticipate all possible problems. Nor may it want to, for rigid delineations of responsibility may impede the organization from acting upon unanticipated situations and problems in the everyday world. The *New York Times* has a rule that any reporter sent outside the United States reports to the international desk. But that desk cannot specify the responsibilities of the traveling reporter to the department charged for the reporter's salary on a yearly basis. During the trip, the reporter probably will locate occurrences of interest to his or her department head, as well as information for the international editor, and may wish to file stories for both editors. Flexible negotiations are an organizational necessity.

In chapter 4, I consider one outcome of the organizational need for flexibility—the maintenance of professional norms. In chapter 7, I explore how those norms lead to reportorial recognition that an occurrence is a news event. Here we need only recognize that the conflicting methods of spreading the news net create a complex bureaucracy whose internal negotiations form occurrences as news events.

Negotiating Newsworthiness

I have argued that a news net is important to news organizations because news is a depletable consumer product that must be made fresh daily and depends upon ongoing activities for its raw material. Additionally, it is necessary to have one person or group of people responsible for knowing what is being captured in the news net. The heads of territorial desks and of specialized topical departments share this responsibility.

However, their individual knowledge of reporters' activities at any one moment is not sufficient for rational planning. The national editor may advise the Denver reporter to file a very long story on a topic, assuming that there will be a lot of space on page one for that item. That editor may not know that the city editor has five reporters covering the explosion of a bomb at a local airport, a story that also demands front-page coverage. That all territorial-desk editors and topical-department editors report to the same person (usually called a managing editor, sometimes an executive editor) mitigates this problem. By coordinating the activities of the major territorial and

topical editors as the day progresses, the managing editor may continually revise ongoing plans for and visions of that day's newspaper
or television news show. As the coordinator and the person responsible for the news product, the managing editor heads negotiations
about which items are truly important news.

The managing or executive editor has several formal tools available that help assess the flow of occurrences and shape the daily
product. The wire services transmit to clients a daily budget, a summary of how their reporters are being used that day.[19] It specifies
each story by a "slug," a one-word identification of the topic, accompanied by a one-sentence elaboration of the story and its expected length.[20] The desk editors prepare similar budgets, each incorporating the transmitted budgets of their individual beats and bureaus. At the *Seaboard City Daily*, a morning paper, the managing
editor kept track of budgets as they were revised. At six each evening
he met privately with the assistant managing editor to alert him to
the potential importance of as-yet unread stories. Together they
assessed the relative importance of stories, discussing which might be
suitable for page one.

Then, sitting down at the copy desk, after some preliminary
work, the assistant managing editor would turn to the local editor
and wire-service editor and ask, "What have you got for me?" Having read the budgets, skimmed some of the copy, and the local editor
having conferred with the city editor, the local and wire-service editors would each mention two or three stories that "looked pretty
good" or might "shape up into something." The assistant managing
editor might inquire about the status of an ongoing phenomenon:
"Anything good on Vietnam today?" Or he might announce, "I'm
getting tired of reading follow-up stories on [Martin Luther] King's
death. Our readers must be, too. We've been giving it a lot of play
for two weeks. Let's wind it down."

[19] Just as a household budget presents a plan for spending and saving resources,
the news budget proposes how its resources—reporters and either column inches or air
time—are to be spent. Newspaper budgets specify the number of "takes" (triple-
spaced pages of copy) each reporter expects to produce; television budgets specify the
number of feet of sound or silent film that each crew anticipates using.

[20] "Slug" is a printer's term for a piece of metal inserted between lines of type.
Newsworkers use the term to apply to a story's label. A story's slug is attached to each
piece of paper pertaining to the story, including the typeset copy. In the composing
room the slug is finally removed and the typeset headline is affixed to the story.
Choosing the slug involves deciding the essence of the story. For instance, in 1967 bat-

Hypothetically, the local editor and the wire-service editor might dispute the assistant managing editor's judgment. Hypothetically, one might say, "That King story is still very important." Hypothetically, the local editor might dispute the priority being given to a Vietnam story over a City Hall story. But such possibilities are more hypothetical than actual.

Sitting in on such discussions at the *Seaboard City Daily* at least twice a week for six months, I never witnessed a dispute over the assistant managing editor's assessment. Nor did the local editor and wire-service editors ever directly challenge each other. Rather, the three men sat amicably side by side evening after evening, even though the local editor had been a competitor for the assistant managing editor's job. The local and wire-service editors always offered roughly the same number of stories, each careful not to step on the other's symbolic toes, even though they occasionally disagreed. (I know of such disagreements only because the local editor would sometimes tell me privately how he would have done something differently from the assistant managing editor or wire-service editor.) Apparently, over time, they had worked out a modus vivendi, a living compromise, for the three men were doomed to sit next to one another, assessing stories together, until one of them was promoted or left the organization. Then, another group might work out another compromise.

The importance of ongoing compromise and negotiation to the assessment of newsworthiness is also captured by Sigal (1973). First, he notes, using Talese's account (1966) of activities at the *New York Times*, that a new editor tries to prove his mettle by getting as many stories from his territorial desk as is possible on page one. Second, Sigal stresses the symmetry of outcomes at the *Times* and *Washington Post* by describing their daily editorial meetings and systematically examining their front pages. At the *Times* and *Post*, determination that an item is important news is accomplished at a daily editorial conference, including the executive editor or managing editor and editors of territorial desks and topical departments.[21] There,

---

tle stories were invariably "Vietnam." Political speeches were slugged by their topic or the name of the politician delivering the talk. As much as possible, ongoing stories receive the same slug from day to day.

[21] This is a loose description of a process that varies from paper to paper or from television station to television station. I have, among other things, introduced uniform titles for editors, since these also vary from one news organization to another.

the merit of occurrences as news is ultimately coded, as together they plan page one.

The film *All the President's Men* captures the flavor of these sessions in its depiction of *Washington Post* editorial conferences during the Watergate crisis. Each editor arrives at the meeting with a list of the stories his or her reporters will file that day. The city (or metropolitan) editor, the national editor, and the international editor take the lead, ticking off for the others items each judges to be important, after the executive editor asks of each one, "What have you got?" Topical editors occasionally may volunteer that they have something special to be considered for the front page. For instance, the sports editor might offer a story about the World Series or the Super Bowl during the appropriate season. The financial editor might offer a story about the gold standard, if Britain were once again considering devaluation of the pound.

Sometimes discussion becomes somewhat heated. *All the President's Men* shows the *Post*'s international and national editors knocking down a Watergate story offered by the metropolitan editor, whose reporters, Carl Bernstein and Robert Woodward, had been assigned to that growing scandal. The film also portrays the national editor as claiming that the story should be reassigned to his reporters, rather than remain the preserve of the metropolitan desk. Each editor tries to get stories by his reporters well placed in the daily news product.

However, there is a limit to the fervor of an editor's arguments. That is, there are mutually determined boundaries about the stories that may be offered for page one. The metropolitan editor of a major daily would be mocked by his colleagues if he suggested front-page coverage for an item about a small fire in a deserted garage, as would a sports editor who suggested page-one placement for a routine collegiate basketball game.[22] Indeed, the possibility of being mocked for poor news judgment (a negative assessment of professional skill from peers) may be one reason that topical-department

[22]These stories would not be newsworthy, *all other things being equal.* For instance, the fire might be more newsworthy if the garage were next door to a hospital in a California town and it was the dry season. Then the fire might typify an omnipresent danger. Assigning importance to stories at legitimated institutions reinforces their position in society, as does the assumption that a small fire or petty crime is not news. Similarly, the general pattern of newsworthy murders—deaths of suburban whites receive more play than those of urban blacks—reinforces social positions: whites are more significant than blacks (cf. Cox, 1977).

editors only occasionally offer stories for page one, as well as the reason they are heard when they do suggest a story from their departmental preserve. In 1976 Joan Whitman, then head of the *New York Times'* family/style department, informed me that she rarely offered stories (perhaps once a month) but had a high rate of success in getting her suggestions on the first page. However, it is also crucial to recognize that these negotiations set the boundaries of what can be considered important news at any particular moment. The boundaries are not absolute or objective standards. By deferring to the claimed importance of stories offered by territorial editors, the topical editors participate in a mutual determination that politics (a territorial responsibility) has precedence over either the home or finances (topical responsibilities).

To avoid discussions' becoming quite heated, the editors must maintain a careful equilibrium, for dissonance interferes with the daily accomplishment of the group's task. Newsworthiness is constituted by mutual agreements accomplished by editors working to maintain this interpersonal balance. Implicit understandings must have been perpetually reaccomplished by all the editors for Sigal (1973) to have found an ongoing symmetry in a test of page-one coverage that he devised.

To understand Sigal's test, assume for the moment the existence of an objective hierarchical ordering of news stories by importance, significance, and interest. And suppose the number of persons an occurrence would potentially affect weighs heavily in the assessment of all three factors. (This supposition is based upon editors' explanations to me of their assessments of stories.) Under such a system, international, national, and metropolitan news would, over time, display a pattern of frequency on page one. International news would appear most often, followed, in decreasing order of appearance, by national and metropolitan news. Or consider the possibility that importance were randomly assigned to news stories. Over time, the laws of probability would predict a roughly equal division of page one by stories from the three desks. But, as Sigal puts it (1973: 30), probability "could hardly explain a tendency toward equal distribution [among the three desks] day after day." Sigal terms equal distribution on any one day an "ideal balance."

To learn whether newspapers maintain no balance, a loose (probability) balance, or an ideal balance, Sigal counted the number of stories on page one of the *New York Times* and of the

Washington Post every day of 1970. He reasoned, "A page one with twelve stories, for instance, would be in [ideal] balance if each desk had four stories; a page one with fourteen stories would be in [ideal] balance with a five-five-four distribution among the desks" (Sigal, 1973: 30). After discarding financial and sports stories and items less than two inches long, Sigal constructed an index of balance variation based on the difference between the actual balance on page one and the ideal balance:

> If, for example, the foreign desk had three stories on page one, the national desk, eight, and the metropolitan desk, five, the ideal balance would be six-five-five and the balance variance, $| 8 - 6 | + | 5 - 5 | + | 3 - 5 | = 2 + 0 + 2 = 4$. In addition, whenever one of the three desks failed to place any stories on page one, the day's page was classified as "imbalanced" [Sigal, 1973: 30].

As arrayed in table 2-1, Sigal's data indicate that the *New York Times'* and the *Washington Post*'s front pages are substantially balanced day after day. That is, more than half the time the balance variation is four or less: If one or two stories had belonged to a different desk, ideal balance could have been obtained on most days. Although knowing the mean number of stories on those pages would facilitate interpretation, one may still infer that this balance results from ongoing editorial negotiation.

TABLE 2-1.   Balance Variation on Page One, 1970

BALANCE VARIATION	NUMBER OF STORIES NEEDING TO BE SHIFTED TO ACHIEVE IDEAL BALANCE	POST ($N = 365$)*	TIMES ($N = 365$)*
0		12.9%	16.4%
2	1	31.0%	37.0%
4	2	26.0%	24.7%
6	3	13.2%	16.4%
8	4	3.0%	1.9%
10	5	0.3%	1.4%
12	6	—	—
14	7	—	—
16	8	—	—
Imbalanced		13.7%	2.2%
		100.1%†	100.0%

SOURCE: *Adapted from Leon V. Sigal,* Reporters and Officials *(Lexington, Mass.: D.C. Heath, 1973), p. 30, by permission of the publisher.*
*Percentages for page ones for the year 1970.
†Error due to rounding.

Sigal's data also permit us to see how the editorial conference sets boundaries. He reports that most cases of imbalance involved no stories from the metropolitan desk. He comments that the *Post*'s special page for displaying metropolitan news could account for this discrepancy between the *Post*'s pattern and that of the *Times*; the *Times* has no comparable metro page highlighting local news. My own observations at the *Seaboard City Daily* affirm Sigal's inference. Page three of the *Seaboard City Daily* was set aside for local (metropolitan) news, including picture displays. Sometimes when the assistant managing editor would reject a city story for page one, he would tell the local editor, "You can do a good display of that [on page three, which you mock up]." On occasion, when the assistant managing editor inquired about a story on the metropolitan budget as yet unoffered for page one, the local editor would respond, "I was thinking of leading with it [on page three]."

Finally, Sigal suggests, the slight overrepresentation of national stories reflects action in bureaucratic channels, particularly one bureaucratic pattern shared by the *Times* and the *Post*. Both have more national than international reporters. I suspect that because of this pattern, over time and on any average day, the budget for the national bureau contains more items than the international budget, for that was the pattern of wire-service budgets I examined while observing at the *Seaboard City Daily*.[23] And both the *Times* and the *Post* offer a wire service to subscribing newspapers that includes, in addition to features and columns, material culled from their first page, so it seems reasonable to assume that they, like other wire services, would offer slightly more national than international news. In sum, the assessment of newsworthiness is a negotiated phenomenon, constituted in the activities of a complex bureaucracy designed to oversee the news net.

One may conclude that the news net not only excludes some occurrences from consideration as news because of a pattern of centralization at legitimated institutions; it also orders priorities by which sort of employee or service produced an item, reporter or stringer, staff or Associated Press reporter. Additionally, the news net is anchored through complex overlapping responsibilities, ordered by a bureaucratic editorial hierarchy. In the act of judging the relative

---

[23]Most American newspapers carry more national than international news, a pattern congruent with that of wire-service coverage. I suspect this congruence arose through mutual accommodation, but I do not know specifically how it did so.

value of diverse items caught in the news net, the editors perpetually create and recreate negotiated standards of judgment. By accomplishing judgments, the editors in turn affirm and reaffirm the validity of the anchoring of the news net as a frame imposing order and coherence on the social world. Just as the young professor and her husband (discussed in chapter 1) mutually negotiate the decision that a particular item is prime news ("You know what that son-of-a-bitch Joe said at the department meeting today?"), the editors make news together.

CHAPTER THREE
Time and Typifications

As competent members of society, we all commonsensically know of the intertwining of time and space. We speak of a family hour, a time when people gather in the same space for a common activity. We measure space in temporal terms when we indicate that some place is within a two-minute drive or a ten-minute walk. We use a spatial metaphor when we speak of a "length of time." Specialists in the study of time-use affirm that we measure distances temporally. They inform us that diverse societies regulate the time it takes to get from home to work, regardless of the distance. That is, people who drive to work in the United States average the same amount of time in transit as do people who use public transportation in some European societies (Robinson, Converse, and Szalai, 1972).

Yet, the metaphor of "spatialized time" is profound, for it emphasizes that the social ordering of time and space stands at the heart of organized human activity. A few sociologists have written on this theme of the social generation of time measurement. In a monograph reminiscent of Thomas Mann's *Magic Mountain* (1946), Roth (1963) considers the generation of timetables by patients at a tuberculosis sanitarium. Even earlier, in a classic article, Sorokin and Merton (1937) point out that the calendar is a social artifact geared to the rhythm of collective activity. Surveying a variety of societies, they find "weeks" of assorted lengths. For agricultural societies, they note, the number of days in the week is related to the frequency of market day. Bringing produce to a central location marks a break in the routine chores of day-to-day agricultural existence. Furthermore, Zerubavel (1977) finds that the generation of a calendar to co-ordinate social activities requires its legitimation by institutions. He points out that the French Republic successfully instituted the metric system of measures and weights but failed in its attempt to impose a rational metric calendar. Although legally introduced, its chronological framework and subdivisions of the day could not replace social rhythms associated with church life, and so the "logical" calendar was ultimately discarded.

The intertwining of time and space as social phenomena is implicit in both the Sorokin and Merton (1937) and the Zerubavel (1977) discussions. The week of non-Christian agricultural communities was set off by physical movement from farm to market place. The week of active French Christians was marked by bodily movement to church services. Indeed, in some religious communities, gatherings with special spatial characteristics also mark the division of the day into discrete units. For instance, Heilman (1976) tells us, members of an Orthodox Jewish synagogue signify their religiosity by gathering to pray together morning and evening. At these morning and evening gatherings they disperse through the sanctuary in a different pattern from that used at the main Sabbath service.

A similar intertwining of time and space is found in the anchoring of the news net.[1] Consider some examples mentioned in the earlier discussion (chapter 2) of the spatial dispersion of reporters and

[1]The examples just discussed suggest that in everyday life, social actors work to link the temporal and spatial characteristics of social activities. (See pp. 185–87 for a discussion of work as intentional consciousness.) This work is accomplished both in everyday talk and thought (as in "It's ten minutes from here") and in observable behavior (for example, the dispersion in the synagogue). Newsworkers as social actors also work at such linkages. Additionally, the news net institutionalizes such linkages as it routinizes newswork. Occurrences that may qualify as news events are not only expected to occur at specific locations, but they are expected to occur at those places at specific times. Or, at least, the rhythm of newswork is designed to catch those occurrences that happen at the appropriate time in the appropriate place. Time and space are accordingly objectified or given solidity by these organizational arrangements.

the activities of editors. First, I suggested that editorial conferences are held because editors are not necessarily aware of occurrences unfolding simultaneously in others' geographic territories, even though those occurrences collectively compete for inclusion in the news product. Second, I suggested, the managing editor keeps track of what's happening or is expected to happen, and where, so that he can revise plans for the daily news product should an important occurrence arise unexpectedly. Similarly, the City Hall bureau chief of one New York newspaper was said to keep tabs on the number of "his" reporters in the City Hall area in case a story requiring the services of many reporters should break. In Schutz' (1962: 69) terms, such temporal planning characterizes social action as project. That is, social action is carried out in the future perfect tense. Action is cast into the future in order to accomplish acts that will have happened, should everything go as anticipated.

Other examples of the intertwining of social time and social space also illustrate news as accomplished project.[2] Until the mid-1970s, the London bureau of the *New York Times* edited European and African copy because its location enabled copy to have been edited before the New York workday began (Adler, 1971). To mix metaphors of time and space, that work could be done in the time zone (geographic location) of the London bureau meant that New York copy editors had some of their work "already out of the way" before their workday formally began. One may generalize that the news media carefully impose a structure upon time and space to enable themselves to accomplish the work of any one day and to plan across days. As is the case with the spatial news net, the structuring of time influences the assessment of occurrences as news events.

The Rhythm of Newsmaking

The Daily Tempo: Just as reporters seek central spatial locations to find potential news events, so, too, reporters are temporally concen-

---

[2] "Accomplished project" has a technical meaning. First, Schutz views action as a project (or projection) of present concerns and past experiences into the future. "Project" thus implies the intentionality of consciousness. Second, as used by the ethnomethodologists, the term "accomplished" refers to the project as a human achievement.

trated. At morning papers, most reporters come to work between 10:00 and 11:00 A.M., after offices likely to generate news have geared up for the day. Most reporters leave between 6:00 and 7:00 P.M., after news sources have closed their offices. One or two reporters check in at 8:00 A.M. at metropolitan dailies "in case something should happen" before the others arrive. A skeletal staff remains until 11:00 P.M. or midnight, anticipating any unscheduled contingencies. Then, usually an assistant city editor holds down the "lobster shift"[3] to revise late editions of the paper and to summon reporters to work if necessary. At 8:00 A.M. the editor on the lobster shift is relieved by an assistant city editor, whose other colleagues arrive at about 10:00 A.M. to start again the news rhythm of the day.

This matching of the news organization's dispersion of reporters to the office hours of institutions extends to weekend scheduling. Then, less than half the desks in the city room are occupied, and some of those are being used by reporters normally assigned to outside beats. The City Hall bureau of one New York daily provides a good example of this temporal synchronization. Monday through Friday, eight or nine reporters sit at bureau desks, including a constant cadre of seven who have weekends off. One of the nine spends Tuesday through Friday at the City Hall bureau and Saturday at the city room; another, Monday through Thursday at the bureau and Sunday at the city room. Since City Hall is closed on weekends, the shifting spatial location of the last two reporters and the temporal arrangement of all nine captures the rhythm of the work week of City Hall politicians.

One consequence of synchronized working hours is that few reporters are available to cover stories before 10:00 A.M. or after 7:00 P.M. on weekdays, and even fewer at those times on weekends. This social arrangement influences the assessment of occurrences as potential news events. According to one New York reporter, anyone wishing coverage for an evening occurrence had better have a "damned good story."[4] For the few reporters available are held in reserve to cover any emergency that might be thought to require their

---

[3]"Lobster" is a reference to the red eyes of tired newsworkers as they come off the night shift.

[4]Coverage of evening stories is even more difficult for television stations. If they use film cameras rather than portable videotape packs to cover the story, the film must be developed. Using either technology, footage must be processed quickly for presentation. Television stations are now using live coverage from new small remote

presence. As the New York reporter put it, "They're there in case someone plants a bomb at La Guardia Airport." Sending a reserve reporter to an evening occurrence depletes the news organization's ability to handle a major story, the very contingency that has determined the reporter's working hours.

Variant rhythms, but similar principles, govern the hours of television reporters. When I first observed news processing at NEWS, I surmised that news was potentially limited to occurrences happening between 10:00 A.M. and 4:00 P.M., the deadline for feeding film into the developer in order to have footage edited by the 6:00 P.M. telecast.[5]

Having available staff also influences the assessment of occurrences during periods when reporters are temporally concentrated. A story justifying the presence of a reporter at 11:00 A.M. might not justify assigning one late in the afternoon. By 3:00 P.M., the few reporters left without assignments are being held in reserve for emergencies, their time filled with writing obituaries and small items, such as rewrites of news releases, that can be handled from the office by making a few telephone calls. And unless the news organization has been alerted in advance that a "good story" will occur late in the day, a high-status reporter will not be available to cover it. By noon, those reporters have received their assignments or enterprised their stories for the day.[6]

Similarly, Gieber (1956) found that the internal scheduling of newswork influences the wire-service editor's assessment of stories to

---

cameras for events occurring during the news program, but problems associated with live coverage have to be ironed out. For instance, passersby may run in front of the camera or harass the reporter.

[5]Epstein (1973) argues that news is also spatially limited. At the time of his study, the networks found it easier to cover stories in Los Angeles, Chicago, New York, and Washington than in other cities because of the placement of connecting cables. Additionally, stories from Vietnam had to have a timeless quality, since the film had to be flown from Saigon to New York for editing. New technologies have created somewhat greater flexibility.

[6]The familiarity of politicians and public relations officers with the rhythm of newswork enables them to manipulate newsworkers and news organizations now and then. A New York political reporter recalls Governor Hugh Carey's and Mayor Abraham Beame's joint announcement of their proposal for the Municipal Assistance Corporation. They unexpectedly called an emergency news conference, scheduling it shortly before the deadlines of morning newspapers and 6:00 P.M. newscasts. The setting, a midtown Manhattan hotel suite, lacked telephones. The timing and lack of telephones accomplished two things: The reporters did not have ample time to check

be included in the newspaper. At a morning paper the wire-service editor selects copy in the evening. Using the wire services' budgets, he quickly sets about filling the columns made available to him. The later the hour, the less space he has left to fill. Accordingly, an occurrence late in the evening must present special competitive merits to be included as a story in the daily news product.

Planning Across Days: Finally, to project work into time and so to control work, the news media plan across days. Consider the following example, a memo addressed to the city editor by a court reporter. It was written in mid-November:

> The grand larceny trial of nursing home owner Bernie Bergman and his son Stanley and accountant Sandak is now scheduled to begin with jury selection January 5. Pretrial motions . . . get under way December 15 before Manhattan Supreme Court. . . . And the federal tax-evasion trial of the Bergmans will follow shortly upon the completion of the state trial.
>
> The grand-larceny trial is expected to be lengthy and time consuming for the reporter. For those reasons, it would be advantageous for the desk to decide in the near future who it wants to provide trial coverage. My view is that the assigned reporter should be free from other responsibilities during the duration of the trial so as not to downgrade the quality of our daily beat coverage.

Or consider the weekly plan of the City Hall reporter whose days off were Fridays and Saturdays. Every Thursday he sought to find a story to file on Thursday and another to write for Sunday, when he worked in the city room, and when it would be more difficult to locate occurrences qualifying as news. Of course, this reporter's foresight meant that to become news, an item found on Sunday would have to be competitive with the item located on Thursday. Otherwise, the reporter would not alter his allocation of his time; he would not change "his" story.

Ultimately, the anchoring of the news net in time and space means that reporters and news organizations suffer from a "glut of

---

the claims made by the politicians, because the story was rushed to meet the deadline. Without phones, the reporters could not inform their editors about the substance of the story. Had the reporters been able to do so, the editors could have assigned additional reporters to double-check the officials' interpretation of the fiscal crisis, and that information could have been available in time to meet the deadline. Reporters both dislike and distrust news promoters who manipulate them too often.

occurrences" with which to fill the news product. Having reporters assigned to beats and bureaus means that they each interpret their task as "filing [at least] a daily story" (Roshco, 1975) about occurrences at their various locations. Some reporters seek to file more, often commenting to colleagues about how many they've written that day. A multitude of stories means that each one cannot be disseminated; choices must be made. The multitude of news releases arriving at reporters' and editors' desks—perhaps fifty a day at New York's City Hall bureau alone—also requires careful winnowing of the use of reporters across time. The process of planning to handle this glut results in a system of classifying occurrences as news events.

Time and the Glut of Occurrences

In chapter 2, I emphasized the need to locate potential news stories to fill the daily product. Now I argue that the news net produces more stories than can be processed. Each one of these is a potential drain upon the news organization's temporal and staff resources. For each occurrence can claim to be idiosyncratic—a particular conjunction of social, economic, political, and psychological forces that formed an occurrence into "this particular occurrence" and not any other existing or having existed in the everyday world.

Accepting this claim for all occurrences is an organizational impossibility. Like any other complex organization, a news medium cannot process idiosyncratic phenomena. It must reduce all phenomena to known classifications, much as hospitals "reduce" each patient to sets of symptoms or diseases, and as teachers view individual students in terms of categories pertinent to learning. Any organization that sought to process each and every phenomenon as a "thing in itself" would be so flexible that it would be unrecognizable as a formal organization. Some means between flexibility and rigidity must be attained (March and Simon, 1958).

Concentrating reporters' working hours does not necessarily provide time to handle the idiosyncrasy of occurrences. A comparison makes this clearer. Providing more doctors than usual in a hospital's emergency room on weekend and holiday nights does not guarantee that the seriously ill and wounded will receive adequate medical treatment, even though that provision takes into account the everyday rhythm of work and recreation. (More accidents arrive in hospitals on weekends because of bar brawls and family disputes engendered by extended intensive interaction.) To facilitate adequate treatment, hospitals institute special routines. For instance, they may schedule all elective surgery before 5:00 P.M. on weekdays. Operating-room schedules also take into account the amount of time customarily required for the expected surgical procedures. What a patient sees as a personal medical emergency is thus rendered routine by the hospital so that it may plan the use of both personnel and physical resources and thus control the flow of work. When allocating resources each week, some hospitals even check lists of critical patients to estimate the kind and amount of work to be expected by the morgue's personnel (Sudnow, 1967).

Just as hospital personnel differentiate among diseases according to their demands for organizational resources, news personnel must anticipate the claims of potential occurrences upon their resources. To control work, newsworkers have developed typifications of occurrences as news stories.[7] (Typifications are classifications arising from practical purposive action.) Anchored or embedded in the use of time, the news typifications characterize stories, much as the anchorage of the news net in space characterizes and constitutes newsworthiness.

The anchoring or embeddedness of typifications in time shares two other important characteristics with the anchoring of newsworthiness in the spatial news net. That is, both news typifications and the assignment of newsworthiness are relatively content free. We have seen that newsworthiness is a negotiated phenomenon rather than the application of independently derived objective criteria to news events. So too, typifications of kinds of news draw upon the *way* occurrences happen, not upon *what* is happening. The typifications are only relatively content free, because some sorts of occurrences are likely to happen one way while others have a different

---

[7] I am claiming that newsworkers develop typifications to control the flow of work in organizations. Generally, though, that aspect of "control" is credited to organizational processes, not professional practices. However, there is theoretical justification for my usage. Zimmerman concludes: "It appears that the 'competent use' of a given [organizational] rule or set of rules is founded upon members' practiced grasp of what particular actions are necessary on a given occasion to provide for the regular reproduction of a normal state of affairs [1970: 237]."

temporal rhythm. For instance, a hospital may generally preplan a specific cesarean delivery; a news organization may preplan coverage of a particular trial. Neither organization can specifically anticipate the work associated with a particular four-alarm fire.

Just as newsworkers claim that there are specific criteria of content against which news is assessed (i.e., how many people are affected by the event), so, too, newsworkers insist that their categorization of news depends upon a story's content.

Newsworkers on Categories of News

At work, reporters and editors refer to five categories of news: hard, soft, spot, developing, and continuing. Journalism texts and informants explain that these terms differentiate kinds of news content or the subject of events-as-news. Asked for definitions of their categories, newsworkers fluster, for they take these categories so much for granted that they find them difficult to define.[8] To specify definitions, newsworkers offer examples of the stories that fall within a given category. They tend to classify the same stories in the same manner. Some stories are cited with such frequency that, viewed as prototypes, they are incorporated in the following discussion.

Hard News Versus Soft News: The newsworkers' main distinction is between hard news and its antithesis, soft news. As they put it, hard news concerns occurrences potentially available to analysis or interpretation, and consists of "factual presentations" of occurrences deemed newsworthy. When pressed, informants indicated that hard news is "simply" the stuff of which news presentations are made. For instance, asked for a definition of hard news, a television editor offered the following catalog of basic news stories: "Hard news is the gubernatorial message to the legislature, the State of the Union Address to Congress, the train-truck accident or the murder, the bank holdup, the legislative proposal . . . and the fire tomorrow."

This editor and other informants voluntarily contrasted hard news with soft news, also known as feature or human-interest stories

---

[8]See Giddens (1976) for a discussion of informants' inability to articulate objectified taken-for-granted classificatory systems.

(cf. Hughes, 1940). Some examples of soft-news stories are: an item about a big-city bus driver who offers a cheery "good morning" to every passenger on his early morning run; a feature about a lonely female bear; a story about young adults who rent a billboard for a month to proclaim "Happy Anniversary Mom and Dad."

Newsworkers distinguish between these two lists by saying that a hard-news story is "interesting to human beings" and a soft-news story is "interesting because it deals with the life of human beings" (Mott, 1952: 58). Or they state that hard news concerns information people should have to be informed citizens and soft news concerns human foibles and the "texture of our human life" (Mott, 1952: 58). Finally, newsworkers may simply summarize: Hard news concerns important matters and soft news, interesting matters.

These separate yet similar attempts to distinguish between hard and soft news present the same classificatory problem; the distinctions overlap. Frequently it is difficult, if not impossible, to decide whether an event is interesting or important or is both interesting and important. Indeed, the same event may be treated as either a hard- or a soft-news story. During a two-year period, the observed television station presented as feature stories some events that its primary television competition presented as hard news, and vice versa.

Spot News and Developing News: Difficulties also appear in the newsworkers' distinctions between spot news and developing news. The most important problem is that the newsworkers partially abandon their claim that the categories are based upon the content or subject matter of events-as-news.

Asked to discuss spot news, newsworkers replied that it is a type (subclassification) of hard news. They cited fires as a prototypical example of spot news. (Occasionally informants added a second example, such as a robbery, murder, accident, tornado, or earthquake.) The subject matter of all examples was conflict with nature, technology, or the penal code.

Asked about developing news (another subclassification of hard news), the newsworkers cited the same examples. Asked, then, to distinguish between spot and developing news, informants introduced a new element, the amount of information that they have about an event-as-news at a given moment. When they learned of an unexpected event, it was classed "spot news." If it took a while to learn the "facts" associated with a "breaking story," it was "developing news." It remained "developing news" so long as "facts" were still emerging and being gathered. When I pointed to previous statements asserting that the subject of the story determined that story's classification, the newsworkers insisted that both statements were correct. In essence, they countered, the subject matter of certain kinds of event-as-news had a tendency to occur in specific ways (fires break out unexpectedly, whereas many demonstrations are preplanned). And so, newsworkers happen to learn of them in certain ways.

Continuing News: Asked to define continuing news, newsworkers reverted to discussing the subject matter of an event-as-news. As the newsworkers put it, continuing news is a series of stories on the same subject based upon events occurring over a period of time. As a prototype, the newsworkers cited the legislative bill. The passage of a bill, they explained, is a complicated process occurring over a period of time. Although news of the bill's progress through the legislative maze may vary from day to day, all stories about the bill deal with the same content—the bill's provisions and whether they will be enacted. In this sense, they said, the story about the legislative bill continues as news. (Other examples cited by informants included trials, election campaigns, economics, diplomacy, and wars. Almost all examples were confrontations within or among recognized institutions, and all are produced by complex organizations.)

Then, once again, the newsworkers partially modified their statements. Maintaining that certain kinds of news content tend to fall under the rubric "continuing news," they added that certain kinds of content (stories about legislative bills and trials, for example) "simply" tend to occur over an extended period of time.

Typifications of News

From Category to Typification: Unfortunately, the newsworkers' definitions of their categories are difficult to apply, even though the definitions, prototypical examples, and lists of stories decrease the variability of the occurrences as the raw material of news, and so reduce their idiosyncrasy. More important, discussing spot, developing, and continuing news, the newsworkers introduce a seemingly extraneous element mentioned in the comparison of hospitals and news organizations: certain kinds of event-as-news tend to happen in certain ways. And so, reporters and editors "just happen" to be alerted to the need to process them in different ways.

The notion of news as frame, particularly the recognition that organizations perform work upon the everyday world to make sense of daily experience, enables the realization that the classificatory scheme is grounded in the rhythm of time use. Schutz' interpretive sociology suggests that the newsworkers' classifications are typifications rather than categories. "Category" refers to the classification of objects according to one or more relevant characteristics ruled salient by the classifiers, frequently by what anthropologists term a "formal analysis." The use of "category" connotes a request for definitions from informants and a sorting of those definitions along dimensions specified by the researcher. "Typification" refers to classification in which the relevant characteristics are central to the solution of practical tasks or problems at hand and are constituted and grounded in everyday activity. The use of "typification" connotes an attempt to place informants' classifications in their everyday context, for typifications are embedded in and take their meaning from the settings in which they are used, and the occasions that prompt their use.[9]

Embedded in practical tasks, the newsworkers' typifications draw on the synchronization of their work with the likely schedule of potential news occurrences. As summarized in table 3-1, the newsworkers' distinctions between hard and soft news reflect questions of

[9]In recent years researchers (Zimmerman, 1970; Cicourel, 1968; Emerson, 1969; Emerson and Messinger, 1977; Sudnow, 1967) have discussed the relationship of typification to practical tasks in people-processing organizations. Examining the production of typifications has enabled labeling theorists to highlight the moral and occupational assumptions underpinning the treatment of deviants. It has enabled them to locate the *practical* considerations that families, police, judges, doctors, and social workers rely on to label offenders and clients (see Emerson and Messinger, 1977). As Schutz (1962) pointed out, typifications help to routinize the world in which we live. They epitomize the routine grounds of everyday life; they enable us to make limited predictions (projections) and thus to plan and act. Schutz's use of the term "typification" is, however, slightly different from that used here. In some contexts Schutz uses the term "category" to apply to social-science constructs. At other times he refers to categories as a subtype of typification whose application depends upon the specificity of the phenomenon being typed (see also McKinney, 1970).

scheduling. Distinctions between spot and developing news pertain to the allocation of resources across time, and vary in their application according to the technology being used. And the typification "continuing news" is embedded in predicting the course of events-as-news.

Hard News: The Flow of Newswork and Scheduling: Because news is a depletable consumer product, newsworkers claim that "quickening urgency" is the "essence of news" (H.M. Hughes, 1940:58; Roshco, 1975). If newsworkers do not act quickly, the hard-news story will be obsolete before it can be distributed in today's newscast or tomorrow's paper. To quote Robert Park (Park and Burgess, 1967), old news is "mere information."

TABLE 3-1. Practical Issues in Typifying News*

TYPIFICATION	HOW IS EVENT SCHEDULED?	IS DISSEMINATION URGENT?	DOES TECHNOLOGY AFFECT PERCEPTION?	ARE FUTURE PREDICTIONS FACILITATED?
Soft news	Nonscheduled	No	No	Yes
Hard news	Unscheduled and prescheduled	Yes	Sometimes	Sometimes
Spot news	Unscheduled	Yes	No	No
Developing news	Unscheduled	Yes	Yes	No
Continuing news	Prescheduled	Yes	No	Yes

*As McKinney and Bourque (1972: 232) note, typifications are flexible and undergo continual transformation. Theoretically, then, as noted by Lindsey Churchill (personal communication), recording typifications in this manner transforms them into components of a typology, for it separates them from the ongoing situations in which they are embedded.

In contrast, soft-news stories need not be "timely." The Sunday newspaper is padded with feature stories about occurrences earlier in the week. Concerned with "timeliness," newsworkers make fine distinctions. They explain that some kinds of content (hard-news stories) become obsolete more quickly than others (soft-news items). This distinction is based upon the distribution of nonscheduled, prescheduled, and unscheduled events as hard and soft news.

A *non*scheduled event-as-news is an occurrence whose date of dissemination as news is determined by the newsworkers. A *pre*-scheduled event-as-news is an occurrence announced for a future date by its convenors; news of it is to be disseminated the day it occurs or the day after. An *un*scheduled event-as-news is one that occurs unexpectedly; news of it is to be disseminated that day or the day after. The type of scheduling characteristic of an event-as-news affects the organization of work.

Most hard-news stories concern prescheduled events (a debate on a legislative bill) or unscheduled events (a fire). Newsworkers do not decide when stories about prescheduled events and unscheduled events-as-news are to be disseminated. Nor do they decide when to gather "facts" and to disseminate accounts and explanations of nonscheduled hard-news stories. Nonscheduled hard-news stories often involve investigative reporting. The publication of the *Pentagon Papers* by the *New York Times* is an example of a nonscheduled hard-news story. The *Times* held the papers for several months before it published extracts, digests, and analyses of them. Processing nonscheduled stories, the news organization copes with the timing and flow of work.

Members of the news enterprise almost always control the timing and flow of work required to process soft-news stories. Few soft-news stories concern unscheduled events, as indicated by the previous list of feature stories. Another example is the "Man in the News" series run by the *New York Times.* Like the obituaries of famous men and women, the "facts" can be, and often are, gathered, written up, and edited in anticipation of future dissemination. Prescheduled soft news also includes such annual "February stories" as items appropriate for Washington's and Lincoln's birthdays and for Valentine's Day. A reporter may be assigned to these stories days in advance, and the specific information to be included in the story may be gathered, written, and edited days before its eventual dissemination.

Of course, there are exceptions to these rules. But news organizations handle those exceptions in a manner that conserves personnel and retains control of the flow of newswork. For instance, "facts" to be used in a feature story about the atmosphere at an important trial cannot be gathered in advance. Nor can feature information about an unscheduled event, such as a fire, be gathered in advance. However, the impact of these events-as-feature stories upon the allocation of personnel is minimal. In the first case, a reporter may be assigned to write the "feature angle" of the trial several days in advance, his name struck from the roster of reporters available to cover the fast-breaking news of the day. In the second case, the same person generally reports both the hard-news fire and its soft-news angle, so that the news organization can conserve reporters.

Spot News: Allocating Resources and Dealing with Technology: As in the case of the hospital, governing the flow of newswork involves more than scheduling. It also involves the allocation of resources and the control of work through prediction. The distinctions among spot news, developing news, and continuing news are occasioned by these practical tasks.

Spot-news events are unscheduled; they appear suddenly and must be processed quickly. The examples offered by informants indicate that spot news is the *specifically* unforeseen event-as-news. For instance, although the staff may anticipate the probability of a fire, they cannot specifically predict where and when a fire will start. This inability to make a definite prediction concerning some events affects the flow of newswork. If a three-alarm fire starts close to deadline, information must be gathered and edited more quickly than usual. If a major fire starts fifty miles from the city room, transportation problems influence the time needed to gather and process "facts" and so influence the allocation of resources to cover the fire.

Some events that newsworkers nominate for membership in the typification "spot news" are of such importance that newsworkers try to create a stable social arrangement to anticipate them—even if the probability that the event will occur is minute. The city desk of most major dailies is staffed around the clock in case a spot-news event should occur. For example, the president of the United States is covered twenty-four hours a day in case something should happen to him. Continually creating stable social arrangements such as these requires both extended allocation of resources (assigning a staff member to sit at the city desk all night) and immediate reallocation of resources (pulling a reporter off another story) if and as necessary.

The different news technologies each have their own varying time rhythms. Film can be shot, edited, and aired in an hour; print technology is more cumbersome and time consuming. Accordingly, as might be expected from the finding that technology influences the organization of work (Hage and Aiken, 1969; Perrow, 1967; Thompson, 1967), as well as my argument that time rhythms influence typifications, a television station's allocation of resources differs from that of a newspaper. The print technology is labor intensive; electronic technology is not. At the *Seaboard City Daily* at least three of the twenty-person staff of general reporters and rewriters sat in the city room from 10:00 A.M. until midnight doing minor but necessary tasks. The observed television station had few reserve reporters and no reserve cameramen, except from 4:00 to 6:00 P.M. and from 9:30 to 11:00 P.M. At these times, reporters and cameramen, bringing their film to be processed, had generally returned from their assignments. They would wait either to cover a spot-news story or to go off shift. Should a specifically unforeseen event occur at any other time of day, the station had to: pay overtime; pull a reporter and a cameraman from a less important story they were already covering; pull a cameraman from a "silent film story" he was covering by himself; hire a free-lance cameraman; pull a staff announcer from his routine duties, such as reading station identification; or assign a newswriter to act as reporter after gaining permission from the appropriate unions. The alternative(s) chosen depended upon the specific situation—the existing dispersion of both film crews and occurrences in time and space at that moment of that day.

Developing News: Technology and the Perception of Events: Practical problems of dealing with a technology and its rhythms are so important that they even affect the newsworker's perception of a spot-news story, especially whether the typification "developing news" will be applied to an event-as-story. In the case of developing news, technology provides a lens through which events-as-news are perceived.[10]

Developing news concerns "emergent situations." A plane

[10]To a great extent, these comments about technology and perception are based on my observations, not the comments of the observed reporters. But they are informed by newsworkers' accounts of encounters with one another, including a NEWS reporter's tale that the "ink" reporters started to treat him respectfully when he joined them in the boring task of waiting for a jury to report its verdict, after having sat through the trial hour after hour, day after day. (Frequently, television stations identify such assignments as wasting the reporter as a resource, for the reporter could cover another story in the morning and "do" the trial in the afternoon.) An ex-wire-service reporter resigned from the writing staff of NEWS (despite improved pay) to rejoin his old wire service. He announced that he missed the excitement of perpetual deadlines designed to feed copy to morning and afternoon newspapers scattered in

crashes. Although this occurrence is unexpected, there are, nonetheless, limitations on the "facts" it can possibly contain. Editors would not expect to run a story stating that those reported dead had come to life. Nor would they expect to run a report of an official denial that a crash occurred. The "facts" of the news story are: A plane crashed at 2:00 P.M. in Ellen Park when an engine caught fire and another went dead, killing eight people, injuring an additional fifteen persons, and damaging two houses. All else is amplification. Since this *specific* plane crash was unexpected, reporters were not present to record "facts" "accurately." "Facts" must be reconstructed, and as more information becomes known, the "facts" will be more "accurate." Although the actual occurrence remains the same, the account of it changes, or, as the newsworkers put it, "the story develops." Ongoing changes of this sort are called "developing news."[11]

Most spot-news stories are developing news. Since both present interrelated work demands, newspaper staffs tend to use the terms interchangeably. Television workers use the term "developing news" in a more restricted sense, identifying some stories as spot news that print journalists term "developing news."[12] Again, technology acts as a key in their formulations, each technology being associated with a different rhythm in the centralized services feeding the news net. The process of covering the death of Martin Luther King, an occurrence that raised different practical problems for the two New England media, illustrates this variation.[13]

different time zones. In both cases the association of variant rhythms with different media were at issue.

[11]Although newsworkers single out only this type of news as being subject to ongoing change, interpretive theories would insist that this process is ongoing for all kinds of news at all times. Suffice it to say that developing news provides a particularly clear example of indexicality (see pp. 188–91).

[12]Howard Epstein (personal communication) notes an additional problem that developing news poses for newspapers: the point at which to "break" a story for successive editions. For instance, should one hold the mail edition for fifteen minutes to include the beginning of a speech, or should one hold the story for inclusion in the later, home-delivery edition? Competition with television makes this decision more difficult and somewhat "meaningless," because whatever the newspaper editors decide to do, the television newscast may carry the speech first.

[13]I observed coverage of King's death at the *Seaboard City Daily*. Activities at NEWS are reconstructed from conversations with the staff held within three days of the assassination.

At the local newspaper, King's injury and subsequent death were labeled "developing news." A continual flow of updated copy needed editing and "demanded" constant revision of the planned format. The assistant managing editor learned of the attempted assassination and plotted a format for the front page. When King's condition was reported as grave by the wire services, the editor drew another format that affected other stories above the fold on page one. When a wire-service bulletin reported King to be dead, all other stories were relegated below the fold. Every story on page one needed a new headline of different-sized type, and lead paragraphs of some stories had to be reset in smaller type. Inside pages were also affected.

The television network, with which NEWS is affiliated, reported on King's condition as a developing story. Periodically, it interrupted programs to present bulletins. But this was a spot-news story for the local television station's personnel. Obviously, the format of the 11:00 P.M. newscast was modified early in the evening. Because of the network's bulletins, the story about King (whatever it might turn out to be) had to be the program's lead. At the newspaper, the production manager and compositors bemoaned the need to lay out the front page three times, each reset accompanying a major development in the story. All production staff worked overtime. At the television station, readjustments in production plans meant less work, not more. By prearrangement, the network preempted the first few minutes of the late-evening newscast to tell the story, just as it had preempted the same five minutes some months earlier to report the death of three astronauts.[14]

Continuing News: Controlling Work Through Prediction: Spot news and developing news are constituted in work arrangements intended to cope with the amount of information specifically predictable before an event occurs. This information is slight or nonexistent, because the events are unscheduled. In contrast, continuing news *facilitates* the control of work, for continuing news events are generally prescheduled. Prescheduling is implicit in the newsworkers' defi-

[14]Used to compare the local media, the concept technology is a gloss, containing the idea that each medium also has different resources associated with its attachment to the national news net. Obviously, as the source of the feed to local stations, the network experienced King's death as developing news.

nition of continuing news as a "series of stories on the same subject based upon events occurring over a period of time."[15] This definition implies the existence of prescheduled change. For instance, the account of the progress of a legislative bill through Congress is an account of a series of events following one another in a continual temporal sequence. An event occurring at any specific point in the sequence bears consequences for anticipated events.

Because they are prescheduled, continuing news stories help newsworkers and news organizations regulate their own activities by freeing staff to deal with the exigencies of the specifically unforeseen. Take that legislative bill. It is to be channeled through the House, the Senate, and the executive office. To cover this series of events-as-news, the reporters must be familiar with the legislative process. Such familiarity may even be viewed as part of a "professional stock of knowledge at hand" (see Schutz, 1964: 29 ff.). The reporter knows the sentiments of pertinent committee members, as well as the distribution of power within both the various House and Senate committees and the House and the Senate themselves. In addition, the reporter also knows the progress being made by other legislative bills. With this cumulative stock of knowledge at hand, the reporter may not only predict the bill's eventual disposition, including the specific route through the legislative process (this bill will be bogged down in the House Ways and Means Committee), but may also weigh the need to cover this bill on any one day against the need to cover another bill about which there is comparable information. That "expert" or "professional" stock of knowledge at hand permits this reporter, other reporters and editors, and the news organization to control work activities.

The continuing news story is a boon to the reporter's ability to control his or her own work, to anticipate specifically, and so to dissipate future problems by projecting events into a routine. Indeed, newsworkers seek out continuing stories because they are predictably and readily covered. The news organization's ability to process continuing stories routinely by predicting future outcomes enables the organization to cope with unexpected events. At the very least, it enables a city editor to state, "Joe Smith will not be available to

[15]See Fishman (1977) for a discussion of how newsworkers constitute "sameness" and a critique of my analysis of news typifications.

cover spot-news stories a week from Tuesday because he will be covering the Bergman trial."

One Consequence of Typifications

Thus far, the examination of time and typifications suggests that newsworkers use typifications to transform the idiosyncratic occurrences of the everyday world into raw materials that can be subjected to routine processing and dissemination. Typifications are constituted in practical problems, including those posed by the synchronization of newswork with how occurrences generally unfold. They impose order upon the raw material of news and so reduce the variability (idiosyncrasy) of the glut of occurrences. They also channel the newsworkers' perceptions of the everyday world by imposing a frame upon strips of daily life.

Yet we do not know whether typifications, as components of the news frame, carry significant consequences when they key occurrences from one multiple reality to another, from the everyday world to the world preferred by the news product. Why do typifications matter? Are they of more than theoretical interest?

Following Schutz (1962, 1964, 1966, 1967), Berger and Luckman (1967) tell us that knowledge may be objectified by institutions. Instead of existing as formulations subject to continual revision and reconstitution, objectified ideas may elicit set ways of dealing with the world. As the product of the intertwining of news time and the news net, the news typifications have become part of the reporter's professional stock of knowledge-at-hand. That is, being a professional reporter capable of coping with idiosyncratic occurrences means being able to use typifications to invoke appropriate reportorial techniques. Again, there is a medical parallel.[16] Being a doctor means having the professional knowledge needed to typify symptoms as diseases and to process patients according to appropriate hospital procedures governing the allocation of resources. Reporters

---

[16]The parallel is not exact, for doctors reign supreme in hospitals and claim the license to control how other members of the medical team do their work. Newsworkers do not "control" the activities of the editorial, advertising, or production staff (see Engwall, 1976; Freidson, 1971).

explain their classificatory system as objective categories, as objectifications.[17] Doctors objectify symptoms as defined (categorized) diseases. In subsequent chapters I will examine the reporter's and editor's professional knowledge as the outgrowth of news organizations' use of time and space. And in chapter 7, I will point to additional consequences of news typifications. For now, one example of the objectification of professional knowledge arising from the use of typification must suffice. For objectification of knowledge may result in errors, much as applying stereotypes about a "criminal appearance" may result in incorrectly labeling someone as criminal or untrustworthy. And in some cases, professional errors in prediction influence the assessment of the newsworthiness of a story.

Put formally, if objectified, typifications can be seductive. Faced with the need to predict and to plan, newsworkers may be seduced into applying what everyone knows—that is, what all newsworkers collectively agree upon. Having a collective stock of knowledge-at-hand concerning how occurrences unfold and a system of typification partially based in the utility of known-in-detail prediction, newsworkers may predict inaccurately. The Wilson–Heath and Dewey–Truman elections are classic examples of such inaccurate prediction.[18]

Inaccurately predicted events-as-news require major unplanned alterations in work processes. Like spot news, they are unscheduled and specifically unforeseen. Like developing news, they are perceived through the frame of a specific technology. Like continuing news, they involve both prediction and postdiction of an event as a member of a chain of events. They challenge knowledge and routines that reporters and editors take for granted.

Reporters and editors cope with the problems of inaccurately predicted events by invoking a special typification: "What-a-story!"

[17]The process of objectification raises two additional issues. At what point and how does objectification become reification? At what point and how do objectified typifications become stereotypes?

[18]It is tempting to identify inaccurate predictions as mistakes. "Mistake" is a lay term (E.C. Hughes, 1964). As Stelling and Bucher (1973) argue, this notion is cast aside in the course of professional socialization, to be replaced by concepts emphasizing the process of doing work. Given evidence of inaccurate *collective* predictions, the newsworkers essentially argue that they are specialists in knowing, gathering, and processing "general knowledge" (Kimball, 1967). If and when their predictions are collective, they are necessarily accurate, for they are based upon shared expertise. The

This typification is constituted in the unusual arrangements that are routinely made to cope with a "what-a-story!" That newsworkers typify these events emphasizes the centrality of typification in their work and the degree to which typifications are constituted in their work.

Symbolically, the degree to which this typification is itself routine is captured by the almost stereotypical manner in which verbal and nonverbal gestures accompany the pronunciation of "*what*-a-story!" "What" is emphasized. The speakers I observed provided additional emphasis by speaking more slowly than usual, adding yet more emphasis by nodding their heads slowly, smiling, and rubbing their hands together, or by enthusiastically touching colleagues.

The extent to which unusual arrangements are routinely made to cope with a "what-a-story" is illustrated by the reaction of the staff of the *Seaboard City Daily* to President Johnson's speech of March 31, 1968. Learning of Johnson's announcement that he would not run for reelection, the newsworkers immediately instituted taken-for-granted routines to handle the what-a-story, and referred to similar situations in the past.

Johnson's speech was prescheduled. The newspaper, like other news media, had an advance copy of the text that omitted, of course, Johnson's "surprise announcement" that he would not run for re-election. As Johnson spoke on television of the deescalation of American bombing, the editors awaited companion stories concerning reactions of political leaders to the so-called bombing halt. These were to be supplied by the wire services. A preliminary format had been drawn for page one. The lead story about the military situation (slugged "bombing halt") had been headlined and edited and was being set into type. Page one was also to include a political story, not

---

newsworkers argue that since their stock of knowledge is necessarily correct, the *situation* is in "error." That is, the situation changed in a way they could not anticipate. The post-hoc explanation of Heath's "surprise victory" over Wilson, as offered in the daily press, supports this interpretation: Confident of victory, Wilson did not campaign sufficiently. Spurred by accounts that he was the underdog, Heath made a special effort to win. A similar process, dependent upon knowledge in detail, might also explain the ability of Agnes, a transsexual claiming to be an intersexed person, to con her doctors (Garfinkel, 1967: 116–185, 285–288). Given their stock of knowledge at hand, the doctors assumed it was impossible for a boy to self-administer the correct dosages of the correct hormones at just the right time to interfere with "normal" sexual development. As a lad, Agnes had done this by taking hormones prescribed for his mother.

placed prominently, about the coming election. Several other assessments of the political situation had already been set into type, including columnists' analyses of the 1968 presidential election to be printed on the editorial page and the page opposite the editorial page; a political cartoon showing Johnson speaking on the telephone and saying "Yes, Bobby"; and a small story speculating whether Robert Kennedy would join Eugene McCarthy in challenging the president as a candidate for the Democratic nomination. The newspaper was in good shape for the first-edition deadline, 11:00 P.M.

And then it happened: bedlam. A prescheduled announcement concerning the continuing "Vietnam problem" and warranting a limited amount of political speculation turned into a major surprise of military, political, and diplomatic importance. An assistant city editor had been watching the speech on the television set of the newspaper's entertainment critic. Excited, he ran, shouting, into the city room. The editor's reaction was perhaps more unprecedented than the president's announcement.[19] The telephone of the assistant managing editor rang. The managing editor was calling to discuss coverage of the speech. Although the managing editor had already made his nightly telephone check, the assistant managing editor automatically said "Hello, Ted," before he had even heard the voice on the other end.[20]

It would be impossible to describe the amount of revision accomplished in a remarkably brief time as reporters summoned by telephone, volunteering editors, and mounds of wire-service copy poured into the newsroom. But the comments of editors and reporters are significant. Lifting their heads to answer telephones, bark orders, and then clarify them, the editors periodically announced, "*What* a story! . . . The story of the century. . . . What a night, what a night! . . . Who would have believed it? . . . There's been nothing like it since Coolidge said, 'I will not run.' "

These remarks are telling. First, they reveal that typification is also based upon taken-for-granted assumptions, a topic explored in subsequent chapters. The paper's top political reporter, when cover-

[19]The newsworkers were particularly proud of the quiet that prevailed in the newsroom. One editor, who had worked at the *New York Times*, claimed that the news of D-Day had spread through the *Times*' city room in whispers.

[20]Neither this incident nor the previous one was witnessed. They were reported to me by five different newsworkers as the evening progressed.

ing the New Hampshire primary, had offered to bet anyone that Johnson would not run for reelection. Few had accepted his challenge, because it would have been like "taking money from a baby."[21]

Second, the remarks emphasize the degree to which work routines can be routinely altered. Johnson's speech of March 31 was said to require reassessing the military situation in Vietnam, the diplomatic situation, especially the possibility of successful peace talks, and the political situation in the United States. The managing and assistant managing editors specifically alerted the copyboys to watch the news services carefully for analyses of these topics. Before any notification came the editors "knew to expect" analyses of these topics. In addition, handling the story required a substantial amount of revision and readjustment of the allocation of resources. Significantly, all the editors took for granted the nature of those readjustments. No discussion was required to decide which political reporters would come back to work. Only minor discussion was required to decide which of the general reporters would be asked to return to work from their homes.

Third, the analogy to Coolidge (the editor who mentioned him thought the others might be too young to remember) alerted the staff to an unusual routine. That is, rules governing the coverage of a what-a-story were invoked by citing another what-a-story. Indeed, the invocation of Coolidge involves an implicit call to reduce the variability of events as the raw material of news, for it states that this event-as-news is "like" that one from years ago.

Fourth, the degree to which an individual what-a-story is typified and thus made routine is indicated by the assistant managing

[21]Similar stories concerning the assumptions about Johnson's candidacy made by newsmen based in Washington, D.C., have circulated in the mass media. A question asked by Kurt H. Wolff (personal communication) prompts a more technical interpretation of the what-a-story. One might say that the content of the what-a-story challenges the newsworkers' taken-for-granted notions of the social world so much that it threatens their ability to maintain the "natural attitude." The routines used to process a what-a-story may then be seen as the process through which the staff work to reestablish the natural attitude. Another approach is also possible. The five typifications previously discussed enable the workers to process other people's emergencies. When faced with a what-a-story, newsworkers are themselves placed in a state of emergency. That they immediately invoke routines to handle the what-a-story again stresses the use of typification grounded in routine to accomplish practical tasks. In this case, the task might be simultaneously processing information and working one's way out of an organizational emergency. See pp. 186–88.

editor's reference to previous what-a-story(ies). He rejected an offer of help from another editor, recalling that that editor had been more of a hindrance than a help in processing a previous what-a-story. Some months later, trying to decide the size of type to be used for a headline about Robert Kennedy's death, he thought back to Christmas and explained, "What a year! What a year! . . . The Tet offensive, Johnson's speech, King's death . . . now this."[22]

Finally, City Hall reporters describe their coverage of the announcement of New York's fiscal crisis and the possibility of default as the "natural" invocation of routines associated with spot coverage, not with those of continuing political coverage. Their daily routines were altered; other modes of coverage were invoked. According to one City Hall bureau chief, "We covered it the way we would cover a disaster—like a hurricane or earthquake. We were [systematically] scattered all over the place," rather than centralized in City Hall.[23] Said the reporter who broke the story for a Long Island paper, "What a story!" Proudly, he explained that he was the reporter who first learned New York's budget was awry. Reporters at neighboring desks firmly attested that they all knew "what to do," how to respond to a story that contravened their professional expectations, how to disperse and what to look for.

In short, as professionals, they knew how to institute routines associated with the rhythm of newswork. And, as professionals, they were familiar with the news organization's need to generate stories and to control the idiosyncrasies of the glut of occurrences by dispersing reporters in a news net flung through time and space. The association between professionalism and the problems faced by news organizations processing idiosyncratic occurrences will be explored in detail in chapter 4.

[22]King's death was retrospectively treated as a what-a-story. At the time, newsworkers greeted it with head shaking devoid of glee, and some quietly discussed the racism of other staff members. How much a what-a-story is subject to routine is forcefully indicated by an incident at the television station on the day of Robert Kennedy's death. Most newsworkers were called to work at 6:00 A.M. Several were not, so that they would still be fresh for the 11:00 P.M. newscast. Coming to work in the midafternoon, one on-camera reporter asked an early-morning arrival, "Did we gather the usual reaction [stories]?" Then, indicating his realization that this question would seem crass to an outsider, he asked me not to include his question in my field notes. (The use of reaction stories as a legitimating device is discussed in chapter 5.)

[23]Dahlgren (1977) points out that economic forces and processes are reified by news, that is, treated as though they were natural phenomena.

CHAPTER FOUR
Flexibility and Professionalism

Ruth Leeds Love (1965) provides an interesting account of network coverage of President John Kennedy's assassination. According to interviews with network personnel gathered by Love and her colleagues at Columbia University's Bureau of Applied Social Science Research, network coverage was "business as usual"—only more so. Business was unusual in that technical facilities were overtaxed and news coverage was continuous. Conditions were difficult:

> Commentators broadcast without scripts, chains of command were ignored or short-circuited, and channels of communication were abbreviated. But, business was as usual in that the news department was covering a story via film, live telecasting and commentary . . . in that virtually everyone carried out his normal duties . . . in that the news division had a bank of accumulated experience to guide its responses . . . and finally . . . the norms and values of the news profession were in force more or less the same way as they are at other times [Love, 1965: 76, 77].

More was involved than typifying the assassination as a what-a-story and getting the news net in place. News professionalism also played a key role in reducing the idiosyncrasy of the Kennedy assassination as the raw material of news.

Not surprisingly, professionalism was a crucial factor in coverage of the assassination; newsworkers describe their activities and judgments that day in terms of professional "instinct" (Wicker, 1965). Sociologists studying organizations and professions tell us that the variability of raw materials, organizational flexibility, and professionalism are interrelated. Briefly put, the greater the variability of raw materials, the greater the organizational flexibility and, accordingly, the greater the professionalism of workers.[1] Here, professionalism connotes the exercise of autonomy, the right of workers to control their own work (Freidson, 1971), frequently by reference to norms developed by professional agencies external to the organizations in which they work (E.C. Hughes, 1964).

For news organizations, reducing the variability of raw materials by developing typifications of events-as-news is not sufficient to maintain control of work. Classifying both a fire and a murder as spot news does not sufficiently specify how information about those occurrences should be gathered. A knowledge of how to cover fires will not help a hard-news specialist to cover a feature story, should one be assigned. Nor will a knowledge of politics assist a topical specialist in covering a fire if that specialist is the only reporter available for assignment when a four-alarm fire breaks out. Finally, because most of the reportorial work of gathering information takes place either outside the newsroom or over the telephone, editors cannot supervise the process.[2] Direct supervision of the work process (rather than the product) would require an expensive organizational investment in more editorial personnel. News organizations maintain flexibility and save money by discouraging a more complex bureaucracy than already exists, and by encouraging professionalism among re-

---

[1] See Stinchcombe (1959) for a discussion of professionalism in the construction industry. Professionalism in newswork should not be confused with a cosmopolitan orientation. See Stark (1962) for cosmopolitan and local orientations among newsworkers. Nor does professionalism necessarily mean that newsworkers at small organizations identify with professional associations. But those smaller organizations serve as training grounds for national reporters. See, for instance, Rather (1977) for a description of the small radio and TV stations he used as a ladder to his job at CBS.

[2] Some reporters resist promotion to an editorial position, such as assistant city editor, because it decreases their association with sources. The longer someone has served as an editor, the less familiarity he or she has with news sources. However, promotions to managing editor and the even higher echelons of newswork bring familiarity with the very powerful. For example, some *New York Times* executives move in the same circles as national political figures.

porters. Among reporters, professionalism is knowing how to get a story that meets organizational needs and standards.

This chapter explores the relationship between news professionalism and organizational flexibility by examining daily activities of nine reporters at their City Hall bureau. It asks, how is flexibility accomplished as a practical daily activity? How does work get done? Examining the activities of a small group of professionals at an economically successful New York daily newspaper highlights the importance of flexibility to newswork, for in that setting one can see how the overlapping lines of territorial, institutional, and topical responsibilities are negotiated by reporters as professionals.

The Bureau

When I observed the nine reporters, in the fall of 1975 and winter of 1976, they were the largest group from any one news organization in City Hall, and they were reputed to provide the best daily coverage of city politics. Four of the reporters had desks in the main press room, five in an auxiliary room in the basement below.³ About twenty-five reporters from eight news organizations shared the main and auxiliary rooms, with reporters from other organizations appearing on an irregular basis. Almost all were employed by newspapers or wire services. From the paper I observed, the reporters and their assignments were:

1. Adams, the bureau chief: assignment of reporters, generation of story ideas, general fiscal and political stories.
2. Butler, bureau manager (former acting bureau chief): copy editing of stories submitted to the city editor, writing of civil-service column and general stories.
3. Calder, reporter: fiscal and economic stories.
4. Dayton, reporter: City Council stories.
5. Edwards, reporter: stories about the Board of Estimate, the

³Two "upstairs" members of the bureau had a different weekday off. When either of them was gone, Edwards, a senior reporter, worked upstairs rather than at his downstairs desk. As in the previous chapters, unless otherwise specified, all names are fictitious. On occasion, I have credited one reporter's actions to another in order to insure further their anonymity.

Planning Commission, various other city bodies, politics in Brooklyn and Queens, and a column based on borough politics.

6. Franklin, reporter: stories about actions of the Board of Estimate concerning Brooklyn, general political reporting; also a subordinate of both the Brooklyn-page editor and the city editor.
7. Green, reporter: same duties as Franklin, but for Manhattan and Staten Island.
8. Hyde, reporter: stories about the municipal courts (criminal and civil), the Water Commission, and the offices of the special prosecutor, the district attorney, and others.
9. Ivers, reporter: general political reporting.

Additionally, three political reporters stationed in the city room had overlapping responsibilities:

10. Jackson: assigned to the fiscal crisis; shared stories with Calder, but primarily responsible for the governor's midtown offices and activities.
11. Louis: the former bureau chief, now a political columnist, and assistant city editor two days a week.
12. Morris: former city hall reporter, also assistant city editor two days a week.

Also (as discussed in chapter 2), the City Hall bureau was responsible for all political events in lower Manhattan, such as hearings of the state legislature held in the World Trade Center, unless claim to a story was disputed by the Albany bureau (the state political beat).

One crucial finding emerged from watching the reporters work: Specialties are ignored when necessary. Everyone must be capable of doing everyone else's work. To paraphrase Calder, the ultimate aim of the bureau, like that of the newspaper, is to get its work done. If everyone stuck to his or her specialty, there might sometimes be a gap in the news net. For all recognizably newsworthy stories to be covered, each specialist must be a generalist, and vice versa. To quote several reporters, each must "be a professional" capable of covering everything and anything, because each may be assigned anything at any time. If Butler is ill, someone else may have to write the civil-service column, as Calder has done. If Calder is tracing an intricate aspect of the fiscal crisis and Jackson is on an assignment, someone else may be put on a late-breaking fiscal story. Morris attests, "We've all done 'fiscal' at one time or another."[4]

Knowing Sources

Being a reporter means knowing how to find stories pertinent to one's placement in the news net. For reporters at the City Hall bureau, locating stories requires having news sources. Although a relatively lowly general-assignment reporter in the city room may be given assignments, beat and senior reporters are encouraged to locate their own. As Green, a young bureau reporter, explained to a former city room colleague at the annual Press Club Christmas party, the City Hall beat is difficult. Not only must one learn who is who in the newsroom, a task necessary for any novice on a new beat, but one must also learn who's who at City Hall.

By knowing enough sources, reporters can maximize their ability to file a story every day and thus demonstrate their competence. That having a story is a matter of competence becomes clear early in the day. Soon after the staff have arrived at their desks, the bureau chief routinely asks the senior reporters, including one senior reporter located in the basement auxiliary room, "What do you have today?" With this question he demonstrates his realization that these reporters have a bevy of sources from which to generate news items. Sometimes the question is redundant. Before leaving the previous evening, the senior reporters may already have reviewed the stories they expect to write the following day.[5]

Knowing sources brings professional status. Hyde said of Louis, "He's the best political reporter in the city. He has more sources than anyone else." New to City Hall, Green commented that she was impressed by the number of sources Edwards had amassed during his decade in the press room. Veterans in the press room, Edwards and Dayton assumed that each knew the names of the other's sources and could drop the last names of relatively obscure politicians in conver-

[4]The impact of who writes a story on the constitution of the story's topic is considered in chapter 7.

[5]Senior reporters also map out which aspect of a running story they will cover over a period of days. For instance, one day Calder advised Butler that he planned to develop one paragraph of that day's story into another story the next day.

sation without needing to provide further identification.[6] The connections, offices, or clubhouses of these politicians (but not necessarily their names) were given when they explained their stories to other bureau colleagues.

The higher the status of sources and the greater the scope of their positions, the higher the status of the reporters.[7] As is well known, news stories, news sources, and reporters are hierarchically arranged. This association of "star" reporters with "star" sources was beautifully captured during NBC's daytime coverage of the Senate's Watergate hearings. During a break in John Ehrlichman's testimony, anchorman John Chancellor, political reporter Douglas Kiker, and judicial correspondent Carl Stern discussed their respective contacts with Ehrlichman and Bob Haldeman, President Richard Nixon's top aides. Of the three reporters, Stern had the lowest status within the NBC news operation, infrequently appearing on the evening news. Anchorman Chancellor appeared nightly; Kiker, several times a week. From his location in the studio, Chancellor introduced the topic of personality differences between Ehrlichman and Haldeman. He noted that he had always found Ehrlichman friendly, helpful, and cooperative, and possessing a fine sense of humor. Ehrlichman returned his phone calls; Haldeman did not, insisting upon retaining a formal distance from newsworkers. Then, Chancellor asked Stern, located in the hallway outside the hearing room, whether he had also found this to be the case. Stern looked startled. Recovering after several seconds of dead air time, he replied that he had never had occasion to telephone either man. Quickly Kiker jumped in. Speaking rapidly from Stern's side, Kiker agreed with Chancellor's characterization of the two Nixon aides. Kiker's manner, when he started talking, resembled that of a man covering another's social gaffe, such as an unintentional insult or revelation of another's failings at an initial meeting of new acquaintances.

A similar phenomenon can be found in the City Hall press room. None of the nine reporters is specifically assigned to cover the mayor, although Calder, the fiscal and economic reporter, had sev-

---

[6]Edwards and Dayton sometimes discussed sources in front of me, correctly assuming that I would not know who they were. Sources also called these reporters at their homes. Rather (1977) speaks of how his superiors would not ask the names of his sources.

[7]There are exceptions to this rule. For instance, secretaries have low status, but know what is going on in their office. Thus they may be a good source of information.

eral questions for the mayor's news secretary almost every day. When the mayor's head news secretary wandered into the press room, at least one of the reporters would ask for information pertinent to a story he or she was working on. Adams did not address questions to him more frequently than Calder, nor did Adams telephone more often. And since many of the mayor's formal news conferences concerned the city's fiscal crisis, Calder almost invariably covered them. Yet, at the end of every year, when the mayor gave a separate one-hour interview to a reporter from each New York daily, Adams represented his newspaper, just as the bureau chief for one of the city's other dailies asked questions for his organization. That other paper's bureau chief was not his group's fiscal expert either. And, as published, both interviews concentrated on the fiscal crisis and the impact of the mayor's and governor's political relationship upon the solution to that crisis.

Gaining more sources works similarly to the distribution of honors in science. To use Merton's (1973) description, the "Matthew Effect" is in operation: The more one has, the more one gets. "Big stories" go to the high-status reporters, even if that means breaching current specialties. When a riot occurred at the Riker's Island prison, the main correctional facility in New York, Adams, a former police reporter, was called in to locate the facts because the "official" police reporter was already busy on other aspects of the case and could not take on an additional angle. Yet he stayed with the Riker's Island story for almost a week, and at one point called upon Franklin to do legwork for him. Although Franklin shared a by-line with Adams, he accepted the story as Adams'. He noted that he got a few really good stories a year but that Adams had them more often.

The frequency with which Adams received good stories filled at least one reporter, Ivers, with envy. Ivers was angry about Adams' handling of the Rikers Island riot. Assigned to do a minor follow-up story of that event weeks after it happened, Ivers wanted to file a magazine-type analysis for the Sunday paper. (Reporters receive extra piecework fees for such work.) Ivers wished to present the prisoners' view that they were held unconstitutionally. Assignment of higher bail than they could pay abrogated the Bill of Rights and supposedly "caused" the riot. However, Adams had already written an article on the riot for the Sunday section. Using police and correctional-department sources, he claimed that the riot was due to conditions at the prison, such as over crowding. Ivers, aware that Adams had more pull with the appropriate Sunday editor, grumbled that he could never get his version printed. Dissatisfied, he explained that no matter how far he advanced in the organization, Adams would always be ahead of him and would always be able to make his version of occurrences carry more weight.[8]

Ivers also grumbled about the number of stories Adams wrote. Each morning, while Bureau Chief Adams asked his senior reporters what they were working on, he leafed through news releases. Senior reporters, including Adams himself, were frequently given two good stories before the junior reporters were given one. Adams grew tense from working on two pieces and answering the city editor's telephoned inquiries while Ivers sat in the auxiliary press room doing crossword puzzles.

Ivers was also annoyed about desk assignments and the way they exacerbated differences in access to sources. Adams developed good sources as the designated bureau chief. Politicians made a special point of meeting Adams—not Ivers. Although both men were simultaneously transferred to the bureau after years on other beats, Adams' contacts rapidly outstripped Ivers'. Seated in the auxiliary press room, Ivers had more difficulty learning who people were, rarely meeting sources who wandered through the press room to say hello.

Knowing sources brings participation in a common reportorial culture. When the state's attorney general, Louis Lefkowitz, made a brilliant and unexpected political move, both the main and the auxiliary press room buzzed about it. Upstairs, reporters referred to "Louie" in praising his past exploits. Downstairs, the junior staff spoke of "Lefky," the nickname employed by headline writers. Using the wrong nickname signaled their marginality and lack of personal acquaintance with the man.

Being a participant in the press room culture brings increased familiarity with sources. Accepted into the culture, reporters may wander over to greet a source who drifts into the room. Participants in the culture may be invited to write for the "Inner Circle," an an-

[8]Ivers was more politically libertarian than the other reporters. Athough reporters tend to be liberal, the atmosphere in the newsroom is not liberal. In every newsroom I have visited, political stickers are affixed to desks. Generally they have indicated past support for the Vietnam war, opposition to gun control, and other conservative leanings. I have never seen a liberal sticker on a desk.

nual musical review, satirizing politicians, staged by New York's political reporters. They may gain more information about politics and politicians' foibles from colleagues from this experience. Or they may be invited to join a friendly game of hearts, played frequently after copy has been filed if there is time to kill before the end of their working day. At least one politician often participated in the game. As head of a powerful City Council committee and a major figure in his borough's political life, this politician was a valuable news source.[9]

Finally, knowing sources simply enables reporters to do their work adequately. After 1:00 P.M. or so, no matter what a reporter's specialty is, he or she may be asked, "Are you up?" (Are you free to cover a story?). One afternoon, the bureau's budget having already been transmitted to the city editor, the Manhattan reporter was assigned a story about Queens, the Brooklyn reporter received a story about Manhattan, and the fiscal reporter was sent out to gather political information for a story being prepared by a city room reporter.[10] Governed by the rhythm of newswork and the association of early assignments with stature, these abrogations of specialties were not viewed as unusual in any way. Indeed, although sometimes zealous to show off his skill, fiscal specialist Calder found it "only natural" that he should be called upon to help a city room colleague that day. After representing the bureau at a briefing luncheon with a presidential aspirant, Calder arrived at his desk in the early afternoon and so had not received or enterprised his own assignment. By assisting someone else, he felt that he was adapting to the organization's need for flexibility. And he could draw on his bank of sources to locate the required information. Late assignments present more difficulties for reporters with fewer sources; having trouble gleaning information, they may miss deadlines.

Hypothetically, if a reporter misses a deadline, the editors will be late in passing the story on to typesetters (if the paper has not introduced computer techniques). If one typesetter must work overtime, according to the union contract, each typesetter gets paid time and a half, as do compositors and printers held past their shift. Trucks bringing the newspaper to newsstands and home subscribers

[9]Again we see the attribution of social meaning to the social distribution of space.

[10]In other words, territorial and institutional assignments within the bureau itself were abrogated.

may leave late, causing readers to buy a competitor's paper. Readers may discover they prefer the competitor's product. Circulation and advertising revenue may drop. To be sure, this reasoning resembles the old hacksaw: for the want of a horseshoe, the horse was lost; for the want of a horse, a kingdom was lost. However, missed deadlines *do* potentially cost money—and newspaper copy does pass sequentially through many hands before it reaches the reader.

Hoarding Sources and Sharing Information

That some reporters have more sources than others also means that some reporters may work in others' specialties, for any privately generated idea or information is the explicit property of its originator. I witnessed several examples of these "property rights." Once, Green generated an idea for a fiscal story despite her paucity of sources. When the Post Office raised its rates, she suggested an item on the impact of the new rates on city spending. Her attitude and the help of others clearly indicated that the story was hers. As she worked, she expressed delight that she had finally enterprised an idea that generated editorial enthusiasm. Calder helped her by teaching her how to read the city budget, a cumbersome document in which the data she needed were encased.

Similarly, Edwards' many sources alerted him to a coming change in the power structure of the City Council, officially Dayton's preserve. Edwards seemed surprised when I asked him why he, rather than Dayton, was writing the story. He virtually shrugged as he explained that he had learned of it before Dayton, and had informed Dayton of the story (as required by professional courtesy), but the story was his. Telling Dayton also reduced the chances of duplicating work. Morris explained property rights with regard to generated information even more clearly. "Suppose," she said, "I find out about a good story involving the City Council. I would tell Dayton. Dayton wouldn't mind. In fact, he would help me get additional information if I needed it." Dayton, all agreed, was a good professional colleague, well versed in the norms of the newsroom.

Of course, while colleagues assist one another, the possibility that someone may poach on one's territory intensifies the competition to maintain one's private bank of sources. When a source has given a story to someone else, even a colleague from the same organization, a reporter will ask, "Why didn't you give that to me?" or complain, "I thought you were going to give that to me." Hyde called a source in Albany to ask why he hadn't received a story. During the annual Press Club Christmas party, Edwards greeted a source and then asked why another reporter had received a prized story. In a second friendly chat at the party he arranged an exclusive interview. In all observed cases, the reporter's manner indicated that the story should be *his*, not simply his paper's. Although employed by a news organization, the reporters presented themselves as autonomous professionals when dealing with sources. Indeed, for one reporter to ask another the name of a concealed source was to violate professional norms (as I unhappily learned from the run around and disapproving looks I received when I violated that norm; cf. Fishman, 1977). I subsequently noted that reporters did not ask colleagues the name of a source when one visited the bureau. Nor did a reporter necessarily introduce the source to his colleagues. Similarly, if a competitor from another organization knew the source, he might say to the visiting source, with a twinkle in his eye, "How are you doing, John?" thus displaying his own professional contacts.[11]

Merely concluding that reporters express their professional autonomy from editorial supervision by hoarding sources and sharing information with bureau colleagues is to understate the matter. Relatively free from editorial supervision, reporters have evolved a complex code that may contravene organizational dictates. If reporters were merely bureaucratic employees operating according to the rules and needs of their organization, they might be expected to hoard information from reporters working for competing media and share with all reporters from their own company. Instead, exercising their autonomy, they may share with competitors and hoard information from other bureaus within their own organization. Identification of information as either bureau or personal property is determined by the reporter's need to maintain control of his or her work.[12]

[11] The familiarity of competitors from other organizations with one's sources is a good reason to use the telephone for extended interviews. Recognizing a source in the press room, competitors may ask themselves what a reporter is working on and make a too-accurate guess. Competition for sources fosters rivalries even in one-newspaper towns. And such rivalries are for status, not economic profit—the motive of competing news organizations.

[12] The many attempts of rivals to learn the identity of Deep Throat, Bernstein and Woodward's prime source in their Watergate investigations, highlight the consideration of sources as private property, as do rivals' printed speculations.

Sharing Information with Competitors' Reporters: Discarding the organizational dictate not to share with competitors, reporters invoke collegiality to exchange some kinds of information with competitors.[13] Readily available information is shared; privately developed information rarely is. Reporters consider it ill mannered either to request privately developed information or to refuse easily accessible material. Consider three examples:

A newspaper had foreknowledge of a committee meeting because its city editor was a member of a citizens' group, appointed by the mayor, to clean up Times Square. Assigned the story, Green walked into the closed meeting and remained a few minutes. She was then asked to leave, and informed that all reporters would be briefed later. While she was out of the press room, a wire-service reporter bemoaned his inability to be in two places at once (he was working on another story) and was reassured by the bureau chief that Green would soon return. Returning to the press room, and without asking whether it was proper, Green briefed the wire-service reporter. He, in turn, gave the information to the competing wire service and a competing New York newspaper. Meanwhile, Green tried to locate the city editor (it was his day off) for an interview about the meeting. Perturbed because she could not reach him quickly, she was reassured by her bureau colleagues that the city editor would call her (as he did within the hour). Green later explained that she had shared the information because everyone would have it after the news secretary's briefing—and her story would be better than her competitors' work, because she could develop exclusive information when she spoke with the city editor.

In another instance, reporters exchanged easily gleaned "facts." A *Times* and a *News* reporter were working on the same fiscal story. The *Times* newsworker called across the press room, "What's the interest rate on those bonds?" The *News* reporter supplied that standard information, voluntarily adding the number of bonds that had been exchanged by a certain hour. The *Times* man noted that he had been given a different figure and had been told to check back later. After making his phone call, the *Times* newsworker gave the *News* reporter the update. The exchange was an example of

[13]Danzger (1975) assumes, as reporters do, that sharing is a form of verification. However, it may be a way of perpetrating inaccuracies. Crouse (1972) points out that reporters denied access to shared information may be forced to develop new lines of inquiry, and so uncover "better" stories.

collegial friendship. A popular reporter, the *News* staff member had been transferred from the press room months before. Asking him for information connoted his sustained membership in the culture of the press room.

The third case reveals a sharp distinction between who is and is not admitted to the professional circle of sharing. Early in the day a press release concerning layoffs in the police department was distributed. Three reporters (from two newspapers and a wire service) collaborated in preparing a statistical summary of the data in the release. Then all three started making phone calls. In the late afternoon a young reporter, filling in for an older man who was ill that day, arrived in the press room and asked for information. A newspaper reporter (A) handed him the summary of the release and said, "You have to call around to get everything else." Ten minutes later a newsroom regular, working for a radio station, asked Reporter A for the first page of his typewritten copy. Reporter A replied, "I'm working on it." When Reporter B, an older reporter from A's newspaper, looked annoyed and disapproving, Reporter A surrendered his copy. One of the boys, the radio reporter would return what was a clear favor some time in the future.

That such sharing is based upon professional autonomy contravening organizational preferences is revealed by the career of Reporter B. Popular with all the reporters, a star performer in the Inner Circle musical reviews, Reporter B had worked in the press room for over fifteen years, first as the employee of a now-defunct newspaper and then as a member of a large City Hall bureau. The radio reporter had been a presence in Reporter B's daily work life longer than he had been associated with Reporter A, his bureau colleague. When Reporter B sent the bureau's copyboy out for coffee, he was as likely to ask the radio reporter if he wanted some as he was to ask Reporter A, who sat next to him.[14]

Reporters from competing news organizations see one another day after day. Together, they participate in and construct a daily

---

[14]Outside the press room, cooperation between media is more rare. In the early 1960s newspaper reporters pulled the plugs of television cameras and walked in front of running cameras. Seeking to maintain the professional supremacy of newspaper work, in Seaboard City they also disparaged TV reporters, calling them "pretty boys." In New York, by 1977, newspaper reporters were tape recording TV interviews held at City Hall to glean more facts. The newspaper reporters stood where they could not be caught by the camera's lens and extended their tape recorders.

work life. They see members of their own organization more rarely (see Gieber and Johnson, 1961). Indeed, reporters recently transferred to the City Hall bureau spoke of their relative isolation from other members of their own organization and, in one case, from competitors at their former beats. At the Press Club Christmas party, Green (recently transferred from the city room) spoke of missing chats with former colleagues and deskmates and delighting in their presence at the party. Another recently transferred reporter used the party to speak with the city editor in an effort to generate a memorable impression. As the reporter explained privately, the city editor's goodwill was essential for career advancement, and he never ran into him. Additionally, fearing the truth in the saying "Out of sight, out of mind," the reporter also planned periodic visits to the city room. Other newsworkers implied that the editors' knowledge of their competence was limited to judgments based on reading unedited copy and on gleaning gossip from the bureau chief, news sources, bureau members who worked in the city room one day a week, and reporters from several news organizations encountered at parties of mutual friends. The editors could not directly observe whether reporters conformed to organizational dictates; they knew only if the copy was professional and if the reporters stayed out of trouble.

Reportorial cooperation must be attributed to more than proximity. In part, mutual assistance is a case of mutual back scratching. Morris explained that if a competitor had gone to the lavatory and a vital news conference was announced, prompting all reporters to scurry out of the press room, she would pound on the lavatory door to tell him where everyone was going. And she would expect someone to find her or leave a note if she were missing at the time of a vital announcement. But more general principles of collegiality are also involved.[15]

In the course of their careers, reporters, like other professionals, move from one organization to another to obtain promotions,

[15]Observing reporters covering demonstrations at Kent State University in summer 1977, Betty Kirschner (personal communication) noted television crews sharing equipment, such as film and video tape. Apparently, not expecting a good story, some crews had not brought enough. Nonetheless, after an event was judged to be over, the reporters would dash off, trying to beat one another to available telephones. In Seaboard City I observed one reporter tie up three phones to prevent rivals from using them while his two colleagues gathered facts. Two rules seemed to be in operation at Kent State: cooperate in areas where you might need help in the future; and get the story to your organization before the competitor.

raises, and increased status. Socializing with one another, attending some of the same parties, reporters know one another by reputation, if not by face-to-face contact. Having a reputation for professional sharing enhances one's occupational mobility and the warmth with which one is greeted by new colleagues. Reporters working out of city rooms share information when they meet competitors at the scene of a story. After returning to their desks, they may telephone one another to seek limited help. And, when all are faced with a dearth of information, they may pool their "facts." Tom Wicker (1965), one of several *New York Times* newsworkers in Dallas when John Kennedy was shot, recalls that during that national and reportial crisis everyone shared everything with everyone else. Ultimately, of course, such professional cooperation enhances adherence to the prime organizational requirement: getting the story in time to disseminate it.

Sharing within the Organization: We have already met one form of sharing within the bureau. When one reporter enterprises a story in another's specialty, the plundered party is expected to follow professional protocol—to approve and to help—just as a replaced doctor is expected to transmit case records willingly to an ex-patient's newly selected physician. Other forms of cooperation are ongoing and informal. A reporter will look up from typing and ask anyone nearby, "What is [so-and-so's] middle initial?" "How do you spell [X]?" "On what street is John Jay College located?" "What is the interest rate on M.A.C. bonds?" Anyone who knows the answer replies, signaling membership in the group and earning a reputation as a helpful colleague, much as academic competitors give one another pertinent bibliographic references. Any reporter could locate the requested information, just as any academician could eventually locate pertinent articles and books. But locating minor "facts" takes time and only breaks the rhythm of writing. And for a reporter, writing is only too often a race against deadlines. Collegial exchange of middle initials and spellings serves the organizational need of getting work done on time.

Ultimately, though, reporters preserve their professional autonomy by jealously protecting their private sources and specialties from others' encroachment—while trying to poach others' material. A bureau regular might advise a novice to interview the head of the

City Planning Commission, suspecting that man would wield even greater power in the future. Calder advised Green to interview the commissioner before he was promoted to deputy mayor, and so helped Green to meet a very visible source.

When promoted to bureau chief, Adams sought to encroach on Albany's territory, much as Sigal (1973) reports that a new metropolitan editor will offer more than his fair share of stories at the first daily editorial conference he attends. Adams instructed a young reporter, Green, to develop a story about an increase in the commuter income tax being proposed by city members of the state legislature at the request of city officials. To accomplish this task, Green followed what she assumed was routine protocol. She telephoned the Albany bureau chief and requested the phone numbers of key state legislators. When scolded by the Albany chief, Green explained that she was new on the beat and following her instructions. After accepting Green's excuse that she hadn't known any better, the Albany chief then phoned Adams and bawled him out in order to reestablish the appropriate intrabureau relationship. Purportedly, he argued: What business is it of the City Hall bureau to call the State Assembly leader? How would you like it if the Albany bureau infringed on you by calling the president of the City Council about a city bill? Protecting his territory, the Albany chief was also protecting his sources as private property and so protecting against possible future poaching.

Some sociologists might object that this last example is not proof of professional autonomy, for complex bureaucracies are often beset by interdepartmental struggles. Particularly in organizations having overlapping bureaucratic responsibilities, one department will try to assume more power at another's expense. Yet the Albany chief handled the conflict in a way that stressed professional courtesy. He telephoned Adams himself; he did not report Adams to their mutual superior, the city editor, whose admonition would have been based on hierarchical organizational authority. Similarly (as discussed in chapter 2), when an education stringer and a sports reporter appeared at a City Hall news conference, the acting bureau chief scolded each editor himself; he did not invoke a higher authority. Indeed, he mentioned the number of reporters on his staff and said he would have one of them cover any City Hall items either editor needed. Although Butler's admonition protected his territorial preserve and facilitated keeping track of his organization's personnel, his offer of future coverage can also be interpreted as a professional courtesy.

Support for the latter interpretation comes from the system of exchanges explicitly favored by bureau chiefs. Like other reporters, they identified explicit and informal exchanges as "contracts" requested when needed information was located in another's preserve.[16] For instance, before Christmas, the Queens bureau chief wanted to run an insert on dangerous children's toys in the Queens edition of the paper. Rather than call the Department of Consumer Affairs for the information, he phoned the City Hall bureau and requested a contract: If a reporter had time, could someone contact the Department of Consumer Affairs and learn which toys were unsafe? In exchange, as was understood but unstated, a Queens reporter would gather information for the City Hall bureau if needed at a future date and if a reporter were available.

Contracts like this are much like consultation and cooperation among medical specialists. Dayton had to place only one phone call to a source at the Department of Consumer Affairs. After a cordial greeting he asked, "Do you remember last year when we ran a story on dangerous toys? The Queens edition would like to do it again. Do you have that information available yet?" The call completed within two minutes, he advised the bureau chief that the list was being compiled and the Department of Consumer Affairs would send it over. Once in the bureau office, it could be transmitted to Queens via telex at three minutes per page. Within a half hour Dayton advised the Queens chief that the contract had been fulfilled.

Although grounded in professional understandings, this cooperation also aids the organization. It is quicker for a representative of Consumer Affairs to bring material to City Hall for immediate transmission to Queens than it is to mail it to the Queens bureau. Whether such contracts qualify as professional courtesy or organizational exchange, these exchanges demonstrate that reporters and bureaus must be flexible. The news net must be flexible if the news organization is to locate occurrences qualifying as news events. Reporters must be capable of covering everything and anything while

[16]The term "contract" was also used when a reporter from a city newspaper asked a reporter from a suburban newspaper if he would ask a printer friend to print up some Christmas cards for the city reporter.

meeting deadlines. They must know where to get information as expediently as possible.

Clearly, whom one asks for information influences what information one receives. Throughout this chapter I have implied that the bureau reporters seek out centralized sources, politicians, and bureaucrats. I never observed these reporters contacting the leaders of social movements. Nor did they search out grass-roots leaders, preferring instead the leaders of local political clubs. They distinguished among political clubs by pointing to the actual power each wields. They contacted the powerful, the politician with the resources to accomplish his or her ambitions, not the merely dissident or dissatisfied. That people with power serve as sources bears consequences for the information newsworkers uncover, as discussed in chapter 5.

Additionally, of course, reporters must know what questions to ask the source, what "facts" to find. Without having some idea of what might be the heart of the matter, the story to be told, each occurrence could maintain its claim to idiosyncratic treatment and thus increase the variability of occurrences as the raw material of news. Knowing what to ask influences whom one asks: The choice of sources and the search for "facts" mutually determine each other. Together, as will be seen in the next chapter, they flesh out the news frame.

CHAPTER FIVE
The Web of Facticity

"What's the story on Sam?" one coworker might ask another, after noticing Sam moping around the office. "Oh, he's hung up on that woman he's been dating, and they're having trouble," is one possible reply. This response presupposes that each worker knows a bit about "that woman," and it could prompt a follow-up question: "What kind of trouble?" or "What happened now?"

As I have constructed this exchange, it is a request for information including interpretation. Set in the context of the news world, however, the conversation would not be a simple request for possibly unvalidated information; it would be demand for facts. By "facts" I mean pertinent information gathered by professionally validated methods specifying the relationship between what is known and how it is known. Other sorts of inquiry, such as philosophy and science, are also concerned with the relationship between phenomena and knowing. But news procedures are neither contemplative nor geared toward determining essence. Nor are they able to predict and confirm axiomatic statements. Unlike more rigorous and reflective approaches to facticity, newswork is a practical activity geared to deadlines. Facts must be quickly identified. But for newsworkers (as for scientists), having witnessed an occurrence is not sufficient to define one's observation as factual. In science, the problem of facticity is embedded in processes of verification and replication. In news, verification of facts is both a political and a professional accomplishment.

Molotch and Lester (1975) offer a case in which the facts offered as news directly contradicted what newsworkers saw and smelled. In January, 1969, President Nixon came to examine a purportedly clean beach in Santa Barbara to pronounce it recovered from a massive oil spill. A hundred yards away, Molotch and Lester claim, lay the oil slick and assorted debris, yet all the national media proclaimed the beaches clean. How could this have happened? Molotch and Lester argue that professional news practices serve political interests.

In contrast, newsworkers state that finding facts entails demonstrating impartiality by removing oneself from a story. Impartiality includes demonstrating that one does everything possible to be accurate so as to maintain credibility and avoid both reprimands from superiors and the omnipresent danger of libel suits. This chapter explores the relationship between finding facts and using sources, particularly the question of whether the practices of newsworkers reinforce the probablility that the dispersion of the news net will eliminate some occurrences from consideration as news events.

Facts, Sources, and Credibility

According to Anthony Smith, a British newscaster, "Credibility in the minds of the audience is the sine qua non of news" (quoted in the Glascow Media Group, 1976: 7). In my first interview with a newsworker, the vice-president of news at NEWS, I quickly learned the importance of credibility. My initial question was, "What should I know to study news?" I was given a text on libel law.[1] Basic introductory jounalism texts include sections on libel. One (Hohenberg, 1962) devotes a chapter to the structure of news organizations, a chapter to leads (first sentences) for stories, and a chapter to libel,

[1]Gans (1972) points out that libel was not a prime concern of the network and national reporters he observed. However, the importance of libel as an aspect of credibility emerges in Friendly (1976), who discusses the importance of replies to slander in the Fairness Doctrine promulgated by the Federal Communications Commission. (I treat this issue tangentially in chapter 8.)

implicitly identifiying libel as an important matter for the novice journalist. In discussion, editors and reporters from the *Seaboard City Daily* and NEWS immediately mentioned libel when asked about problems confronting news organizations. They also volunteered information about libel suits when asked about difficulties encountered during their careers. Copy thought to be particularly vulnerable to a libel suit, such as an article on the reputed head of the local Mafia, was shown to the *Daily's* lawyer before it reached the copy editors. News organizations routinely save copy in case someone should sue for libel, in order to answer possible questions of intention and in the event of the story's having been cropped for publication.

Libel suits, a hazard of the trade, cost money. Although they are relatively rare, when they do occur they may place the news organization in financial jeopardy. Equally important, the invocation of libel expresses a concern with the paper's reputation for maintaining credibility. If libel suits become widely known, they may endanger an organization's credibility and so potentially decrease sales and profits. The need to maintain credibility explains why most libel suits are settled out of court, even if the news organization believes it could prove its innocence. Additionally, a libel suit disrupts newsroom routine by requiring some staff members to appear in court, thus depleting the news net.

Asked how to avoid libel, *Seaboard City Daily* reporters implicitly cited a key factor in the maintenance of credibility—the mutual determination of fact and source. They asserted that the newsworker must question facts by going to the source. In this context the word "source," unquestioned in the last chapter, is suggestive, connoting a font or point of origin. One may ask how one determines the appropriate point of origin of information—the particular social location that deserves characterization as a source. And how can such sources enable the rapid identification of facts so that deadlines can be met?

Viewing all sources as questionable, news reporters must spend time verifying their statements. Consider the following absurd and hypothetical story produced by questioning the veracity of a source: "Robert Jones and his alleged wife, Fay Smith Jones, yesterday held what they described as a cocktail party at their supposed home, 187 Grand Street, Seaboard City, purportedly in honor of a woman claiming to be Mrs. John Smith, commonly thought to be the aunt of the self-described hostess." Verifying the first fact, that Robert Jones is married to Fay Smith Jones, entails the time-consuming task of checking with one possible source, the appropriate marriage registry. Or the newsworkers could identify the couple as a reputable source and accept their statement that they are married.

Clearly, identifying the appropriate source of information and deciding whether verification is necessary are situationally determined. For instance, if a woman identifying herself as Gloria White Jones, the wife of the same Robert Jones, crashed the party and charged Jones with bigamy, a phone call to the bureau of marriage licenses would be in order. However, in this alternative, the topic of the story would be the alleged bigamy, not a cocktail party. The accusation of a crime, bigamy, requires substantiation because of its potentially libelous nature. Furthermore, writing that Fay Smith Jones is the "alleged wife" of Robert Jones might prove libelous if both Joneses verify the marriage: Use of the term "alleged" imputes their veracity and their social (moral) reputation.

Rules requiring unimpeachable sources and identifying those sources are embedded in socially structured understandings of the everyday world and its institutions. One extreme example, Carl Bernstein and Robert Woodward's investigative reporting of the Watergate conspiracy, highlights this embeddedness. Bernstein and Woodward (1974) write of an editorial ruling that each alleged fact had to be verified by two independent sources. Clearly, that level of substantiation, relatively rare in newswork, was required because of the political power of the web of conspirators, as demonstrated by the subsequent revelation that White House personnel discussed the possible revocation of television licenses held by Bernstein and Woodward's employer, the *Washington Post* (Porter, 1976). A defensive strategy to protect the newspaper and its television stations, this extreme use of verification reveals once more that professional practices meet organizational needs. Equally important, the Bernstein–Woodward reportage reveals that the identification of facts is grounded in everyday methods of attributing meaning to social reality.

Let me contrast the Bernstein–Woodward reporting with the first hypothetical story about Robert Jones and Fay Smith Jones. The Joneses are identified as married, rather than as allegedly married, because they have mutually accomplished a history congruent with that self-presentation. As long as their actions conform to societal notions of how married couples act, there is no apparent reason to verify their claims of being married. But, in and of itself, any one fact uncovered by Bernstein and Woodward contradicts the self-presentation and common understanding of powerful politicians. Viewed as a referent (or as an indexical particular, to use the ethnomethodologist's term), a fact pointing to the identification of the president as a crook contradicts other referents signifying responsibility and power.[2] Furthermore, "crook" and "president" are commonly held to be mutually exclusive identities, each constituted in mutually exclusive particulars. Since the fact that "the president is a crook" goes against common sense, additional verification of additional facts must be amassed to cast the president in his newly proposed identity.

Put somewhat differently, to flesh out any one supposed fact one amasses a host of supposed facts that, when taken together, present themselves as both individually and collectively self-validating. Together they constitute a web of facticity by establishing themselves as cross-referents to one another: A fact justifies the whole (this story is factual), and the whole (all the facts) validates this fact (this particular referent). Mutually validating one another, the facts establish how one can talk about the president-as-crook merely by talking about the president-as-crook. The intermeshed and internally consistent facticity obtains to the president as a person, not to the presidency, an office; to this crook, the president, as an example of crookedness (a complex of moral attributes).

Consideration of an alternative way of viewing the president-as-crook reveals the intermeshing of fact, source, and common understandings. Rather than amass mutually self-validating facts about this president, one could, hypothetically, recast the social and moral attributes of the presidency. One might delegitimate the presidency by robbing it of the sanctity of high office; one might identify the presidency as just another political office (albeit a more powerful one), akin to the office of Democratic club leader in a Chicago ward.[3] In this desanctified context one sees the president as ward

[2] For a discussion of methods of attributing meaning to social reality, see pp. 188–91.

[3] President Nixon experimented with this tactic, distributing information to discredit the political actions of Presidents John Kennedy and Lyndon Johnson.

heeler. And, in this alternative, facts would be used to protect one-self from the powerful, not to maintain credibility while countering everyday understandings of the president as legitimated leader.[4]

In both modes of reporting, the actual Bernstein-Woodward method and the proposed possible alternative, reporters are engaged in the theoretic activity of making sense of the world by constructing meanings. But the second alternative, delegitimating the presidency, threatens the very basis of newswork. Challenging the legitmacy of offices holding centralized information dismantles the news net. If all of officialdom is corrupt, all its facts and occurrences must be viewed as alleged facts and alleged occurrences. Accordingly, to fill the news columns and air time of the news product, news organizations would have to find an alternative and economical method of locating occurrences and constituent facts acceptable as news. For example, if the institutions of everyday life are delegitimated, the facts tendered by the Bureau of Marriage Licenses would be suspect. One could no longer call that bureau to learn whether Robert Jones and Fay Smith had married. In sum, amassing mutually self-validating facts simultaneously accomplishes the doing of newswork and reconstitutes the everyday world of offices and factories, of politics and bureaucrats, of bus schedules and class rosters as historically given.[5]

The examples just contrasted are admittedly extreme and beg the argument that facts are held necessary to maintain credibility and to meet deadlines.[6] To argue that one would not challenge the mar-

---

[4]Facts about the powerful are treated with more care than those about the powerless. Rather (1977: 119) recalls covering the death of John Kennedy: "What did I have? Well, I had a doctor at the hospital who said the President was dead. A priest who said, definitely, he was dead. And the hospital's chief of staff, who had told Eddie Backer [a colleague] he was dead. If you were working the cop shop in Houston, Texas . . . what you had was a dead man." But talking to CBS headquarters in New York, Rather had second thoughts about disseminating that news on national radio and television. He continues, "But this [allegedly dead man] was the President of the United States. . . . If I had been given, say, two seconds to think about it, if someone had asked, 'Do you want us to announce that the President is dead and play the national anthem?' I would have said, whoa, better run that past someone else."

[5]Following Berger and Luckmann's (1967) interpretation of Schutz (1962, 1964, 1966, 1967), one might say the reporters thus objectify those phenomena. See pp. 186, 187, 195-97.

[6]The following letter to the editor (*Newsweek*, 1977:16) is a good example of the association between facts and credibility: "You have continuously lacked a display of objectivity in your reporting on Pakistan. Opinions may differ—as yours certainly do with mine—but the facts are indisputable. The army take-over . . . came on the eve of

riage of the Joneses but would require mutually validating facts to report that the president is a crook is to belabor the obvious. And the Bernstein–Woodward stories on Watergate were primarily investigative *nonscheduled* items, not spot news. Yet the contrast highlights a dependence upon accepted understandings of the social world intrinsic to news.

Taken by itself, a fact has no meaning. Indeed, even "two and two equals four" is factual only within certain mathematical systems or theories. It is the imposition of a frame of other ordered facts that enables recognition of facticity and attribution of meaning. This specific understanding of facts, captured in the Bernstein–Woodward stories, runs through deadline journalism, as seen in the following two examples. In each, the provision of supplementary evidence was said to lend facticity to a story.

One evening the assistant managing editor of the *Seaboard City Daily* informed the city editor that he wanted "more objective obits" after reading an obituary of a deceased "master musician." He asked, "How do we know" the deceased was a "master musician" as opposed to a "two-bit musician" playing with the town band? The city editor replied that several paragraphs into the story one learns that the deceased had played with John Philip Sousa. The additional fact, both editors agreed, justified using the term "master musician" as a statement of fact.[7]

In the second case, more facts were also called for to validate an alleged fact. A reporter criticized the news editors for "bad [nonobjective] editing" when a published story referred to "communist propaganda" seen at a 1968 student demonstration. She claimed the article should have included more "facts," such as the titles of specific observed works. While recognizing that the label "communist propaganda" might not be an accurate characterization of

a government-opposition accord, and not when the talks 'foundered,' as you reported. And as Bhutto's daughter, who was present on the scene, I can assure you that the Prime Minister was not looking 'tousled' and wearing night clothes when he was arrested, the news of the coup was not brought by a military man and Mr. Bhutto did not pace 'across the lawn of his residence.' Nor does he own spaniels. When you cannot report verifiable accounts correctly, it is both regrettable and sad to contemplate the degree to which you have misinformed your readership on Pakistani politics. [Signed] BENAZIR BHUTTO, Karachi."

[7]Note that the editors confused objectivity with a fair assessment of the meaning of indexical particulars. The relationship of objectivity, facts, and fairness is discussed in chapter 8.

each individual piece of literature, she insisted that such a presentation would be more "objective." It would offer "facts" (titles) supporting the initial truth-claim. Furthermore, the titles would presumably enable the reader to assess the degree to which the description "communist propaganda" was accurate and thus "factual."

One wonders, of course, which titles would validate the label "communist propaganda": *Das Kapital*, *The Communist Manifesto*, SDS pamphlets? But even to ask that question is to support the everyday assumption that supplementary facts entail an assessment of truth. Why else would titles validate or invalidate the claim that communist propaganda was seen? Furthermore, to ask about titles, accepts, implicitly, the existence of communist propaganda as a referent for information opposed to American or capitalist interests. If American and capitalist (or anticommunist) interests were not assumed to be identical, the presence of communist propaganda at a student antiwar demonstration would not be a pertinent fact. Rather, students selling SDS pamphlets at a rally would be of no more news interest than worshippers selling Bibles at a church bazaar.[8] Mentioning communist propaganda becomes a device for discrediting *these* college students, who are harboring an AWOL soldier opposed to the Vietnam war, just as cumulative facts discredit Nixon, but not the presidency, in the Bernstein–Woodward Watergate stories.[9]

Nonverifiable Facts

The emphasis on accumulating facts also presupposes that facts can be verified. One can learn whether the Joneses had married, what the Watergate conspirators said and did, with whom the deceased musician played, and the specific titles of observed literature. But newsworkers must also cope with nonverifiable facts, facts that could be verified in theory but not in practice—and certainly not in time for deadlines. Dealing with this problem in the approved pro-

---

[8]The Bibles and other sale items might be noted by a village newspaper.

[9]Note that I just used the reporter's method of adding supplementary information to make this assessment seem credible. That is, I noted that these students were harboring an AWOL soldier.

fessional manner, newsworkers explicitly recognize the mutual embeddedness of fact and source. For rather than recognize a nonverifiable statement as fact, they intermesh fact and source. In the course of accomplishing this copresentation, newsworkers create and control controversies as news.

Relocating Facticity:[10] Suppose a senator claims that America lags behind the Soviet Union in the development of a specific type of missile. Reporters certainly cannot check the claim in time to meet their deadlines. Probably they could never locate adequate information to assess whether the claim is a fact. The reporter can only record (in print or on film) that the senator stated "A." For newsworkers, that Senator X said "A" is fact, even if "A" is false.

This method of reporting creates problems for both the newsworker and the news organization. First, the news consumer supposedly wants to know whether statement "A" is a "fact," and news purports to tell the news consumers what they want and need to know. Second, since the senator's claim to truth cannot be verified, news consumers may accuse both the reporter and the news organization of bias (of "favoring" the senator) if an opposing opinion is not presented. For instance, if the senator is a Republican and the president is a Democrat, some news consumers might accuse the newspaper of bias favoring the Republicans because the only "fact" reported was the Republican senator's statement. If the charge is made, the reporter's and newspaper's claims to credibility in the face of anticipated criticism have been endangered.

Although a reporter cannot himself confirm the truth of the senator's charge, he can contact someone who can. For instance, in this hypothetical case, the newsworker can ask the secretary of defense (a Democrat) if the senator's charge is true. If the secretary states that the charge is false, the reporter cannot prove that the secretary's assessment is "fact," but the reporter can write that the secretary of defense stated "B." Presenting both truth-claim "A," attributed to the senator, and truth-claim "B," attributed to the secretary of defense, the reporter may then claim to have been fair by presenting "both sides of the story" without favoring either politician or political party. Furthermore, by presenting both truth-claims, the profes-

[10]In Goffman's (1974) terms, the following discussion concerns a key by which information is transcribed from one multiple reality to another.

sional reporter theoretically allows the news consumer to decide who is telling the truth. Like doctors who offer a service by telling patients the probable success of different medical options, reporters absolve themselves of responsibility by structuring the alternatives. As previously argued, that necessary framework is implicit in the context of assumed legitimacy.

Extending the example helps clarify the context of assumed legitimacy. While asserting truth-claim "B," the secretary of defense may charge that the senator is playing politics with national defense. The chairperson of the House Arms Committee, a Republican, may then counter the secretary's charge, stating that the Democratic administration is endangering national safety through inadequate intelligence and cavalier treatment of the budget for arms development. The next day, the national head of a peace group may call a press conference to accuse all parties to the controversy of militarism, claiming that the politicans are overemphasizing weapons development to the detriment of a determined exploration of a diplomatic search for world peace and security. A spokesperson for the president may then condemn the leader of the peace group as a communist sympathizer trying to undermine the American political process. At this point there are five persons (the senator, the secretary, the committee chairperson, the peace-group leader, and the presidential spokesperson) making nonverifiable truth-claims, each presenting one possible reality. Four of them are representing legitimated institutions with access to centralized information. Only one, the head of the peace group, is challenging the context in which news is generated. Thus, at one and the same time, the newsworkers are creating and controlling controversy. That is, they have presented four versions of the same legitimated reality: Democrats versus Republicans; Congress versus the executive branch. Even the representative of the peace group has quasi legitimation. The group's claims are undercut by a lack of information pertinent to the specific debate: How does the group know what diplomatic channels have been tried and abandoned? But the group's representative holds a recognized status as a national leader of concerned people. The group's leader is not merely one dissident.

Editors are particularly apt to invoke the distinction between legitimation and quasi legitimation. For instance, during the social ferment of the 1960s editors asked one another, "How many people does that guy represent?'' as they purposively played down coverage of some civil-rights leaders and antiwar groups. NEWS stopped broadcasting films showing leaders of the Student Nonviolent Coordinating Committee and of Students for a Democratic Society. Aware that airing the different groups' activities constituted quasi legitimation, the editors feared that the telecasts would recruit more followers for groups questioning the premises of the American political system. The editors' model for determining quasi legitimacy depended upon numerical accretion: the more members, the more legitimate their spokesperson.

This reasoning was also invoked in a beat reporter's comparison of the importance of covering the women's movement and of covering city politics, both assignments she had held. The New York chapter of the National Organization for Women has perhaps 10,000 members, she said. In contrast, the city government employs 300,000. That the reporter mentioned NOW is itself significant, for she did not touch upon any of the smaller feminist groups that challenge the legitimacy of the American political system.[11]

Most important, in all the time I've spent observing reporters and editors, I've never heard them challenge the right of an elected or appointed official to make news. Rather, the assumption is that the holder of a legitimated status speaks for the government. All others must demonstrate their relationship to a more amorphous entity—the public. Indeed, Gieber and Johnson (1961) argue that this distinction is built into the very language of reporters and reporting. At the City Hall bureau of a California town, they observed that "the city" was used as a referent for politicans (as in "The city is trying to balance its budget"). Citizens were "the public" (as in "The public must pull together in this crisis, as the city does its best to balance the budget").[12]

Working distinctions among legitimate newsmakers, quasi-legitimate newsmakers, and the amorphous public imply gradations in whose truth-claims may be reported and framed as fact. Again the power of legitimate sources comes into play.

[11]Similarly, political reporters deal with Democrats and Republicans (and in New York, with the Liberal and Conservative parties). They do not report on the Trotskyites, the Progressive Labor party, and other such groups that challenge the legitimacy of the political system.

[12]Again there is an exception. During a crime wave, the "city" is the populace, as in "the city, terrorized by the 44-caliber-killer. . . ."

Imputing Facts: Located in an institutionalized news net, reporters and editors accumulate experience with complex organizations and interorganizational relationships. On the basis of that experience, identified as the arcane knowledge implicit in news judgment, newsworkers make three generalizations:

1. Most individuals, as news sources, have an axe to grind. To be believed, an individual must prove his or her reliability as a news source.
2. Some individuals, such as committee heads, are in a position to know more than other people in an organization. Although they may have an axe to grind, their information is probably more "accurate" because they have more "facts" at their disposal.
3. Institutions and organizations have procedures designed to protect both the institution and the people who come into contact with it. The significance of either a statement or a "no comment" must be assessed according to the newsworker's knowledge of institutional procedures.

Each generalization emphasizes a key assumption about the organization of newswork and finding facts. The first generalization, proven reliability of sources, necessarily favors sources met through institutionalized beats. To prove reliability one must at some time have ongoing contact with reporters.[13] The second generalization, that some sources have more facts than others, draws on the professional assumption that facts are mutually self-validating. The more facts one has access to, the better one's chances of knowing what is going on. The third generalization builds upon the other two and, additionally, assumes the inherent rectitude of legitimated organizations.

Newsworkers lump these three generalizations together, speaking of how "something makes sense" intuitively. The following example illustrates the preference for institutionalized sources rather than information offered by the average or involved citizen.

A father who had been advised that he might be charged with child neglect resulting in the death of his daughter from cystic

---

[13]Shibutani (1966) reports that newsworkers ignored the information that a Nazi war criminal, scheduled for execution, had already died in his cell. The guard who reported the death to reporters waiting outside the prison walls was not a known and tested source. (See also Goldenberg, 1975.)

fibrosis visited the city room of the *Seaboard City Daily* to protest his innocence. A story concerning the father's protestations was approved by the suburban news editor but rejected by the local news editor and the assistant managing editor, who insisted that the suburban news editor should have known better than to approve the story. These dissenting editors based their rejection on two factors: the story contained too many unanswered questions, and the editors' imputed meaning of the police department's behavior. As one of them put it, "When the police and the district attorney put up a flap, you know something is wrong." He insisted, "Newspapers have to follow the legal steps as they appear in a normal arrest–indictment–trial sequence, unless the newspapers are convinced there has been a miscarriage of justice. . . . Then newspapers can pull out all the stops and crusade for the accused."

This case involved too many unanswered questions. For instance, the submitted story did not say if the child had been under medical treatment. The editors asked if the child would have died if not neglected. More importantly, when the local news editor phoned the police, seeking additional information about the father, the police "clammed up." On the basis of their experience with police procedure, these editors assumed that the police were considering arresting the man. Since the "police would not arrest" without the legal evidence required to prove a case in court, the editors concluded that "there's something fishy about this." To run the story, the men felt they had to get "more facts" that countered a logical assessment of police procedure. Presenting supplementary evidence, the newspaper could claim it had been objective. As one editor put it, "The story is similar to one about a man whose wife has been murdered, and the man has not been arrested, but he has been told not to leave town. The man goes to all the newspapers and tries to clear himself of an accusation not yet made. If a week later the man is indicted for murder and we have printed his story, *how do we, the newspaper, look?*"

A similar gradation of sources is found in coverage of civil disorders and demonstrations. Kapsis et al. (1970) find that news reports of riots draw heavily upon police versions of occurrences rather than citizens' accounts.[14] Similarly, news reports of student

---

[14]At issue again is the importance of centralized sources to newswork and how newswork legitimates those sources. (See also Glasgow Media Group, 1976.)

strikes use university sources (public-relations officers and administrators) to estimate how many students attend classes—despite the obvious self-interest explicit in the official account. Estimates of the effectiveness of union strikes are taken from such legitimated officials as union heads and industry spokespersons to present conflicting truth-claims, rather than from workers or shop stewards.[15] Similarly, coverage of the Senate Watergate Committee centered on the remarks of Democratic chairperson Sam Erwin and ranking Republican Howard Baker rather than on the other senators.

The Judicious Use of Quotation Marks: Ultimately, the use of graded sources who may be quoted as offering truth-claims is converted into a technical device designed to distance the reporter from phenomena identified as facts. Quotations of other people's opinions are presented to create a web of mutually self-validating facts. Again, a discussion among *Seaboard City Daily* editors provides an example.

A slum building, owned by an absentee landlord, had been without heat for several days in near-zero-degree temperature. When contacted, the landlord claimed that someone was fixing the furnace at that moment. When the local news editor called the building, no one was working on the heating unit, a "fact" he added to the reporter's story. Checking the story, the assistant managing editor told his subordinate local editor to contact more tenants of the building and to increase the number of names mentioned in the story. The assistant managing editor said, "If you can get me more [quotations from tenants] we'll [print] it." After a while he repeated that he wanted more people quoted, because "I've had too much trouble." Without supporting evidence, the story may be libelous.

Adding more names and quotations as mutually determining facts, the newsworkers may achieve distance from the story by getting others to express desired opinions. For example, the reporters may remove their own opinions from the story by getting others to say what they themselves think. Thus a reporter covering a concerned group's visit to a federal attorney, to request action on the killing of black students in Orangeburg, South Carolina, asked a

---

[15]To be sure, some workers are occasionally interviewed, but they are treated as symbols. See chapter 6 for a discussion of representativeness, representation, and symbols.

minister for his reaction to the lawyer's behavior. The minister answered, "We have a great deal of concern for what is going on. It's unfortunate that our concern was responded to in a way that really didn't recognize that when people have been killed, a great deal of emotion evolves, which is not taken care of by telling people to hurry along." The reporter then asked, "To put it briefly, are you dissatisfied?" The minister replied, "I think there was unnecessary harshness." After a pause he concluded, "Rudeness is the word." As we left, the reporter explained to me that he had interviewed the minister specifically to get those statements so as to avoid editorializing that the federal attorney was rude.

Quotation marks do more than remove the reporter's voice from a story and signal "This statement belongs to someone other than the reporter." They also may be used to indicate "so-called." For instance, in the 1960s the New Left (*without* quotation marks) was the name of a specific group. The "New Left" (*with* quotation marks) indicated a group calling itself the New Left; in this case the legitimacy of the group is questioned.

Impressed by a draft-resistance demonstration, a reporter used quotation marks in all possible ways to appease his editors, whom he knew to be opposed to the demonstration. He wrote:

> Some [thousands of] persons swarmed to a sunny [city] Park yesterday where an "incredibly successful" antidraft, antiwar rally was climaxed when more than [several hundred] youth turned in their draft cards.
>
> The tenor of the 2 1/2-hour demonstration was that a "New Left" movement is growing and must be enlarged to erase present American policy and "build an America we won't be ashamed to live in."
>
> The Park protest was the [Seaboard City] segment of coast-to-coast demonstrations in 60 cities called National Resistance Day. The two-day event concludes today with "political workshops" in the [city] area.
>
> The [city] Park rally was relatively free from violence considering the huge throng, mostly young people. City Deputy Supt. [John Smith], in charge of the police detachment, said, "Only two or three fights, quickly broken up, marred an otherwise perfect day."

Quotations in the first three paragraphs were taken from speeches given at the rally, although their source was not identified in the story. Although the reporter personally agreed with all the statements and terms enclosed in quotation marks, the quotation marks enabled him to claim that he had not interjected his opinions into the story. A professional's technical device, quotation marks, made the story factual and protected the reporter from his superiors. This reporter received most of the demonstration assignments, although he was sympathetic to the demonstrators and his editors were not. Had his sympathies been perceived, he would not have been sent to future demonstrations, or his stories would have been substantially altered. They were not heavily edited. Rather, among themselves, the editors praised this reporter's work. In effect, the reporter manipulated his superiors, interjecting his own views, by following professional procedures for finding facts.[16]

Of course, the use of quotation marks is embedded in the news net. It presupposes having a source to quote. Yet just as facts may be nonverifiable, so, too, sources may not produce appropriate quotations. Additionally, news organizations may wish to present analyses of the facts, stories sustaining an argument independent of an interlocking web of mutually validating facts. The bureaucratic dispersion of newsworkers through time and space, formalized as a feature of the news product, permits explicitly interpretive analysis to be accomplished.[17]

Facts and the Form of News Presentations

The dispersion of reporters by territory, institutional specialization, and topic is formalized in the division of a newspaper or newscast. A newspaper is divided into sections and pages. Its first pages contain factual (objective) general stories, potentially drawing from anywhere and everywhere in the news net. Specialized topical subjects, such as sports, women's, and financial news, appear on clearly delineated pages placed together in separate sections. General stories in which the reporter stands as the source of facts are placed on

[16]The scheduling of shifts enabled the reporter to protect his political views from editorial supervision. The reporter came to work at 8:00 A.M. and left before 6:00 P.M. The copy desk and make-up editors handling his work started their shift at 6:00 P.M.

[17]I use the phrase "explicitly interpretive analysis" to differentiate these stories from others. All stories are necessarily interpretive analyses, because the identification of facts is always an interpretive and pretheoretic enterprise. (See Garfinkel, 1967; Zimmerman and Pollner, 1970; and chapter 9 of this volume.)

either the editorial or the "op ed" page (the page opposite the editorial page). On newspapers there are only two exceptions to this rule. One is the soft-news feature story explicitly immune from the professional requirement of presentation through a web of facticity. On some newspapers the feature story is only a partial exception. For instance, the *New York Times* runs general soft news on the first page of its second section. The other exception is the "news analysis" that may be published on the general pages, if accompanied by the distinct formal label "news analysis."

Television news shows contain similar formal distinctions. Local news shows schedule specific time slots for sports and weather. Some set aside two minutes for editorials and editorial replies, directly following the newscast. Hour-long newscasts and those lasting two hours (like WNBC's weekday evening program) carry recurring features at prescheduled times. Included are movie reviews, consumer reports, and an investigative story (an exploration of a single topic carried for five minutes on each of five consecutive days). National telecasts also use timing as a formal device. For instance, the evening news (like some local programs) frequently ends with a "kicker," a feature story designed to keep the audience smiling. Charles Kurault's "On the Road" stories serve this function for the CBS program. Special labels may identify stories in which the reporter is presented as the source. For instance, when Eric Sevareid intoned his wisdom on CBS, the words "news analysis" or "commentary" were superimposed on the television screen. Walter Cronkite's introduction explicitly stated that Sevareid was offering "*his* analysis" or "*his* comments."

Such formal devices place a barrier between the problematic story and other stories. Just as quotation marks theoretically establish a distance between the reporter and a story, signaling that the materials enclosed may be problematic, the label "news analysis" indicates that the material neither represents the opinions of the management nor is necessarily "true." The presentation is the reporter's interpretation of the "facts." Readers or viewers should trust and accept the reporter's information according to their assessment of his or her qualifications and attitudes, as revealed in the reporter's general work and previous news analyses. Labeling some items as other than "objective facts" also reinforces the claim that most stories present facts, for it signals, "This news organization is seriously concerned with distinctions between factual and interpretive materials."

As with the distinction between hard and soft news, newsworkers find it difficult to distinguish between fact and interpretation. When I observed reporters in Seaboard City, my question, "How is objective reporting different from news analysis?" was the most difficult for newsworkers to answer. Several reporters and an assistant city editor indicated their reluctance to put their "professional instinct" into words by saying they did not know. The managing editor of the Sunday paper smiled and patted the local news editor on the back when I asked the local news editor that question. An adjunct professor of journalism at a local college, the local news editor tackled the question. After rambling for several minutes without being able to focus on the key distinction, he said:

> News analysis implies value judgments. Straight news has no value judgments whatsoever. . . . You can't eliminate the label "news analysis" and say anything. No, I'd say an alarm goes off in the editor's mind who thinks, "This is loaded and I want to get off the hook." [Although] the reader thinks the label . . . [is] weighty and ponderous, the key point is the number and degree of value judgments undocumented at the time.

But he could not say what invariably determines the "number and degree of value judgments undocumented at the time." Like achieving the identification of facts, determining value judgments was said to rest on professional instincts, including reliability of sources and the nature of the story itself.

It is not surprising that newsworkers found the "intuitively obvious" distinction between fact and value judgment difficult to explain. First, facing the problem means considering how much all identification of facts is embedded in specific understandings of the everyday world. As we have seen, those understandings presuppose the legitimacy of existing institutions and are the basis of the news net. To examine the distinction between fact and value judgment, then, is to be willing to examine seriously the indexical and reflexive nature of news as knowledge. It is to acknowledge that news frames strips of everyday occurrences and is not a mere mirror of events. And it is to acknowledge that the activities of American news professionals are geared to maintaining the American political system as much as the work of Soviet journalists is geared to preserving that nation's political system. It is also to cast aside the identification of news as a crusade for truth.

Second, examining the distinction between facts and value judgments challenges existing professional techniques for telling stories. Those techniques simultaneously confirm the existence of a distinction and enable a distinction to be made. Newsworkers identify facts with hard news and one mode of storytelling. They associate soft news with quite a different mode.

Gitlin (1977) parodies the mode of hard news by comparing it to a line from an old television show: "Just the facts, Ma'am." The parody works because it takes off from the old journalist's lead sentence or sentences concerned with who, what, where, when, why, and how—the basic material for a news story. For instance, the reporter who used quotations to write the story on the antidraft demonstration explained to me: "First I'll lead with the most material things. . . . How many people were there—that's the story . . . the number of draft cards turned in. . . . In the second [paragraph], I'll set the tone. Then I'll go into the speeches. The hard facts go first."

This reporter realized that someone else might identify different facts as central to the story. After skimming an account of the demonstration in an afternoon paper, he called it "biased." He complained that "there were thousands of people there [at the demonstration] and maybe all but a few were peaceful, yet [the other paper's reporter] led with an incident about violence." But both stories could claim hard-news facticity so long as both followed professional storytelling devices. For instance, the stories could be structured lead followed by documentation in decreasing order of judged documentary importance, the classic "inverted pyramid" of journalistic narratives (a style common to many forms of non-fiction).[18] Or the stories could be structured in block style, with a series of leads, each immediately followed by pertinent supporting facts serving as documentation. As explained in journalism texts (e.g., Hohenberg, 1962), each form carries facticity and each facilitates professional newswork by enabling editors to omit paragraphs in ascending order of importance working from the bottom to fit the story into the available space.

[18]The stories may also be viewed as formal narratives. Although the popular culture uses "narrative" to refer to a fictional account, any story is necessarily a narrative exposition as it structures items and has a beginning, middle, and end.

The soft-news genre, nonscheduled news, is presented in a more varied narrative, divorced from the lead–documentation structure. The lead sentence may turn on a twist of words. It may back into a story by presenting an unattributed quotation or generalization that is subsequently specified. The article may have a surprise ending, like a short story by Edgar Allan Poe. It may attribute motivation or human qualities to animals and inanimate objects. It may parody. It may move from one narrator to another, building suspense and leading to a denouement. In short, eschewing the mode of lead–documentation, the mode of facticity, such an article may be difficult to edit. These pieces are often removed from the routines associated with deadline journalism and demand nonscheduled editorial care. Significantly, because feature stories evoke a different mode of narration, they are said to require special professional skills, particularly a light touch as opposed to the heavy hand of amassed facts.

The special skills identified with feature stories supplement the claim to professionalism rather than challenge it. General editors may take pride in their ability to edit features; headline writers in their ability to write a complementary parody or joke; film editors in their ability to construct finely tuned sequences lasting seconds. Indeed, as stories prompting special professional skills, feature stories are much like topical departmental news carried on page one. Giving me an avuncular lesson in newswork, the assistant managing editor of the *Seaboard City Daily* explained that particular editorial care must be taken with fashion, sports, or financial news carried on page one because the general reader might not be familiar with the special vocabularies, assumptions, and ongoing contexts in which topical news is framed. This similarity to feature stories confirms the characterization of general news as a web of mutually self-validating facts, for it confirms intermeshed facticity, embedded in everyday understandings, as an accomplished feature of general news.

Finding Facts

The notion of different modes of narrative serves as a method of guiding reporters to locate appropriate facts. Questions to be asked are contained in the form of presentation.[19] Consider two seemingly disparate stories. In the first, a toddler fell out of an open tenement window. In the second, the governor's first grandchild died of an infant pulmonary disease. The stories are intrinsically different in the way they become news: The death of an infant of ordinary lineage from a common disease is not intrinsically newsworthy, but the death of the governor's first grandchild is. In contrast, telling of the death of the tenement child constitutes a public warning to news consumers to safeguard open windows during hot summer months. Also, the tenement death was handled by a general reporter, the death of the governor's grandchild by a political reporter.

Yet Jane Morris, the political reporter in this instance, implies that the frame used to handle the tenement death guided her ability to write about the governor's grandchild. Reading the newspaper, she, like other reporters, asked herself, with whom did my colleague speak to get this information? And why is this information here? Upon reading the story of the tenement death she noted that the reporter had asked neighbors about the child to detail aspects of his personality. She particularly noted the technique, because asking a parent about a just-deceased child is a most unpleasant task. Assigned to cover the death of the governor's grandchild, she called his friends and members of his "political neighborhood" to ask about the infant's physical characteristics and personality.

Similarly, using the frame of facticity, reporters may lump even more disparate events together. For instance, any sort of spot news may be called a "fire story," indicating that routine techniques of finding facts are used. Addressing a Columbia University interdisciplinary seminar about United Nations coverage, one New York daily's UN reporter bemoaned the set themes of coverage, particularly the persistence of the cold-war sports drama—the United States versus the Soviet Union. He spoke of the need for in-depth background treatments, for interpretation and analysis. Yet, when asked if he ever covered other sorts of stories, he beamed as he told of tracking information pertinent to the explosion of a bomb at La Guardia airport. Despite the clear divorce of his present assignment from on-site destruction, he enthusiastically proclaimed, "I love covering a fire!" His exclamation echoes newsworkers' professional critiques of one

[19]Scientific articles may also be seen as narratives guiding the location of facts (Gusfield, 1976).

another: "He can't even cover a fire" or "He can only cover a fire."[20] For a fire is a basic spot-news story, standing near the center of the hard-news narrative repertoire. Dealing with a known form, the reporter knows which facts to seek from which centralized sources, even as the reporter searches out that story's idiosyncratic angle (Altheide, 1976).

As known story forms (lead–documentation) demanding facts and sources, "the fire," "the trial," "the political convention," "the lost child," "the death of the president" reduce the idiosyncrasy of occurrences as news. Accepted as professional tools and extensions of news typifications, the different approaches to set story forms may, of course, lead the reporter to the wrong conclusions, and so hamper coverage. Assumptions about the power of the presidency, implicit in news narratives and gradations of sources, led newsworkers to predict, as a matter of course, Lyndon Johnson's victory in the 1968 Democratic primary in New Hampshire (Tuchman, 1972: 673, 674). Those same assumptions led them to believe that Johnson would run for reelection despite his defeat. Ultimately, of course, Johnson "violated" those assumptions by declining to run for reelection. In so doing, he produced a "what-a-story."

In the processing of that what-a-story, described in chapter 3, one sees the reliance on known narrative forms. While ordering the web of facticity, known routines were instituted. The invocation of Calvin Coolidge; reporters writing about the responses of legitimated and quasi-legitimated leaders (selected by gradations of power and representiveness); the expectation that the wire services would produce specific stories—all attest to professional knowledge of the appropriate questions to ask appropriate sources. All these confirm that the omnipresence of the web of facticity (including its implicit validation of existing social and political institutions) both guides the search for news and perpetually reconstitutes itself as the frame for news.

---

[20] A newspaper reporter made the first comment about a colleague. The second comment, a criticism of a cameraman, was made by two other cameramen at the observed television station.

CHAPTER SIX
Representation and the News Narrative

Attributing to news narratives the power to raise certain questions and to ignore others may seem to digress from this book's argument. Rather than demonstrate that news is a product of specific ways of organizing newswork, it suggests that the formal characteristics of the product of newswork guide inquiry. The power of forms cannot be dismissed. Consider a relatively self-contained example involving language: A conversational gambit frequently used by women and children, "Guess what?" mandates the attentive reply "What?" and so structures some conversational interactions among spouses as well as exchanges between parents and children (P. Fishman, 1978; West and Zimmerman, 1977). And both art and literary critics have long demonstrated that conventions associated with forms guide perception as inquiry. Not only do art and literature reflect the culture in which they are produced, they also speak directly to the history of art and literary traditions.

News narratives have their own history. The use of film and videotape in television news has evolved over two decades, announcers

An earlier version of pp. 110–21, 131–32 appeared in "The Technology of Objectivity: Doing 'Objective' TV News Film." *Urban Life and Culture* 2:1 (April 1973): 3–26. Reprinted by permission of the publisher, Sage Publications, Inc.

having switched from reading hand-held copy on-camera to a more artful integration of sound and visual image.[1] Similarly, the language and format of newspaper reporting have evolved and grown since Benjamin Day introduced the *New York Sun* and, with it, the popular press. Since the 1920s lead sentences have grown shorter. There has been an increased use of techniques associated with magazine writing, including dramatic lead sentences, as Hohenberg (1962) points out. In television the evolution of news conventions has been prompted by the medium's capacity to involve viewers and, once they are involved, to sell the viewers' attention to advertisers.[2] For newspapers, the slow transformation to more open space over the past twenty years—shorter sentences and lighter (whiter) pages—has been an effort to combat the news consumers' increasing dependence upon television news. However, in both media newsworkers identify contemporary formal conventions with professionalism—knowing how to tell a story with a minimum of supervisory guidance.

This chapter explores some contemporary conventions of news storytelling to learn how they support organizational and professional needs to control work. It also asks how those conventions maintain the web of facticity. Thus, instead of viewing formal attributes of news stories as self-contained phenomena, it places them in the context of the organization of work.

Constructing Narratives as an Accessible Craft Skill

To newsworkers, the ability to build narratives is a professional skill, learned in an earlier day through years of craft apprenticeship. City Hall bureau reporters over the age of forty-five speak of having spent five to ten years learning those skills as copyboys. Among the younger reporters, specialized college courses or graduate training

[1]The best history of electronic journalism is Barnouw's (1966, 1968, 1970) three-volume work.

[2]Television executives were slow to realize that news could be profitable. But by the 1970s news was being designed with the aid of consumer research. The "happy talk" of on-camera newscasters is a product of that research, often decried as nonprofessional. See Schudson (1978) for a discussion of similar conflicts in journalism during the 1880s.

honed writing abilities.[3] For both groups, the proof of skill is the ability to rise above accepted narrative forms, such as the inverted-pyramid or block styles, and still create a story that maintains the web of facticity and builds drama. Creative professional writing may be represented by a lead sentence that backs into an inverted pyramid. Omitting the "what" and "when" from the lead may serve to whet the reader's curiosity. Professionalism may mean breaking those rules that serve as bibles for hacks.[4]

For some reporters, professionalism means lightly edited copy. For others, it means rarely reading their published articles, since they find editing either offensive to their autonomy or destructive to their intent. Editors see their professionalism as the ability to rework reporters' sentences so as to improve upon their intent and to locate still unanswered questions. For both editors and reporters, professionalism means following the dictates of their organization's style, sometimes formalized in a style book, as at the *New York Times*.

What makes the news narrative intrinsically different from other narrative forms? Some characteristics of news writing are obvious. Stories are written in the past tense, headlines in the present. Paragraphs are short, perhaps one to three sentences. Sentences generally contain fewer than twenty words and avoid words of more than two syllables. Word order is different from that of spoken language: "Vice-President Spiro Agnew earlier today condemned the news media at a conference of . . . in Des Moines" rather than "Earlier today, Vice-President Spiro Agnew condemned the news media, while speaking at a conference of . . . held in Des Moines."[5] As the Committee on Public Doublespeak of the National Council of Teachers of English frequently points out, newswriting is often "news-speak," full of awkward lengthy sentences, packed with nouns connoting facticity, and replete with such hackneyed transitions as "meanwhile" and "elsewhere." That we are all immersed in news-speak, even though newsworkers often condemn it, makes that language even more difficult to describe and analyze. The analyst is

[3]The distinction between college-trained reporters and apprentices was also found in the 1880s.

[4]Hacks, of course, may see themselves as professionals. Here I am using the term "professional" to refer to those who have reached the summit of their occupation. In contrast, "hacks" refers to those whose work is denigrated as routine by these professionals.

[5]These examples are *not* direct quotations from news accounts.

placed in the position of the protagonist of Moliere's *Le Bourgeois Gentilhomme*, discovering that he has been speaking prose all along. Yet, clearly, the language of news prose contains a special relationship to the everyday world, for, like any other language, it both frames and accomplishes discourse. It is perception and it guides perception; it reconstitutes the everyday world.[6]

The language of television news film is a recently evolved foreign tongue we have all learned to translate but that few of us speak. Precisely because that language is quickly grasped, it makes accessible some presuppositions of news. The visual rendition of the web of facticity, it also serves the interests of news organizations in controlling work by decreasing the variability of raw materials, and it serves the newsworker's professional interests by enabling autonomy and protecting his or her intent.

Unlike written copy, film and videotape maximize the reporters' and cameramen's intent. One can change the written word, but cannot easily alter the recorded spoken word to insert a new phrase. Nor can one change the distance between camera and speaker, the framing of the picture, short of filming again. Some alteration is, of course, possible. One can reorder sequences of film to create an argument unintended by the person filmed or the one filming. But there are distinct limits to the alternatives possible without refilming. Those limits mean that the rules governing the visual language of news film must be more explicit and hence more accessible than the rules governing the written and spoken word.

Unfortunately, analysts of news do not customarily treat news film as a visual language. Rather, they naively suppose that news film captures reality without imposing its own rules. To be sure, echoing an early essay by Lang and Lang (1953), analysts may ask what has been omitted from the camera's frame. But since news film is a moving picture, critics give in to what might be called the "representational temptation." Worth describes that temptation this way:

> It would, of course, be tempting to argue that pictorial events—at least those on a "representational" level—are meaningful because they are signs that have an iconic relation to the "real world"; that, in contrast to verbal events . . . recognition of pictures is physiologically easier; and that, therefore, assumptions of existence are more reasonably

[6]See Giddens (1976) for a discussion of language use as the constitution of the social world (see also Turner, 1974).

made. Given this tempting argument, one can then continue by saying that when we look at pictures, meaning is developed by . . . a simple "natural" process of recognition without codes, conventions, and social schemata [1978: 19, 20].

However, as Worth points out:

Gombrich (1971) has forever spoiled this temptation by calling our attention to Alain's brilliant *New Yorker* cartoon. . . . [O]nce we are confronted with the "person" on the modeling stand and the different "people" doing the drawing, it is difficult to take the position that what we call "representational" drawing is in fact representational *because* it is the way the eye sees [1978: 20].

Rather, the term "representational," whether applied to drawing, photographs, or news film, must refer to codes, conventions, and social schemata, identified as representational by members of a specific culture (see figure 6-1).

Anthropological work on conventions of documentary filmmaking in nonindustrial cultures suggests that television news film builds upon conventions of representation. Adair, Worth, and their students have instructed Navajos, deaf-mutes, and ghetto adolescents on the operation of cameras and editing devices. Left on their own to discover shots and sequences, these filmmakers produced cinematic variations of their verbal languages and storytelling traditions. For instance, Navajo silent films contain a plethora of walking sequences, recreating the role of walking as a connective between two activities, as in Navajo oral narratives. The makers of these films go out of their way to avoid close-ups of faces. And, interestingly, the films are far more accessible to Navajo speakers than to English speakers. Worth and Adair (1970: 22) report the reaction of a monolingual Navajo to a *silent* film made by a bilingual Navajo artist. She said, "I cannot understand English. It was telling all about [the subject of the film] in English, which I couldn't understand."

This Navajo's reaction to the silent film warns us to avoid the representational temptation, and suggests that we should regard television news film as professionally and organizationally produced patterns of news culture. To be sure, news film presents itself to us as actual representations, not as symbols and signs manipulated by set conventions. This self-presentation is specifically contained in the word used by newsworkers and filmmakers to indicate film taken of events in progress. Applied to demonstrations, wars, public meet-

FIGURE 6-1
Drawing by Alain; © 1955 The New Yorker Magazine, Inc.

ings, and other sorts of seemingly nonstaged gatherings, that term is "actuality." Following the Navajo's warning, though, one must understand the claim to actuality and actual representation as a claim to facticity and as a visual rendition of the web of facticity. To paraphrase Goffman (1974: 450), the acceptance of representational conventions as facticity makes reality vulnerable to manipulation. Identifying those conventions as artful manipulations enables one to regard filmed events as social accomplishments—the product of newswork.

News Film and Cultural Definitions of Facticity

News film casts an aura of representation by its explicit refusal to give the appearance of manipulating time and space. Instead, its use of time and space announces that the tempo of events and spatial arrangements have *not* been tampered with to tell this story. By seeming *not* to arrange time and space, news film claims to present facts, not interpretations. That is, the web of facticity is embedded in a supposedly neutral—not distorted—synchronization of film with the rhythm of everyday life. Like the construction of a newspaper story, the structure of news film claims neutrality and credibility by avoiding conventions associated with fiction. To associate distortion (lack of neutrality) with the conventions of fiction both limits the filmic vocabulary and defines fact by contrast, much as the label "news analysis" on a specific newspaper article reinforces the facticity of stories presented without that label.

Consider the dimension of *time*. In film, time is captured by shooting sequences of frames at a standard number of frames per second. (Videotape uses a related phenomenon of electronic pulses.) The number of frames shot per second can be altered to achieve special effects. For instance, fast motion may introduce humor, as in silent-movie chase sequences or the classic newsreel of the family of time-motion-study experts Gilbreth and Carey (1963) described in *Cheaper by the Dozen*. Slow motion may introduce tenderness or love.[7] Sequences of this sort are so common in television commercials that they approach a cultural cliché: lovers with soft, shining hair and/or glistening teeth gamboling in slow motion across pastoral settings.

When cameramen[8] at NEWS erred by shooting in fast or slow motion, they were scolded by their superiors. If the rhythm of the film could not be corrected during projection, as a rule, the film would be discarded because it might impugn the credibility of the news organization. But there are exceptions to this rule.

One obvious exception is sports film, in which slow motion is used to enable viewers to see and judge for themselves a player's technical skill or a referee's acumen. Significantly, sports film is encased in its own segment of the news telecast, and traditionally, in

[7]It may be difficult to eliminate the implication of tenderness from slow-motion film. Appearing on television, George Roy Hill, the director of *Butch Cassidy and the Sundance Kid*, discussed the filming in slow motion of a scene in which the "heroes" kill for the first time. Originally the scene was shot from several angles. The director had planned to weave together short segments of these takes. But he could not use the resulting sequence; it was too beautiful.

[8]All the persons operating cameras at NEWS were men. Men also monopolize the new minicam technology.

that segment, announcers may interpretatively analyze the activities of sports figures and teams and may favor the home teams. Like citing the titles of the "communist propaganda" (as discussed in chapter 5), slow-motion sports film provides documentary evidence, lending an aura of facticity.

A second exception occurs in news film proper. When entering a building, a criminal or dignitary may cross from car to doorway in as little as five seconds. Yet the reporter may need ten seconds to explain why the person was entering the building. In this case the cameraman will adjust his equipment to slow motion, taking care not to film the subject's arms and legs or the moving arms and legs of anyone else on-camera. The dignitary or criminal seems to require ten seconds to cross to the doorway or run out of a courthouse, and the program will have a sufficient amount of film to "cover" the ten-second explanation offered by the news announcer. Television newsworkers justify this practice by noting that the viewer cannot perceive the time distortion, and that since the essence of TV news is film (showing the dignitary smiling and hopeful, or serious and determined), storytelling requires this practice. Implicit in the second justification is the idea that the film is a neutral transduction of images, enabling viewers to "see for themselves." Yet newsworkers reject this assumption on other occasions; they differentiate among newsmakers by specifying who provides good and who "dead" footage.

A third exception concerns two related stories, the John F. Kennedy assassination and the murder of Lee Harvey Oswald. CBS tried to obtain amateur film of the Kennedy assassination to run in slow motion, in order to show "what actually happened." It could not obtain that film. However, having its own film of Jack Ruby killing Oswald, the network did run that in slow motion. As presented by Dan Rather (1977: 123–29, 139–40), the justification for the latter was to squelch rumors about the Oswald murder. In slow motion, one could "see the facts" more clearly, and the reporter could specify that this was "regular" film projected in slow motion to assist viewers in determining their analysis of this *actual* event. Like the label "news analysis," identification of the film as "slow motion" also serves to set it off as different from other news film.

News film's arrangement of *space* also eschews dramatic conventions to create an aura of facticity. In cinema various angles are used to forward the dramatic action. For instance, low camera placement may emphasize suspense. This technique, common in the 1930s, was used in *The Maltese Falcon* to intensify Sidney Greenstreet's forbidding girth. The camera may be placed above an action to suggest danger, as often is the case in the perennial police chase across rooftops. This type of wide-angle shot may also be used to emphasize the physical distance of one event from another.[9]

Television news film is rarely shot from above when recording *animate* objects, but towns, forests, escape routes of bank robbers, tornado paths, and battlefields are often filmed from a helicopter. For a news cameraworker, facticity is produced by meeting an event "head on," with camera placement fixed to simulate the angle of a person of average height confronting another person eye to eye. All else is condemned as "distortion," and the team responsible for the affronting footage is likely to receive an official reprimand.

Head on

Bird's-eye   Worm's-eye

FIGURE 6-2

Historically, use of the alternative perspectives sketched in figure 6-2 was not viewed as a "distortion" of reality, since these are variations upon a fixed-point perspective. When perspective was re-

---

[9]The camera may also be placed so as to give a limited view of the action. Clearly, news film eschews a limited view of an action, for it aims "to capture accurately" an event. Although it has been suggested that TV news film may show a limited view of an action, giving the "wrong" impression of what happened, as in the telecasting of MacArthur Day (Lang and Lang, 1953) or of riots (National Advisory Commission on Civil Disorders, 1968: 363), newsworkers claim to have recorded the crucial events.

discovered, during the Renaissance, these variations were held to be another way to capture reality. Mantegna's painting, "The Dead Christ," rendered schematically in figure 6-3, is an apt example in support of this interpretation.

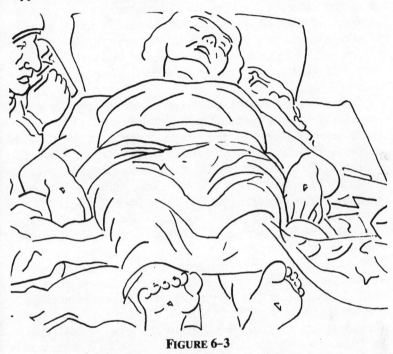

FIGURE 6-3

The significant factor is that television newsworkers call alternative perspectives "distortion." Distortion is said to hamper the viewers' perception of the central figure or event, and hence the facticity of news. For instance, after viewing figure 6-2, a cameraman for NEWS recalled seeing a sequence of Adlai Stevenson during the 1956 presidential campaign. A photographer had knelt and captured Stevenson's hand as it extended to grasp a supporter's. The cameraman recalled that the hand coming toward the camera appeared "as large as Stevenson himself. You couldn't even see Stevenson, for God's sake." Since a hand is as much a part of a person as his head, "seeing" must mean seeing clearly from a head-on perspective. This connotation imparts an aspect of facticity to the accepted perspective.

Cameramen see little variation in the way stories are photographed. As the head cameraman at NEWS explained, one sets up the camera, lines up the reporter and the persons to be interviewed, and then shoots. Although prodded, he saw no variation on this simple procedure, and I never observed a significant variation in either an interview or a press conference. On the contrary, public-relations officers arranged the typical press conference to facilitate this procedure, and the room in which the governor held his press conferences was constructed to enable the head-on, fixed-point perspective.[10]

Significant variations upon this procedure are found only when nonscheduled events of a noninterview nature are being filmed. Then the cameraperson must battle to maintain control of the allocation of space. This may occur at a fire, a demonstration, a riot. Dan Rather (1977) reports that when covering a demonstration, one seeks the safety of height; in war one may shoot while crawling on the ground, or from helicopters entering or leaving battle areas.

Significantly, since "bird's-eye" and "worm's-eye" perspectives are generally reserved for inanimate objects, shooting participants in demonstrations, fires, and riots from these perspectives symbolically converts the participants into objects. Rather than individuals, they appear as components of some quantitatively portrayed mass. That is, just as statistics on crime are presented as independent phenomena (in news accounts the murder rate increases or decreases for unanalyzed reasons, as though having a life of its own [Dahlgren, 1977]), the mass-as-thing takes on a life of its own. Like a tornado or crime rate, the mass seems independent of its individual components.

[10]The governor sat behind a desk on a raised podium. A platform near the back of the room was provided for television news cameras. From the platform, cameramen could shoot over the heads of reporters and record the governor from a head-on perspective. Designing a room suitable for all newsworkers presupposes a familiarity with newswork not yet available to most radical social movements.

One might counter that a film frame of a man sitting behind a desk represents a variation on this perspective, because the desk is in fixed space and thereby influences camera placement. However, the cameraworkers retain the power to rearrange space for their own purposes, including use of the appropriate perspective. They may alter the spatial relationship between desk and desk chair, rearrange items on the desk top, or choose to film the newsmaker sitting in an armchair rather than at his desk. They may suggest the angle at which the newsmaker faces the camera and the point toward which the newsmaker directs his or her eyes. Having exercised this power, a cameraperson frequently lowers the tripod to make sure the sitting person will be filmed in a head-on perspective.

This view of the conversion of numbers of citizens into a mass is supported by other professional preferences for the representation of neutral renditions of space. Film that is jumpy is dramatic; it captures a feeling of tumult. News reporting supposedly avoids rendering feeling by its use of time and space. Accordingly, as Dan Rather (1977) mentions, at a demonstration, where a jostled camera might result in jumpy film, the camera is placed on a nearby roof or in a suitable window. There, the otherwise avoided bird's-eye view provides steady film and a wider angle. Significantly, in this situation, the cameramen working at NEWS frequently had to explain to editors why this camera placement was used. Typically, one cameraman said, "I had to go upstairs to shoot it; there was so much pushing." However, cameramen never search out a high spot when other shoving newsworkers interfere with their shooting a single individual, as is frequently the case when dignitaries arrive at an airport or courtroom. In filming one person, the head-on perspective is maintained. Neither the dignitary nor the newsworkers are transformed into a tornadolike mass. Filming the newsworkers-as-mass would show that newsworkers (not the flow of occurrences) create views, and so would challenge the credibility of news. Such an overview would reveal that much of the excitement of the event has been generated by newsworkers. And just as newspaper reporters use quotation marks to claim impartiality and credibility, so, too, news footage must avoid implying that newsworkers and organizations generate both occurrences and their rendition as events. Supposedly, to imply involvement is to undermine the web of facticity.

News Film and Social Roles

Cameramen use the head-on perspective for individuals, and in news footage those individuals are generally legitimated and quasi-legitimated officials. Those whose activities break the social order—rioters and demonstrators, like tornados and floods—are filmed from a different perspective. In general, news film's adaptations of social roles stress neutrality. By neutrality I do not mean the refusal to take sides in a dispute, for the anchoring of the news net in time and space necessarily involves the news organization in the process of legitimation. Rather, I mean that the visual portrayal of roles stresses noninvolvement: Reporters filmed at the scene of a story are clearly portrayed as being removed from, and uninvolved in, the action sequences. Both reporters and newsmakers are framed as officials and professionals, as one would see them if one sat in front of their desks. These social meanings—seeming representations—are achieved by filmic conventions regarding camera range. The framings are designed to be neither intimate nor distant.

Drawing upon the work of Grosser, a portrait painter, Hall (1966) attributes social meaning to the use of height, width, and depth on a horizontal and vertical plane, applicable to a painting or a frame of film. Hall describes four categories of space and their social meanings. One of these is public space, defined by Grosser's statement that bodies perceived from a distance of more than thirteen feet are seen "as something having little connection with ourselves." Hall's other classifications are social distance (four to twelve feet) and intimate distance (zero to eighteen inches). Each is divided into a "close" and "far" phase, whose cultural usage Hall describes.[11]

Hall (1966: 112-15) suggests that, at close personal distance, "one can hold or grasp the other person. . . . A wife can stay inside the circle of her husband's personal zone with impunity. For another woman to do so is an entirely different story." Hall goes on to discuss "keeping someone at arm's length away." That far personal distance "extends from a point that is just outside easy touching distance by one person to a point where two people can touch fingers if they extend both arms. . . . Subjects of personal interest and involvement can be discussed at this distance." Far personal distance melts into close social distance: "[I]mpersonal business occurs at this distance, and in the close phase there is more involvement than in the far phase. People who work together tend to use close social distance." Far social distance is, according to Hall, "the distance to which people move when someone says, 'stand away so I can look at

[11] According to Grosser, "At more than thirteen feet away . . . the human figure can be seen in its entirety as a single whole. At this distance . . . we are chiefly aware of its outlines and proportions. . . . The painter can look at his model as if he were a tree in a landscape or an apple in a still life. But four to eight feet is the portrait distance. . . . The painter is near enough so that his eyes have no trouble in understanding the sitter's solid forms, yet he is far enough away so that the foreshortening of the forms presents no real problem. Here, at the normal distance of social intimacy and easy conversation, the sitter's soul begins to appear. . . . Nearer than three feet, within touching distance, the soul is far too much in evidence for any sort of disinterested observation [in Hall, 1966: 71-72]."

you.' Business and social discourse conducted at the far end of social distance has a more formal character than if it occurs inside the close phase [of social distance].'' In sum, Hall suggests that different dis-

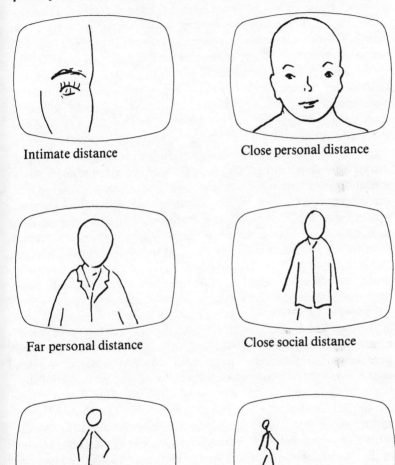

Intimate distance

Close personal distance

Far personal distance

Close social distance

Far social distance

Public distance

FIGURE 6–4

tances have different social meanings; more specifically, he implies that patterned role relationships are expressed through physical distance.

Newsworkers' use of social distance conforms to Hall's descriptions, sketched in figure 6-4 as they would appear on a television screen. Of these six possible framings, three are commonly found in television news film. These are far personal distance, close social distance, and far social distance, all of which, according to Hall, are used in our culture for discussions ranging from "personal interest and involvement" to more formal "business and social talks." I refer to these three as "talking distance," and to close personal distance and intimate distance as "touching distance."

The meanings that newsmen attribute to talking and touching distance are demonstrated by considering frame arrangements rarely found on television news presentations. On screen A of figure 6-5, the subject is framed as in the customary television close-up technique. On screen B, the subject is framed as in a dramatic close-up technique. Both screens present a "talking head," the newsworkers' term for film showing someone speaking in the studio or at least removed from any action. By providing a greater distance between the camera lens (viewer) and the subject, screen A is supposedly more impartial; being farther away, it literally seems more detached. "Coming in tight" on the talking head, as screen B does, is not seen as neutral. The framing sketched in screen B is used to capture moments of drama, which newsmen do not associate with "straight, hard news." As one cameraman–informant explained, screen B is used for dramatic impact when someone with an "interesting face" is expressing emotion. An example he cited was Rose Kennedy discussing her dead sons. Here, the camera would come in on her face and try to capture a tear. Again, the exception is interesting. As the NEWS cameraman noted, Rose Kennedy "occupies a special place" in the "hearts of Americans." Rendering her in an involved manner can still connote neutrality, since that framing captures her particular role in American society. Supposedly, admiration for her is "above politics."

Significantly, the cameraman volunteered that he would *absolutely* never use that range technique on the talking heads of reporters. Indeed, when one unfortunate cameraman framed a TV reporter in touching distance (to compensate for a previous error in the filming), the work was scornfully disparaged by colleagues. As news-workers, television reporters must be shown as nonparticipants whose role is to comment and describe neutrally. The camera may not suggest that the TV workers have emotions or ideas about the story they are reporting, that the reporters get "too close."[12]

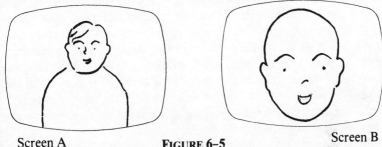

Screen A   **Figure 6–5**   Screen B

Public distance is all but forbidden in recording events involving "individuals," even though those events may normally be seen from a public distance. One might suppose that television news film would use public distance to give viewers the illusion of having attended an event or speech. This may be called neutral because, theoretically, it would decrease the emotional involvement between viewer and speaker. However, public distance precludes the personal and social contact that is the hallmark of television news. Public distance *de*personalizes,[13] and is used only to show masses, not individuals. Since news portrays individuals (as participants in or symbols of events) and individuals' opinions about events, the use of public distance is "unnewslike." Furthermore, public distance greatly limits the ability of news film to capture emotions. As Hall (1966: 117) points out, "Most actors know that at thirty or more feet, the subtle shades of meaning conveyed by the normal voice are lost, as are the

[12]Occasions prompting newsworkers to show emotion become professional gossip and sometimes cause conversation among audience members. One example of this break in emotional distance was Walter Cronkite's self-presentation during reports on President John Kennedy's assassination. The reporter's ability to contain emotions and so create social distance may be particularly striking to his or her intimates. Rather (1977) recalls his wife's amazement that he reported on that presidential assassination without showing sorrow or grief.

[13]Conversely, intimate distance is said to capture emotion at the cost of objectivity.

details of facial expression and movement." Recording at public distance, the film might gain exaggerated neutrality, but it would lose the other central characteristic of television news film, emotional impact.

Usage of talking distance depends upon who is talking. Anchorpersons and commentators appear in standard torso shots, emphasizing their head and shoulders and initially including their hands holding the program script. The camera operators attempt to project friendliness to the audience through this framing, and to maintain neutrality by keeping the torso framing standard throughout a sequence of stories. The consistency of the camera work serves as the visual correlative of the newspaper's news-speak, symbolically proclaiming neutrality by announcing, "We treat one event the same way we treat any other."

The head and shoulders of a talking head, whether that of a mayor, senator, or secretary, may be similarly framed or presented at a greater distance from the camera lens (varying between Hall's far personal and close social distance). All newsmakers are presented from this same distance or combination of distances, again connoting neutral presentation.[14] The anchorperson, commentators, and newsmakers may be portrayed in a tighter (closer) shot than the TV reporter at the scene of a story, who appears in close-social or far-social distance. When a reporter is shot interviewing a newsmaker, at least the reporter's torso appears on-screen. More frequently, and as a general rule, the reporter is portrayed standing in front of the scene of a story, the camera moving in, eventually focusing on the reporter from the waist-up. The event in the background is shown at "depersonalizing" public distance. But the reporter is "farther" from the camera lens and viewer than either an anchorperson or newsmaker. This technique includes the events in the background and shows the reporter detached from the event and not part of it.[15]

[14]Sometimes I witnessed the filming of exceptions to these generalizations. On every observed occasion, though, the affronting footage was the only available method of filming, and the crew was quick to tell the managing editor why they had filmed the way they did.

[15]When reporters break the association between patterned role relationships and camera range by getting involved in an event, other newsworkers consider it newsworthy. One example of this is John Chancellor's hasty exit from the 1964 Democratic Convention. He spoke on the air as he was being carried out of the hall.

The distinction between cinematic detachment and participation connotes neutrality. A movie actor would be shown acting in a crowd, despite the extent to which such a shot might initially block the viewer's clear identification of him. The movie director would want to portray the hero acting with others to show his involvement, in contrast to the intentional portrayal of the uninvolved reporter. A newspaper reporter, hired by NEWS despite his lack of television experience, quickly learned his "role" in on-film reporting. Editing his footage, the technicians told him before the editors could, "Next time you cover a story like this, stand in *front* of the picketers."

To state that television newsworkers customarily use certain framings to convey social roles is to suggest that television news film employs a lexicon of standard shots. Compiling that lexicon, the Glasgow Media Group (forthcoming) has reduced television news images to about fifty shots and variations. Such limitation strongly suggests that television news speaks through codes. The visual detachment of reporters from the phenomena placed in the background may be seen as a code for detachment. Additionally, news film codifies places and events.

Standard Shots of People, Places, and Events

Consider some standard shots commonly used in television footage to claim representational facticity. First, by framing reporters in front of easily identified symbolic locations, news film informs viewers that the reporter is actually *at* the scene of the story. For instance, a White House correspondent is framed against the portico of the White House; a London reporter, in front of Big Ben; a Soviet correspondent, against Red Square; a reporter in Prague, on a bridge overlooking the Old Town. Alternately, as in the last example, if a story concerns general activities in a city, news film may show a slow panorama of the skyline, sometimes drawn from files or, if the film library is so disordered that retrieval is expensive or if construction has made old footage "inaccurate," the skyline may be shot again. Similarly, exteriors of buildings set the stage for interviews and "actuality" once the reporter is inside the building.

Second, events are coded by the supposed essence of the ongoing activity. For instance, a union strike is symbolized by picketers milling outside an uncrossed plant gate. Or, if access to the plant is made available by the management, the film may show shut-down machines, or simply a locked gate (see Glascow Media Group, forthcoming). Similarly, strikes by farm workers are symbolized by pictures of unpeopled fields, unused machinery, and crops described as growing too ripe. Jungle wars, such as in Southeast Asia, are symbolized by soldiers cutting their way through dense growth, helicopters removing the wounded, and shots of trenches, fortifications, and of soldiers resting, crawling, or throwing themselves on their bellies to avoid the enemy's fire. Murders are symbolized by blood on sidewalks and by car windshields splayed with bullets. Drug busts result in film of piles of packets, displayed on a table in the room where they were found or in the locked storeroom of the police property clerk. Police stakeouts are symbolized by officers on roofs, in windows, and crouching in doorways or behind cars.[16] In all these examples, one quick look tells American viewers what the story is.

Third, people are presented symbolically. Not only are they garbed in the clothing appropriate to their occupation, but also nonlegitimated individuals are made to typify all members of their particular group or class. NBC's coverage of a strike at an automobile plant during the Vietnam war provided a particularly apt example of this phenomenon, especially since Detroit had experienced racial violence. A correspondent interviewed a black striker, his wife beside him, in his home, and asked about their financial problems due to the strike and their feelings about their son, then on combat duty in Vietnam. Similarly, stories about fluctuations in agricultural prices feature an "average farmer." Stories about rising homicide rates in small cities and towns are set in a "typical American small town," where a "typical citizen" tells of his or her life style and fears.[17]

Said to lend drama and human meaning to the news (E.J. Epstein, 1973), symbols accomplish two factors associated with the web

---

[16]Jay Ruby (personal communication) speaks of what he terms "the Kissinger plane ritual," footage of diplomats arriving at and leaving airports. The viewer assumes that each airport is in a different city, but airports are so similar that they could all be the same stage set. Such footage seems designed to provide reassurance that American diplomacy is actively seeking solutions to impasses.

[17]The person interviewed may also be a local official.

of facticity. They provide "actual" supplementary evidence: People as symbols tell of the impact of news events upon their lives so that the reporter need not present interpretations. The symbols thus "protect" reporters from presenting themselves as being involved in the story. And the use of symbols strengthens the distinction between legitimated newsmakers and "just plain folks." The talking heads of congresspersons and senators, mayors and chairpersons, cabinet members and generals, offer their own opinions and demonstrate their own expertise.[18] Although they are said to be representatives of the people by dint of their legitimated positions and power, they speak for themselves. But symbols are only symbols: people whose ideas and opinions are not news in and of themselves. They are not representatives but are assumed to be *representations* of others who are coping with a mutual dilemma. When the dilemma has passed— the strike has ended or the town has started to recover from the hurricane—the symbol loses all news value, and once again is merely an ordinary person undifferentiated from the mass of ordinary people, i.e., a member of the public.

When someone is a symbol, he or she is framed at talking distance, but is rarely shown seated behind a desk or conference table.[19] More likely settings are the home, supermarket, a blue-collar worksite, or some scene of common recreational activity. Again, by the use of such settings, the symbol is set off from other persons interviewed on the news. The symbol is also differentiated from legitimated newsmakers by occasional variations in camerawork. If the symbol is speaking about a particularly emotional topic, the film may sometimes approximate touching distance. Tears and other displays of emotion are welcomed by the now more intimate camera. These displays do not function as an attribute of the individual. They are social indicators of the plight of a group, whether the group is parents with incurably ill children, wives of soldiers missing in action, or families made homeless by a natural disaster. Similarly, the joy of returning prisoners of war and their families, whether cap-

[18]Unless, of course, the story concerns the daily routines of an "average" member of Congress.

[19]In a recent documentary shown at the 1977 independent film seminar sponsored by the Public Broadcasting System and Film Seminars, Inc., at Arden House, Alfonso Beato framed a peasant analyzing the economic history of Puerto Rico as though he were a reporter. After the viewing, the first question asked by seminar participants was, "Who was that guy that you framed him like Dan Rather?"

tured at touching or talking distance, symbolizes the joy of all in that situation.

Why does television news use such symbols as well as the other described framings? Identifying these devices as professional skills lending an aura of neutrality to the web of facticity does not suffice. For by serving as basic components of news-film narratives, these frames also place professionalism in the service of organizational flexibility.

Assembling a Television News Narrative

Unlike major metropolitan dailies, few local television news-rooms are organized around a system of beats (although some reporters and cameraworkers are recognized as having specialties). At NEWS, one reporter consistently covered the state government. The anchorman, when acting as a reporter, drew the day's best story, generally a political item. Five other reporters covered everything and anything that came along. Frequently, several of the reporters covered more than one story a day, and it was always possible that a crew would finish one story and be assigned another. (Crews in the station's cars kept in continual contact with the assignment editor by shortwave radio to coordinate their lunch hours and locations with the unfolding occurrences of the day.)

Epstein (1973) points out that network correspondents could never be sure of supervising the editing of their stories. Frequently thousands of miles from the facilities where their raw film was assembled into a narrative, they were required to send material others could process. So, too, local television crews could never depend upon transforming their material into a finished story; the probability of one more assignment was too great. Because of this probability, it would be foolish for a crew to turn in idiosyncratic film or videotape. Facing idiosyncratic material, film and videotape editors and those supervising their work would have to spend more time than usual working on the material; they would have to decipher the crew's version of the story and match that decoding to their own vision of what the story should be.

The problem of decoding would be particularly acute if the film or videotape eschewed the narrative form in favor of a more poetic or symbolic treatment. Sol Worth (personal communication) reports an experiment at the University of Pennsylvania's Annenberg School of Communication. Subjects viewed three silent films, a narrative, a "poetic" treatment, and a collage of random film clips, and were then asked to tell each film's story. The narrative was the easiest to handle. Respondents also found it easy to construct a story about the collage of random clips. The poetic treatment gave respondents the most trouble. Worth explains that the narrative draws on traditions of storytelling accessible through participation in the American culture. Respondents could project their own stories onto the random clips. But the poetic treatment was clearly recognizable as one person's vision, requiring respondents to decode that vision rather than formulate their own story. Neither cultural forms of storytelling nor personal projections could be easily used to decipher the poetic treatment.

A television crew that turned in idiosyncratic material would risk seeing its conception of the story transformed by editors facing a crush of stories to be edited and aired. Taking extra time to work on the idiosyncratic footage, the technician assigned the material might develop a backlog of work. In both cases, the film crew and technician face organizational problems. If the idiosyncratic footage cannot be deciphered, the reporter's superiors might call him on the carpet for filming segments that "could not be worked with." The cutting team (a technician and writer) might be reprimanded, introducing friction and, ultimately, incompatibility among staff members. Incompatibility is dysfunctional for the television station, as work tasks are so heavily interrelated. Disaster may result for the reporters: Editors who remain inside the newsroom all day determine the reporter's story assignments. On occasion, the editors consult the writers with whom they are friendly. Dissatisfied, they may inflict punishment by rewarding "good" stories to other reporters, thus decreasing the offender's status in the newsroom. The film cutter may approach the reporter's work in a less respectful fashion and in the future may not recommend inclusion of optional pictures of the reporter to other members of the cutting team. At many American television stations, reporters earn an extra fee when this optional picture is shown. By angering the technician, a reporter reduces his or her potential income.

Film or videotape that conforms to the accepted narrative form facilitates work by other staff members. Although it may take as long as an hour and a half to perfect a complex three-minute story, I have seen a story cut in as little as five minutes when it arrived a half-hour before the nightly newscast. Stories cut this quickly may not live up to all the professional–technical standards. But in the case of a just-breaking occurrence, it lives up to a crucial organizational concern: getting the story on the air before it becomes obsolete, "mere history," old news.

The use of film and videotape sequences easily assembled into narrative form remains important in later stages of production. The story must be aired, but the director and his assistant may not receive the program's script until five minutes before air time (although they generally have a copy a half-hour before the program's start).[20] They rarely rehearse the film and almost never have time to make a video-tape of complex stories with many segments before the program (whenever possible, New York stations and the networks try to make a videotape of edited stories before air time to decrease the possibility of such errors as cues being mistimed or splices of filmed frames breaking during the broadcast). Especially when a story has been put together very late, the director has no idea what is on the film. Using symbols ("translated" here), his copy of the script format merely reads: "Color sound film with the sound on tape, concerning crime records, lasting two minutes fourteen seconds, with the last words, 'This is Tom Evans at City Hall for NEWS.' When the sound film has been running fifteen seconds, air the accompanying silent film racked on another projector for twenty seconds, and then return to the picture on the sound film."

The format informs the director what he can expect to see as he sits in the control booth and gives orders to the following persons: the assistant director; the two or three engineers handling sight and sound levels; the technician(s) running the several movie projectors and videotape equipment; cameramen; the studio floor assistant; the newscaster; and the announcer who introduces the program and reads prespecified lines in commercial advertisements. Although engineers sitting in the control booth may receive orders directly, the others, scattered in different rooms, must be sequentially contacted via headsets.

With the format before him, and aware of the standard forms, the director knows what to expect. If silent film seemingly unasso-

[20]The directors I observed were male. There are very few women directors employed in major markets, as far as I know.

ciated with the story appears on his TV monitor, the director knows something has gone wrong, and can immediately institute appropriate corrective procedures. Similarly, the appearance on the format of key words associated with standard forms tells the director whether split-second timing is mandatory or is merely optional. (The director's clock is divided into fractions of a second.)

The usual narrative form is associated with professionalism, satisfies organizational needs, and is familiar to the average Western television viewer. Using "facts" purposely unincorporated in the film or videotape, an anchorperson introduces the story and then either continues to narrate as silent film is aired or allows sound film to deliver its own information. Or the viewer may be treated to a complex mixture of these elements (as shown in table 6-1).

TABLE 6.1.   Some Standard Television Narratives

BASIC UNITS*	
Unit A, silent film:	beginning / middle / end
Unit B, sound film:	newsmaker talking / x / newsmaker talking / x / newsmaker talking (*x* indicates silent film showing reporter's hands, notebook, or head)
COMPLEX NARRATIVES	
Type 1:	introduction (*y*) / Unit B, sound film / closing (*y*) (*y* indicates sound film of the reporter describing what has happened, or will happen, in Unit B)
Type 2:	introduction (*y*) / sound film of an event (B') / closing (B' indicates a variation of Unit B, sound film)
Type 3:	introduction (*y*) / Unit A' silent film / closing (*y*) (A' indicates that Unit A, silent film, is being shown from one projector while a reporter's commentary is from a separate recorded source)
Type 4:	introduction (*y*) / Unit A' / Unit B' (demonstration) / Unit B / closing (*y*) *y* / Unit A' / Unit B / *y'* Unit B' / *y'* / Unit B / *y* (*y'* indicates sound film of the reporter introducing information pertinent to the next segment of the package)

*Diagrams are not to scale. Basic units last from 15 to 45 seconds. Complex narratives last from 1 to 8 minutes.

For the television staff, professionalism connotes following the narrative forms in a way that satisfies notions of continuity and variation, each of which has a technical and a contextual application. That is, the staff wants to present a story that is both technically and textually continuous, but they wish the story to have sufficient filmic variation to interest the viewer. Consider the following hypothetical complex example:

> Reporter in studio: "City Hall buzzed today with talk of a possible solution to the fiscal crisis, as Tom Evans reports":
>
> Tom Evans (on film from steps of the City Hall) describes City Council proposal for five seconds.
>
> Evans' voice continues giving information about City Council's discussion. Silent film shows Council meeting.
>
> Evans' voice introduces chat with key Council member as silent film continues.
>
> Sound film shows Council member talking about the new proposal, including views of its opponents.
>
> Evans' voice, explaining depth of opponents' anger, accompanies silent film of demonstration against the proposal outside the City Hall.
>
> Evans interviews a demonstrator on sound film.
>
> Evans, on steps of the City Hall, sums up the story.

The example includes pictures of people sitting and standing. It tells of two "related occurrences" sharing temporal (and spatial) proximity. Verbal transitions take the audience from one locale to the other. And it would probably include visual transitions (cut-aways) as well.[21]

For our purposes, this example has at least three interesting components. First, providing filmic variation to interest the viewer (whether that variation occurs in one story as above or involves pacing over a series of stories) serves the interests of the news organization. By keeping viewers from turning off the program, the station

---

[21]Because of the mechanical structure of the camera, on standard television film, the sound accompanying the visual image on a specific frame is not attached to that exact frame. The sound track may be "off" by as many as twenty-six frames. This discrepancy presents a technical problem when film is cut. Two frames of sound film cannot be spliced together without creating an audio-visual disjuncture. To combat the lack of synchronization (a jump-cut), the film cutter inserts twenty-four to twenty-six frames of silent film (cut-aways) between the two recorded statements that are to be joined. A typical cut-away is the face of the reporter listening to the newsmaker. Sound film of the reporter asking a question (filmed after the formal interview) may also be used as a cut-away.

maintains its ratings and its advertising revenue. Second, providing visual variation by juxtaposing Council members and demonstrators in the same (or adjoining) stories states (or strongly implies) that the two groups are interconnected. It thus forces them into the same context, or frame, and negates the claim that the actions of either group are independent, idiosyncratic phenomena.

If the cited example had been a complex story about four different demonstrations, each held on the same day and each about a different issue, then each would be viewed as merely one more demonstration in a string of demonstrations. And thus each would lose its claim to idiosyncrasy. In actual practice, though, idiosyncrasy has already been lost to conventions governing consistency and variation. I have observed television editors choosing not to cover a demonstration because they already had "demonstration film" for that day's program. The first demonstration was intended to provide visual variation from the talking heads of reporters and those interviewed. Covering a second demonstration would supposedly endanger the program's visual variation by providing too much of the same thing. In both cases, the invocation of visual variation forces demonstrations into a common frame by foisting the same formal concerns upon discrete occurrences (much as Reporter Morris imposed a common frame upon the deaths of the tenement child and the governor's granddaughter by interviewing the governor's political neighbors, as discussed in chapter 5).

As a third component of our example, visual variation as a framing device leads film crews and other personnel to "think visually," as they put it. The newsworkers dislike running too many stories comprised of talking heads. To avoid such visual boredom, they introduce other visual elements whenever possible. As a television reporter explained, "You know, this is a strange medium. . . . You have to consider a lot of things: time, picture possibilities, action movement in the appropriate setting. . . . You begin to think this way." The reporter provided an example:

> Last Christmas, a cameraman and I did a story involving a little bit of information. We interviewed [a doctor] at the State Mental Health Center about Christmas parties, and he started talking about beads in ornaments, that they are detrimental to man if eaten but kill dogs if dogs eat them. Well, we walked outside the hospital and saw beads on the Christmas tree of an organization across the street. Just shooting those beads meant the story could [incorporate visual variation].

In the example, the film of the beads provides visual illustration of the talking head's comments. But sometimes visual material contradicts the audio track. Epstein (1973) points out that Vietnam footage had to have a timeless quality because film had to be shipped from Vietnam to New York. Timelessness was achieved by the nightly parade of symbols: Americans foraging through jungles, American bunkers, Americans walking through Vietnamese villages, American helicopters evacuating American troops. Meanwhile, the sound track spoke about the progress of a Vietnamese war. According to Gitlin:

> TV did not probe for the purposes of the antagonists. It did not, for the most part, measure administrative claims and vocabularies ("Viet Cong") against observed actuality. It accepted the official American version of a patriotic war against North Vietnamese invaders. That's what it *said*, for the most part, if not in so many words. But what it *showed*, night after night, was American soldiers slogging it out with an invisible enemy, without any *visible* purpose or trajectory. Here was a tension between the political line (represented mostly in the voice) and the journalistic code (represented mostly in the picture). . . . One key result was that the war was represented as senseless, unwinnable, bogged down. . . . So TV helped bring about *war-weariness* in the population: not coherent reasons for opposition, not any sensible analysis, but simply a blur of exhaustion [1977: 794].

The pictures Epstein and Gitlin mention provide visual variation to the narration by invoking standard shots, symbols of war. Generally, of course, standard symbols both provide visual variation and complement the sound track rather than contradict it. A quick shot of picketers outside an airport, during a story about officials visiting an airport to assess the sound pollution of the SST, connotes opposition. A talking head inside an office or in front of a bank of microphones indicates a legitimated official or spokesperson. Shots of people in a rowboat, framed against the roofs of submerged cars and the upper stories of two-family houses, alleviate visual boredom and symbolize flood damage. The invocation of visual variation relies upon the lexicon of television news framings, any of which, if shown long enough (at least ten seconds), can register its claim to represent the web of facticity.

Just as newspaper editors may look for a bright story to liven up the heavy news on page one, so, too, television news may employ a second method to provide visual variation. That method is the airing of upbeat feature stories, including "kickers" at the program's end.[22] Newspaper feature stories require more careful editing than hard news because they are frequently built upon twists of newspaper narrative style. On television, too, soft news requires more editorial work, because features often aim to incorporate a poetic, not a narrative, vision. The use of narrative forms applied to hard news is suspended. For instance, photographers and editors may either shoot or edit in sequences of one to five seconds, rather than the ten-second minimum associated with the display of symbols in hard-news stories. Equally important, the camera may discard news conventions about time, space, and distance. Features assembled at NEWS provide some examples.

In one feature story, a reporter commented on the rerouting of traffic around a congested city square. The city had erected a maze of signs, including "one way," "bear to right," "bear to left," and "do not enter," as well as a plethora of markers indicating the direction toward specific streets. The reporter appeared in the opening of the story and, as he talked, signs and cars appeared on the TV screen, forming a jumble of images. Suddenly the camera focused on one large sign, and the reporter's head popped from behind it as he signed off, "This is Pat Trenton from Maywood Square for NEWS." The closing of another feature story, this one on an electronic music concert, broke rules by framing the reporter at intimate distance and by using a worm's-eye perspective. The reporter's head was also bathed in green light.

On another occasion the TV team did a feature story about the city's red-light zone, a district of seedy movie houses, "nonacademic" bookstores, and bars for dancing frequented by a variety of "deviants." As part of the feature, the film showed feet walking down the street without focusing upon the bodies attached to them. Dancing inside one of the bars was filmed in silhouette, partially so that faces could not be identified (as the cameraman explained, so that a wife would not spy her husband, who had supposedly been working late), but primarily for the photographic effect of people

[22]The term refers to humorous stories that either the newsmakers or the audience will "get a kick" out of. Because kickers are the last story in a program, the term is sometimes used to refer to the story in the last spot even if it does not display or evoke warmth or humor.

dancing in a dark room to the sound of hard rock music and background conversation.

"Distortion" involving special lighting effects and music was used in other features. NEWS did a Christmas feature about tree lights and bells, with a sound track carrying bells pealing a Christmas tune. Neither the lights nor the bells on-screen were in clear focus. They appeared as diffuse shapes and colors moving in an organized whirl synchronized to the music. The cameraman's description of his work is most pertinent here. Talking about range and perspective shots, he used the word "distortion," stating that news film "never, never, never" used lighting and distortion such as that incorporated in the swimming-pool scene of the then-current movie, *The Graduate*. Yet, when I mentioned the Christmas bells-and-lights feature, he replied, "That's different!" Significantly, this cameraman preferred to shoot features and was later hired by a network to do so. He explained that "you can do more" cinematically with soft than with hard news. This cameraman's statement underscores television's identification of the news narrative with the web of facticity. It tells us that the news narrative raises some questions and ignores others specifically because its style and format are visual incorporations of themes dominating the organization of newswork.

The news media's bureaucratic organization of time and space is reified in the news narrative's organization of frames of film. And the use of filmic conventions and narrative forms enables reporters to insure that their rendition of stories will not be mauled by editors. It facilitates the news organization's ability to be flexible, to move reporters from story to story during the day. It enables film crews to cover any assignment, to be generalists who can transform any idiosyncratic occurrence into a conventional news event.

CHAPTER SEVEN

The Topic of the Women's Movement

Throughout this examination of news, I have emphasized the impact of the social organization of time and space upon newswork. I have argued that both news organizations and newsworkers, beset by deadlines, actively work at developing the ability to transform any occurrence into an event. Yet, ironically, the achievement of that ability to reduce the idiosyncrasy of occurrences often blinds newsworkers: It prevents them from seeing some occurrences as potential news. More technically, one might say that the organization of newswork prevents newsworkers from constituting some phenomena as public topics, as "resources for discourse in public matters" (Molotch and Lester, 1974: 103).

As discussed in previous chapters, the anchoring of the news net shapes access to the news as a stratified social resource (Tuchman, 1976; Goldenberg, 1975). The news media are more accessible to some social movements, interest groups, and political actors than to others. Those who hold recognized reins of legitimated power clearly have more access to the media than those who do not. Lower-class groups in particular are cut off from the media as a resource unless they recruit middle-class supporters who have routinized media contacts (Jenkins, 1975), attack those who attract media coverage, or recruit reporters to join their cause as "advocate journalists." After studying the access of four community groups to Boston's three daily newspapers (excluding the *Christian Science Monitor*), Goldenberg put it this way:

> The reporter is the key media person for resource-poor groups, the major filter in the access process. However, the reporter is also an organization person who works for a newspaper with goals, structure, standard procedures and policies that somewhat limit and shape the discretion that individual reporters have in news-gathering and reporting [1975: 145].

If a social movement can recruit advocate journalists, how do those reporters constitute the issues raised by the group as news topics? This question is important theoretically for several reasons: First, social movements pass through distinct phases (Oberschall, 1973), progressing from informal groups or networks to complex voluntary organizations able to lobby corporations, unions, and legislative bodies. Inasmuch as news organizations coordinate their news nets with legitimated institutions, one would expect the coverage of a social movement to change as the movement evolves.

Second, newswork is a daily *practical* activity. The tempo of newswork, including covering a different story every day, mandates an emphasis on events, not issues. Events are concretely embedded in the web of facticity, the who, what, when, where, why, and how of the traditional news lead. Issues are not; they are based in analytic explanations of the everyday world as a socially experienced structure. For example, the idea and so the issue of institutionalized racism entails a description of social processes involving the interrelationship of a host of institutions and social problems; it eschews an examination of the prejudices of specific individuals. But newswork emphasizes the primacy of the individual: the individual as source, as legitimated representative, as incumbent, as power broker.

Events are discrete, said to have a beginning, a middle, and an end. Even events (occurrences) that continue over time, such as the course of a legislative bill or a trial, are said to begin and to end. A bill is introduced into committee. A trial is called to order. Issues do not have the same sort of temporal anchoring as events. Did sexism begin when Betty Friedan (1963) called attention to it as "the problem with no name"? Or is sexism an ongoing phenomenon, present in all human history, and so to be dismissed as unnewsworthy?

Phillips argues that the nature of newswork creates "craft-related habits of mind" that blind newsworkers to issues. She explains:

> Craft-related habits of mind, such as dependence upon [professional] "instinct," the logic of the concrete, a present time orientation, and an emphasis on contingent events rather than structural necessities, serve to [structure] the presentation of news. Externally imposed constraints (e.g., regularly scheduled telecasts) and organizational pressures to routinize work combine with the journalist's tendency to view the day's events as discrete, unrelated facts to produce the news mosaic of surface reality. . . . Linkages between events are not suggested. . . the news gives the feeling that there is novelty without change [1976: 92].

At best, innovative delegitimating social movements are novelties—unless they portend violence and are recast as potential disruptions. As Molotch and Lester (1974) point out, to make news, members of social movements may have to assemble at an inappropriate time in an inappropriate place to engage in an accordingly inappropriate activity.[1]

Equally important, proponents of an issue may make their case by offering a world view alien to reporters' event orientation. Halloran, Elliott, and Murdock (1970) report that British media anticipated that a major antiwar demonstration would be violent and covered the actual occurrence as unrealized violence. They note also that London peace marchers protesting British support of American involvement in Vietnam carried signs about inflation and higher taxes, problems they associated with that British foreign policy. Rather than interpret those signs as components of a sophisticated analysis, reporters read them as indications of a haphazard (non-event-oriented) approach.

The discrepancy between the approaches of newsworkers and members of social movements is a conflict between craft as consciousness and the more analytic consciousness of the social movement. For, as Schutz (1962) points out, consciousness is constituted in daily activity, and as Bensman and Lilienfeld (1973) add, today consciousness is constituted in occupational and professional activities.[2] The activities and temporal orientations of newswork and

[1] This formulation again stresses that social actors work to lend meaning to uses of time and space. The activity is deemed inappropriate because of its ongoing associations with the social meaning attached to "this space" at "this time."

[2] Bensman and Lilienfeld (1973) contrast craft consciousness with class consciousness, but crafts are themselves class based. They attempt to apply phenom-

those of social movements are antithetical. Necessarily, then, just as newswork transforms occurrences into news events, so, too, it must transform the thrust of issues (as defined by proponents of a social movement) as it shapes them into news stories. Coverage of the women's movement offers an example of that transformation, accomplished in slightly different ways as the movement grew more powerful.

The Early Coverage: Ostracism and Ridicule

From its unofficial inception with the White House Conference on Equal Opportunity in 1965 and the official birth of the National Organization for Women in 1966, the women's movement has not been a resource-poor group. Most of its original members, drawn to a Washington meeting to pressure government to improve women's lot, were professional and upper-middle class. Early press releases were cranked out on congressional mimeograph machines by well-paid executives whose contacts enabled them to "borrow" these facilities. The press releases were designed by top women in public relations in New York, especially recruited by Betty Friedan to convert the news media into a movement resource. On the suggestion of these advisors, the news conference announcing the formation of the NOW was held in the living room of Friedan's home. Because news conferences are generally held in offices, the public relations experts felt that the novelty of the setting would attract all the New York-based media. But by stressing novelty rather than timeliness, the setting transformed NOW into soft news.

Friedan, a former reporter, had fairly extensive media contacts, in part developed during a promotional tour for *The Feminine Mystique*. Subsequently hired to write a monthly column in a women's magazine, she learned to call press conferences about the "controversial" topics treated in her column when she wanted a public forum. Friedan, in turn, was backed up by groups of talented freelance writers, hawking articles about the ideas of the nascent move-

enological treatments of time to craft activites. Unfortunately nonreflexive (see chapter 9 of this volume), their argument fails to explore fully recent developments in interpretive theories. (For a discussion of Schutz' [1962, 1964, 1966, 1967] concepts, see pp. 185–88 in this volume.)

ment to the New York–based magazines. Like any professional community, the world of New York free-lancers and staff writers is essentially a small one. It extends from the magazines, and their continual search for new topical materials that "everyone is talking about," to the world of daily news. Those worlds overlap, for some daily reporters also write magazine pieces. Feminism became one topic circulated and assessed by this group.

Instead of suffering from a dearth of contacts, the women's movement was beset by an excess of editorial and reportorial jibes. The movement's members complained that male editors refused to take "women's lib" seriously—and the women felt their argument proved by that slighting nickname conferred by the media. As Morris (1973: 527) points out, news treatments characterized by ridicule and ostracism indicate public definition of the women's movement as peculiar.[3] The *New York Times'* coverage of the 1965 White House Conference on Equal Opportunity provides one well-known example of ridicule. Hole and Levine report that, at the conference:

> One person wondered if the law required Playboy Clubs to hire male bunnies. Almost immediately [a section of Title VII providing for valid exceptions from the law] became known as the "bunny law." A *New York Times* front-page story on the conference was headlined: "For Instance, Can She Pitch for the Mets?"; the bunny problem was referred to throughout [1971: 34].

Editors at the *New York Post* had proposed the headline "It's Ladies Day on Fifth [Avenue]" to characterize the mammoth march of August 26, 1970, although they were discouraged by the newsroom's feminists (according to a *Post* reporter interviewed in July 1975).

Sometimes the "jokes" were invented by women reporters to satisfy the attitudes they attributed to their editors. Lindsy Van Gelder of the *New York Post* regrets her coverage of the 1968 Atlantic City demonstrations at the Miss America pageant. Although she was "really turned on" by the WITCH (Women's International Conspiracy from Hell) group and "could identify with" the demonstration, she told me:

[3]Turner and Killian (1957) suggest, as Morris (1974) reminds us, that ignoring revolutionary ideas may be a means of social control. This goes beyond the mechanism of social control described by Lazarsfeld and Merton (1948), but see Milliband (1969).

> It didn't occur to me at the time that I should insist upon its being taken seriously. [Other demonstrators] were burning draft cards at the time and I featured overmuch the burning of bras, girdles, and curlers. I tried to be light and witty so it [the story] would get in [the paper]. I was afraid that if I reported it straight, it wouldn't get in at all.

By being "light and witty," Van Gelder, like other reporters, eschewed the web of facticity and constituted the women's movement as novelty—as soft news. Indeed, as historians of the women's movement have pointed out, bras, girdles, and curlers were never burned at the Atlantic City demonstration; they were thrown into a wastebasket.

Getting in the Paper: Being Noticed

To become news, an occurrence or issue must come within either a reporter's or a news organization's purview. Being "merely" physically and temporally part of a reporter's "here and now" (Schutz, 1966), that is, being accessible to the news net, is not sufficient. Rather, an issue or event must be sociologically or psychologically pertinent to a reporter's grasp of the world—and the issue or event must resonate with the reporter's purposes and practical activities (Molotch, 1978). Public definition of the women's movement as something peculiar tended to limit coverage of the movement, since male editors shared that view and tended to reinforce it by their patterns of selective blindness toward women (Morris, 1975). Bernard (1973) points out that power, politics, and stratification are male concerns and, traditionally, they are also "first-page" concerns. That is, the professional ideology to which "newsmen" subscribe identifies male concerns as *the* important news stories, and accordingly relegates topics traditionally characterized as "female" to a peripheral status as news.

Dorothy E. Smith (1973; 1975; see also Daniels, 1975) has argued that today's dominant ideologies are male. As Smith puts it:

> The control by men of the ideological forms which regulate social relations . . . is structured socially by an authority they hold as individuals by virtue of their membership in a class . . . as men, they appear as representatives of the power and authority of the institutionalized structures which govern the society [1975: 362].

Smith's notion may be extended to the professional ideologies that govern the behavior of reporters, who operate to maintain male authority by insisting upon the rectitude of male concerns.

As we have seen, the craft consciousness of newswork identifies events, not issues, as the stuff and substance of hard news. And hard news is itself the stuff and substance of daily news coverage. Deemed factual, hard-news stories about occurrences take precedence over other stories, both in their evaluation as potentially newsworthy items and in their internal processing through a news organization. Particularly during the period when the so-called radical wing of the women's movement emphasized consciousness raising (Carden, 1973; Freeman, 1975), much of the movement's political emphasis was on "changing people's heads" about such issues as women's place in the world. To say the least, this is not an observable political occurrence, as are such traditional activities as canvassing, caucusing, campaigning, and voting. Because the thrust was not observable, it was relatively easy to dismiss as "not newsworthy." As one New York reporter who covered the movement in the late 1960s put it, "I think that news is what's in people's heads. But that's not the traditional view." A reporter for another New York paper was more explicit: "There were a lot of interesting things going on, but I couldn't nail things down. There was formless kind of talk. . . . I could see things changing, but it was hard to put my finger on it and say to the metropolitan desk, 'This is what's happening.' And, to be covered by the metropolitan desk, a story has to be of general interest to everyone." In other words, the reporter could not draw on narrative forms embedded in the web of facticity to frame seemingly "formless kind of talk" as a topic—a news story she could tell.

To be more explicit, consciousness raising does not provide observable events that may be held to symbolize the progress, purposes, or problems of organized institutions. It does not provide, for instance, speeches that may be predistributed, quoted, and analyzed for new (but not radically new) statements about the condition of the world. Inasmuch as the consciousness-raising groups were militantly egalitarian in their efforts to eradicate traditional "male" leadership roles—including the role of public spokesperson—no one consciousness-raising group could provide the name of one woman who could *always* speak for the group about women's issues. More important, nobody could speak for *all* consciousness-raising groups. If a reporter wanted to know what members of such groups thought and who or what they represented, there was no one person elected to speak for the groups or recognized as their legitimate spokesperson. Representativeness could not be quantitatively determined.

Nor could consciousness raising and its "issues" be covered by professional formulas. Yet the craft consciousness of newswork insists that social transformation must be located and brought to the attention of the news consumer. To mediate and to satisfy these seemingly conflicting expectations, newspersons turned to established practices for locating sources. Some of these practices tended to elicit critical assessments of feminism. Newspersons would interview a "first" (the first woman to head a coed university, the first woman to head a multinational corporation, the first woman professional jockey) and ask her opinions about issues raised by the women's movement. Particularly in the early days of the movement, politicians and "firsts" rarely gave more than moderate approval to some of its aims. As research on professional women who have achieved greatly has demonstrated, they tend to view themselves as exceptional individuals who have succeeded because of their abilities. These women tend to have little sympathy for the plight of those whom they see as less talented (Hochschild, 1974).

Another professional practice, the "reaction story," encouraged reformist statements by media-nominated leaders. When editors judge an occurrence to be unusually newsworthy, particularly if it might reasonably be expected to affect future occurrences, they seek to learn the "reactions" of public figures. (See the discussion of the coverage of President Johnson's decision not to seek a second elected term in chapter 3 of this text.) Gathered in a reaction story, these opinions may introduce issuelike elements (controlled conflict and controversy) to the coverage, especially if the reporters interview people who are known to disagree with one another.[4] Thus a leader of the women's movement might be asked to give a "feminist" reaction, while the opinions of legitimated political and civic leaders are also being sought. Publishing the views of a quasi-legitimated leader undermines the radicals' attempt to remain leaderless. It imposes structure on the movement.

Moreover, to ask a leader her view, the reporters had to locate someone who would at least admit to being a leader, a role eschewed by some radicals. Frequently, those who were noticeable to news-

---

[4]Cater (1959) gives an example of a reporter who created an issue by searching for a senator willing to criticize a bill most senators were thought to favor.

workers had satisfied the requirements of accomplishment applied to men as spokespersons. To use the traditional sociological distinction between "to do" and "to be," such women as Betty Friedan, Kate Millet, and Germaine Greer had *achieved* their status rather than "merely" being wives and mothers, and so newsworkers could notice them as individuals. Each of these women had written best-selling books. Millet's was written as her doctoral dissertation at a major American university; Greer taught at a well-known British university; Friedan had founded NOW. The nature of each woman's accomplishment would encourage her to accept the publicity garnered by a media-nominated leader: Publicity sells books as well as ideas.[5]

That the media's nomination of spokespersons favors reform rather than radical ideas is indicated by the fate of two women whom the media once exploited. Millet (1974) abandoned her media-created leadership role after finding that the constant publicity not only estranged her from radical friends, but also interfered with her ability to maintain her radical life style. In the mid-1960s Betty Friedan thrust forward the then well-dressed and ladylike Ti-Grace Atkinson to speak to the press at demonstrations. But by the mid-1970s Friedan and Atkinson had quarreled about NOW's position on lesbianism; Atkinson had participated in founding the Radical Feminists and declared herself a lesbian. She was abandoned by the media, which could not condone such untoward conduct by a quasi-legitimated spokesperson.

Craft consciousness also contributes to a male vision of the women's movement by inadvertently disparaging events disruptive of social order. The practical task of locating a spokesperson again dominates. Easy access to the news media requires ongoing contacts between a reporter and a news source, such as those provided by beats. Those who plan disruptive events do not have these contacts, because they are frequently suspicious of the media or may have other reasons, such as possible arrest, for *not* cultivating contact.[6] In such cases, to learn about the event, reporters turn to their routine

[5] I do not mean to imply that greed motivated these women. Millet (1974) writes about being overwhelmed by media attention. Friedan (interviews, 1975) sought publicity for NOW.

[6] Thorne (1970) reports that members of social movements suspect that many persons identifying themselves as reporters may be government agents. NEWS reporters identified some "reporters" seen at news conferences as "ringers"; they were believed to work for the FBI or other investigative agencies.

sources of information—those who, because of their institutional status, are in a central position to know what is going on. Such routine sources are, of course, the very people in power who are being attacked, and they are more than willing to disparage their attackers. Again, standard reportorial practice legitimates those with institutional power.

Finally, inasmuch as reportorial procedures favor sources with power, they may transform the revolutionary potential of such groups as the Women's Political Caucus into a reformist thrust. To cover a caucus is to cover an event. Since a caucus is explicitly concerned with the distribution of political power or with other facets of legitimated institutions, reporters can rely on standard methods of covering conventions. As one informant put it, "Take the Women's Political Caucus; they [the men] are used to covering things like that.[7] They can do it from the old formulas, but [the only change is that they] talk about women in front instead of men." Both powerful (free to choose her own stories) and very professional (according to colleagues), a reporter who has covered such conventions gave an idea of those formulas in her critique of coverage by a Texas newspaper. "My favorite horrifying example of coverage of the caucus is from 1974 in Houston [a national convention]. Three thousand women were there for three days. Sissy Farenthold, a hometown girl, was elected head of the whole shebang. Everyone was there—black, white, Friedan, Chisholm." But, rather than cover the "hometown girl," the celebrities in town, the racial angle, the internal scuffles for power and for unity—all known narratives—"their only story on page one was a two-column box about a workshop on sexual privacy—a codeword for lesbianism."[8] To this reporter, at least, nonprofessional coverage (the kind produced by what she terms "rotten rags") ignores issues in favor of sensationalizing; professional coverage focuses upon leaders, their interactions, and con-

[7]Traditionally, men have covered politics; women doing so have been few and far between.

[8]At least one feminist reporter sought to protect the movement from charges of lesbianism. She said (interview, August 1975) with pride, "We did not capitalize on differences within the movement. The lesbian thing . . . it could have torn the movement apart. We haven't turned it into something divisive." This reporter justified her action by invoking the professional identification of news as information of general interest. She was proud to have protected the schisms in the movement from male editors, because "internal divisions in the movement are not of general interest." Whether such an assessment is correct is irrelevant to this discussion.

crete group actions. Again, the professional emphasis is upon events, not issues. And, significantly, the reporter has drawn a contrast between soft-news treatment—a two-column box on an oddity—and the hard-news narrative she favors.

Of course, reportorial craft consciousness can sometimes be used to serve a social movement. For instance, women reporters, whom their male colleagues recognize as subscribing to professional ideologies, may make issues in the movement noticeable as stories. Grace Lichtenstein, then chief of the *New York Times* Rocky Mountain bureau and first female head of a national *Times* bureau, gave an example of one such story:

> Several months ago, I initiated a story carried on page one about changes in the rape laws across the country as it looked in every state. I used Colorado, where it was being discussed in the legislature, as a peg and it got a lot of space. There have been times when I found editors unaware of things happening, like the rape laws. Only women think in terms of rape laws; the men [who are editors] know about capital punishment [interview, August 1975].

Lichtenstein credits Eileen Shanahan, then the *Times'* Washington-based economics reporter, with instituting coverage of the fight for the Equal Rights Amendment, NOW conventions, and Women's Political Caucus meetings. Shanahan explains:

> In 1971, the first time E.R.A. was in the House, I became aware of it, and I became aware that no one else was interested in covering it and they thought it peculiar that I was interested. If you volunteer for work, you're allowed to do it. I created a national women's rights beat here.

Of course, Shanahan is a very well-established reporter. Proud of the professionalism of her paper, she can also state:

> I have never, well very rarely, done a piece that didn't run pretty much as I wrote it and the length I wrote it. [The national editor] is happy to have me telling him, "This is good, we have to cover this." My ability to define stories is because of professionalism [interview, August 1975].

Ironically, feminist reporters whose stories are noticed because of their professionalism frequently ask hostile questions of feminists at news conferences to prove their reportorial neutrality. Judy Klemesrud (interview, July 1975), another *Times* reporter, explains,

"The hardest part of the job [of covering feminists] is not sounding like one of them. I have to be objective, a gadfly." Put another way, she must demonstrate her acceptance of the web of facticity.

Getting in the Paper: Making Deadline

Even when recognized professionals, like Shanahan or Lichtenstein, can make women's issues noticeable as stories, difficulties occur in using the newspaper as a movement resource. One problem is converting an issue or even a sequence of issues and stories into a beat—a routine round of institutions and persons to be contacted at scheduled intervals for knowledge of events. Shanahan, in part, was able to run her self-created women's beat while continuing to cover economic news because the Washington women's groups are heavily institutionalized. Like other lobbying operations, the coalition for the Equal Rights Amendment and the National Women's Political Caucus each has an office, open at specified hours. They are administered, so to speak. When taking over coverage of the equal-rights provisions of Title 9 from Shanahan, the *Times*' Washington-based education reporter had the time available, some sources who would be routinely familiar with the bill, and a knowledge that political activities and lobbying activities in Washington fall into temporal patterns that can be made convenient for newswork.[9]

However, particularly in the early days of feminism's reemergence and to a large extent today, the scheduling of the activities of feminist groups is in conflict with the schedules that govern newspapers. In one interview after another, New York–based feminist reporters insisted, "I find a lot of feminists are ignorant of the realities of working in a newsroom." In part, they were referring to the scheduling of newswork (as discussed in chapter 3). Beat reporters for morning papers report for work in the late morning and leave in the early evening. To make the early edition, their copy must be filed by the early evening. Deadlines for the mammoth Sunday papers are even earlier, at some papers early Saturday afternoon. However, many members of the women's movement have jobs out-

[9]Needless to say, politicians and their news secretaries do not hesitate to use their familiarity with news routines to manipulate reporters and news organizations.

side the home, just as these feminist reporters do. Consequently, the movement tends to schedule evening meetings, after work when baby-sitters are available. Conferences, including, for instance, the convening meeting of the New York chapter of the Women's Political Caucus, are held on weekends. Like other working people, most reporters are off on weekends. Those who go to cover women's weekend activities must have their stories filed Saturday afternoon. The activities themselves may have barely started by that time. A general-assignment reporter told by her *New York Times* editor to "keep an eye on" the women's movement (as opposed to having it as a beat) insists, "My main problem was Sunday, weekends and night meetings, conferences and things like that."

To be sure, newsrooms are geared to handle late-breaking news. As noted, as much news as possible is processed as early as possible in order to provide for "emergencies"; staffing patterns also anticipate the transformation of other institutions' crises into newsroom routines. In addition, special provisions are made for perennially late standard items, such as theatre reviews. For example, a hard-news story judged to be of only marginal news value may be run in the first edition to occupy the space saved for a review. Provisions, including an elaborate system of stringers, are also made for the sports department, since many scores are not final until the late evening and important games are played on weekends. But to make those expensive provisions, the publisher and editors must be convinced that the expected coverage is vital to the newspaper as a consumer product. Reviews of cultural events and sports coverage are held to be of clear economic value to the news as product—not so news of the late-breaking events of the women's movement.

There is, however, one place in a newspaper that seems at least topically related to news of the women's movement and can be geared to handle those stories. That is the women's page, in particular the women's page of such major dailies as the *New York Times* and the *Los Angeles Times*.[10] On each of these papers, an alert editor with an adequate budget runs an alert staff that produces its own copy; it does not draw from syndicated items and wire services. Although no longer called the women's page (rather, they are labeled "life style," "people," or "food, family, furnishing, fashion") such

[10]Each of these papers runs its own wire service and includes stories from its women's pages in its distribution.

pages are a clear outgrowth of the traditional women's page that Van Gelder (1974; see also Guenin; 1975; Merritt and Gross, 1978) still finds typical of American newspapers.[11] They may be seen as a resource for the women's movement.

Getting in the Paper: The *New York Times*

Drawing on interviews with female editors and reporters for the *New York Times*, the rest of this chapter considers the *Times'* "family/style" section (its women's page) as such a resource. The data also include discussions with New York feminists about *Times* coverage. The *Times* was selected because it is a nationally prominent newspaper whose women's page is said to have introduced a new type of journalism in the 1960s.

One of the *Times'* women's page reporters characterizes that section as "the most feminist oriented in the country," although she notes that the paper goes through "periods when the [page's] editors say, 'We've had too many women's lib stories lately.' " (Again, the reference is to maintaining a stance of neutrality.) Credited by her staff as believing that the section is not to be written by feminists for feminists, Joan Whitman (interview, July 1975), then the section's editor, insists that it should carry "news about women, not news for women." That necessarily includes some news about the women's movement, in particular some news about "the changes in women's lives and the effects of the women's movement." Whitman says that her section covered the movement "by my choice." When she replaced Charlotte Curtis, who had been promoted to editor of the op ed page, Whitman asked neither the managing editor (her boss) nor her colleague, the metropolitan editor, if she could assume responsibility for the movement's coverage. She explains, "I just started to do it," in part because the women's page could provide better coverage than the general pages. The *Times'* women's page is a movement resource because its editor chose to make it one. An experienced professional, she may be likened to the professionally respected women reporters who introduce movement news into the general news col-

[11]She suggests that a Martian reading a traditional page "would conclude that every female earthling spent at least several days every month getting married."

umns. So long as her page met professionally respected criteria, like having an interesting layout, it was hers to run.

The woman's movement was not a general story because other editors did not choose to make it one. A metropolitan reporter assigned to keep an eye on the women's movement complained that her unofficial beat was a ghetto. Other reporters would continually give her items on women, including financial-department news about women's promotions in corporations and a diversity of other "firsts." Since the professional practice is to poach on others' preserves, not to enhance them, one must surmise that these gifts were prompted by other reporters' anticipated or experienced inability to get those items approved by their own bureaucratic superiors.

Besides the willingness to cover items about the women's movement, Whitman, members of her staff, and members of the metropolitan staff were all quick to cite four characteristics that make the women's page an ideal spot for such news; the most important is that these columns don't cover much "breaking" or hard news. Although an occasional story (perhaps ten or twelve per year, to use Whitman's figure) may be so topical or so tied in with that day's world events that it starts on page one and jumps to "family/style," most news on that page is "soft." The women's page can ignore late-night and Saturday deadlines and hold a story over for another day's edition, if desired.

In practice (as discussed in chapter 3), classifying any one occurrence as hard or soft news may be difficult. In 1966 the *Times* women's page ran a brief story in which Betty Friedan announced the formation of NOW. Placed between a recipe for turkey stuffing and an article announcing that hairstylist Pierre Henri was returning to his job at Saks Fifth Avenue, material in the NOW article clearly indicated that Friedan had been interviewed at least several days before the story's printing. The founding of NOW was treated as soft news.

A women's page reporter was assigned to cover a press conference held by Julie Nixon Eisenhower when she was scheduled to serve as Barbara Walters' television replacement for a week. After Eisenhower made comments about her father, the story was reassessed as hard news and moved to page one.

Another ambiguous example involves *Times* coverage of International Women's Year. Some stories about it were written by the

UN correspondent (who reports to the foreign editor) and carried on the general pages. Some were written by Judy Klemesrud, then one of the two women's-page writers keeping an eye on the movement, and were carried on the women's page. Coverage of the Mexico City conference, provided by Klemesrud, appeared on both general and women's pages.

By agreement, the women's page does not handle stories of daily urgency. But once, for any reason, an item becomes part of the preserve of the women's page, it may be reconstituted as "soft news." The page's editor may exercise her autonomy to treat a story as hard news or she may offer it to another editor to be treated as hard news. Each day Whitman attended the department editors' conference with the managing editor. At those meetings (described in chapter 2), the department editors assess their available material and may offer stories for page one.

As a second favorable characteristic, because most items on the women's page are seen as feature stories, news of the women's movement takes on added news value. Not only do reporters compete to be assigned to good stories and editors compete to get their own reporters' stories in the paper, but also the occurrences themselves are said to vie for attention. On her page, Whitman noted, stories about the women's movement don't have to "compete with Watergate." To be sure, Whitman has chosen to compare copy on the movement to a story that newsworkers identify as one of the most important of the decade. But others echo her assessment. Klemesrud says, "If the feminist stories didn't run on our page, they wouldn't run anywhere." Van Gelder of the *New York Post* says, "Whitman ran a story on that woman minister in France; if she didn't run it, it wouldn't have run at all." Lichtenstein suggests, "Half of where a story goes has to do with the kind of news day it is. If it's slow, the story [one of her feminist stories] may be on page one." But "if it's heavy [if the story must compete with many others], it goes inside and may be offered to the women's page."[12]

Defined as important on the "soft-news" women's page, a story may take on two more valued characteristics, informants note. It can be longer than it would be if run on the general pages, and it can receive a better display, including pictures. National bureau reporters, Washington reporters, and metropolitan reporters are all oriented

[12]She continues, "Perhaps it's unconscious discrimination."

toward page one. Indeed, a Washington reporter for the *Times* may pay more attention to page one of the *Washington Post* than to the women's page of the *Times*. Yet, a national reporter volunteered, the women's page "is the most revolutionary page in the paper. I never mind a story of mine appearing there [instead of page one]. You get good play, sensitive editing, and it will be well read." One women's page reporter points out, "There are space limitations for other [pages]." The coverage of International Women's Year offers a good example. The UN correspondent filed a story about a conference at the United Nations. It was terse, ran on an inside page, and was primarily a "shopping list of speakers," a catalogue of facts. Klemesrud filed a story on that same topic for the women's page. It occupied several columns, discussed the content of speeches, and analyzed the political interaction among conference planners, American feminists, and Third World women.

In this context, Whitman's assessment of her page's role becomes pertinent theoretically. She says, "I always get flack from women in the movement [who think stories about their activities should be run on the general news pages]. I just think they're wrong. It's better to have lots of space and good display [pictures] than to be in a four-paragraph story and," to repeat an example, "compete with Watergate" for editorial and reader attention. Indeed, Whitman's assessment raises a key issue: How does the eventual site of publication constitute an event as a topic?

Constituting the Movement as a Topic

A newspaper is a bureaucracy. A major metropolitan daily, like the *Times*, not only has such gross divisions as "advertising" and "editorial," but also its large divisions are subdivided into areas of discrete responsibility, each with its own department head (or editor) and, most important, its own budget. Department heads may jockey among themselves for power within the bureaucracy, as documented by Talese's account of the *Times*. This jockeying may include sexual politics. Talese (1966: 111) reports that an assistant managing editor mocked the "wasted" columns of the women's page to criticize a more highly placed editor's notion of importance. An informant advised me that Charlotte Curtis was one of two powerful women who refused to join the *Times* women's caucus when it started. According to the informant, Curtis' promotion from editor of the women's page to editor of the op ed page was being considered during that period. Jockeying and negotiations also affirm the primacy of the territorial editors over the topical departments. Yet Whitman notes that in 1975 her page had more stories starting on page one than in the recent past, at least in part because the growth and institutionalization of the women's movement have had an impact upon male editors.[13] According to Whitman, "There's greater interest in some things; [the other editors] are realizing the importance" of topics covered by the staff of the women's page.

On rare occasions the national editor may offer the women's page editor a story he "thinks will be good" for that section of the paper.[14] The placement of an article, written by a national reporter, on the impact of the recession on the divorce rate is one example of that practice. The coverage of the Mexico City conference of International Women's Year is another. In the first example, offering a story to the women's page "buys" more space elsewhere in the paper. (That is, it leaves more room for stories on the general pages.) In editorial conferences Whitman would argue that stories about women and the changing family belonged on her page. She said, "I fight for these stories. I request of whatever [province it may fall into], this is coming up and I would like to cover it for my page." Whitman requested that one of her reporters, Klemesrud, be assigned to International Women's Year after Klemesrud had asked Whitman for the assignment.

The location of the International Women's Year conference in Mexico City makes clear how the disposition of a story helps constitute its topic. At the *Times*, travel arrangements for a reporter assigned to a story outside the United States are charged to the foreign

[13] A member of the staff estimated three or four such stories a month.

[14] It is in the interests of the metropolitan, national, and international editors to have their stories jump to the women's page. Such "jumps" leave free columns in the general pages, which the editors share. The women's page has its own space budget. However, appearance on the women's page may be viewed as decreasing the article's importance and the writer's glory. Klemesrud acknowledged this past prejudice against appearing there when she suggested that reporters who "mind" when their work is on that page "don't like women." Her comment implies recognition of a common finding in the study of gender roles: Western societies accord less prestige to the activities of women than to those of men.

desk's budget. A member of the national editor's staff had filed some stories on International Women's Year. Klemesrud had filed more and longer stories on events and issues relating to International Women's Year. An award-winning journalist who also writes for magazines on a free-lance basis, Klemesrud could claim expertise on women's politics and some familiarity with the diplomatic problems that had surfaced at previous IWY meetings and might be expected to crop up again. Faced with Whitman's recommendation, the managing editor and foreign editor agreed that Klemesrud should cover the Mexico City event. But, it was specified that it was to be "the foreign editor's story. He would get all running-news stories about the conference and tribune [a special meeting for feminist nondelegates]. We [the women's page] would rake off stories that were not hard news, like stories about delegates." Some of Klemesrud's continuing-news stories started on page one and were fairly lengthy. All of her women's page stories received a "good display."[15]

The principle of territoriality and budgetary priority continued to be invoked to explain the *Times*' coverage after the Mexico City conference had ended. Jill Ruckleshaus, head of the American delegation, and other American delegates called a news conference to protest the stories carried by the American media. They noted that the stories had emphasized the disorganization of this woman's conference without the qualification that all international conferences are disorganized. Thus, the delegates claimed, the stories blamed women for the disorganization. Klemesrud, who felt the delegates' critique to be justified, covered the press conference, a hard-news story, for the *Times*. Her story was on the women's page; hard news connected with the conference had ceased to be the foreign editor's preserve when Klemesrud returned to her desk at the "family/style" department. And, as hard news carried on the women's page, the story received a large amount of space.

The practical reasoning associated with bureaucratic bargaining and bureaucratic budgets helps to constitute a topic. For just as any occurrence in the world may or may not be constituted as a story, depending upon whether it is noticed and deemed newsworthy, so, too, the practical reasoning associated with bureaucracies may determine: which aspects of a phenomenon are noticed and deemed news-

[15]Who chooses the pictures to be used on a page is an indicator of power. The women's page editor selects her own. Other departments have picture editors.

worthy; how those aspects are treated; the written style; and the display, including length and use of eye-catching pictures. These attributes may be considered the essence of a topic. Indeed, one might even say that an occurrence serves as the occasion of a topic. One informant claimed that editors will do a story on the women's movement if "they think a story on that topic is due and an event comes along."

By identifying a hard-news "general" story on International Women's Year with a story on the women's page, one may not notice that each story concerns a different topic: The event may occasion different accounts (Altheide, 1976; Lester, 1975), different plots (Darnton, 1975; Hughes, 1940), different treatments—in short, different stock narratives. That different topics should result is particularly probable since reporters tend, over time, to adopt the outlook of the news sources with whom they are associated: They ask the questions appropriate to their sources' world.[16] Inasmuch as questions contain their own answers, guiding where one may look for an answer and thus what one may find, these questions may be said to reconstitute not only a topic but a world.

The Institutionalized Movement: The Tyranny of Success

Ironically, yet logically, the successful institutionalization of the women's movement limited its ability to carry forth radical issues. As canons of neutrality were applied, feminists' views were balanced against those of members of the Pussycat League and, later, the

[16]Several examples involving President Nixon are pertinent. Reporters unaccustomed to covering the president noted items designed to be ignored. Noticing them changed the topic of each story.

Thus Wise (1973) reports that Latham of the *Washington Post* metropolitan staff was sent to cover Thanksgiving dinner at the White House, at which Nixon was scheduled to host wounded veterans from the war in Southeast Asia. Since Latham had never covered the president, he did not have a White House identification card and was kept waiting for twenty minutes at the building's gate. "As a result, Latham missed the opening glimpse of dinner afforded other reporters and cameramen; by the time he got through the gate, they were back in the White House press room watching football on TV [Wise, 1973: 13]." They were bored by this routine event; Latham was excited. So he requested the list of men who had sat at the president's table, phoned them about the dinner conversation, and learned that the president had discussed an American raid on a military base near Son Tay. The existence of that raid had previously been denied by the State Department.

forces of Phyllis Schlafly. And journalists who were also feminists had a limited view because of their membership in the middle class. Exposed to one another's activities as members of their respective news organizations' women's caucuses, in the early days of the movement they could try to turn their colleagues and professional friends into the basis for a news story. But other components of the women's movement, the activities of black groups, Puerto Rican groups, and ethnic working-class groups, were not as readily visible to them. By writing about what they saw, they helped to generate and to perpetuate the put-down that the women's movement was made up solely of the white middle class.

Furthermore, although the movement's bureaucratic establishment of central offices facilitated beat reporting, it also helped to redirect the social movement. As is common in the later stages of social movements, bureaucratic offices are used to lobby legislatures and government agencies. The women's offices helped to and were intended to turn the thrust of the movement from a concern with consciousness to a concern with politics and law. The avowed purpose of the National Women's Political Caucus and its member chapters is to elect feminists and lobby for legal change. The location of its office in Washington is not a symbolic or fortuitous gesture but a practical choice. However, once laws are introduced and activities are sponsored and funded by governments, they are not as likely to come under the purview of the women's page. Instead, laws about education become the concern of the education editor. Legal challenges to affirmative action become the affair of court and labor reporters. Proposals for constitutional amendments forbidding abortion become the concern of political reporters. In short, stories about issues raised by the women's movement are made into routine occurrences covered by specific (nonwomen's) beats and bureaus or assigned to general reporters.

Some feminists, notably Cynthia Epstein (1978), argue that this reassignment of responsibility is as it should be. Placement of news of the women's movement on the segregated women's page classifies

---

Bernstein and Woodward (1974) attended a Nixon news conference some time after their disclosures had crumbled some of Nixon's power and enabled them to request assignment to the news conference in the place of the regular reporter. Toward the end of the story they wrote, they noted that Nixon's hands shook throughout the news conference. Beat reporters accustomed to the White House routine omitted this observation from their stories, although they confirmed its accuracy. In both cases, the *Post*'s editors rescued Nixon by editing out the remark.

those stories among food, fashions, and funishings, not among the pressing affairs of the day. It tells men, Epstein argues, that the ideas and activities of the women's movement are not their concern. Since the official founding of NOW, feminists have debated whether it is more advantageous to be carried on the women's pages or the general pages of newspapers (Betty Friedan, personal communication, 1975).[17]

Yet both proponents of the women's page and proponents of general news placement, such as Epstein, ignore a key issue. By becoming the responsibility of beat and general reporters, issues and occurrences generated by any social movement are necessarily subjected to the frame of the conventional news narrative. Movement leaders may participate in the created and controlled controversy implicit in the web of facticity but, by dint of this participation, stories cannot propound the leaders' analysis of issues as factual statements about the social structure. The leaders may recommend practical reforms—subject to juxtaposed refutation and debate. But stories about their statements must center on who, what, and where, and the mechanics of why and how. Once framed within the web of facticity, a social movement cannot undercut the news net by challenging the legitimacy of established institutions.

To repeat an example from the work of Halloran, Elliott, and Murdock (1970), when British demonstrators against the Vietnam war carried picket signs about inflation and taxes, British journalists identified those concerns as irrelevant. Unlike the demonstrators, they did not analytically link Britain's economic problems with support of the war. Like the British demonstrators, American leftists failed in their attempt to have reporters notice a link between inflation and war. And the women's movement's identification of constricting undergarments as symbols of social constriction still brings smirks. Similarly, the feminist analysis that sexism is constituted in language regularly elicits journalistic parodies about congresspersons, chairpeople, and ombudspersons; folks named Johnsperson, coffee branded Martinoffspring and sayings like "Ecce persona." As Phillips put it, craft consciousness, "the logic of the concrete, a

[17]That debate has not centered around ghettoized women's television talk shows versus nightly TV news, because the structure of television programming does not necessitate a choice. Theoretically, both are possible; for a description of actual practice, see Cantor (1978).

present time orientation, and an emphasis on contingent events rather than structural necessities" (1976: 92) shapes news.

Ultimately, as we see in the next chapter, such "craft-related habits of mind" (Phillips, 1976: 92) are more than professional practices in the service of organizational needs. Indeed, sometimes they conflict with organizational preferences and mandates. But even when professionals conflict with their organizations and news organizations crusade against local and national governments, news practice is an ideology in action.

CHAPTER EIGHT
Facts, Freedom of Speech, and Ideology

Theorists have consistently argued that a society's mass media necessarily legitimate its status quo. Gerbner (1972: 51) suggests that today's mass media "are the cultural arm of the industrial order from which they spring" and so are in all ways political. Enzensberger (1974) characterizes the media as "the consciousness industry," whose "main business is to sell the existing social hierarchy" (Glascow Media Group, 1976) to consumers. Enzensberger (1974) extends that metaphor, speaking of contemporary communications processes as "the industrialization of mind." All argue that the mass media limit the frames within which public issues are debated, and so narrow the available political alternatives. Those limits may permit the expression of some dissenting opinion. But as Milliband (1969: 238) notes, the mass media "still contribute to the fostering of a climate of conformity" by containing dissent, "by the presentation of news which falls outside the consensus as curious heresies or . . . by treating [dissenting views] as irrelevant eccentricities which serious people may dismiss as of no consequence."

Despite the empirical support (introduced in preceding chapters), problems remain before one can apply the theorists' statements to my data. First, my analysis is based on data gathered over a ten-year period in the United States, and so do not permit historical or cross-cultural generalization. The theorists emphasize that news, like all cultural phenomena, develops in conjunction with socioeconomic and political institutions. But I have not demonstrated that contemporary news frames develop in concert with other institutions and are historically linked to them. Without reviewing the history of American news, it is impossible to affirm that the news media are "the cultural arm of the industrial order from which they spring."

Second, newsworkers would decry my generalizations. Both newsworkers and news organizations insistently present themselves as the fourth branch of government (Cater, 1959), the "fourth estate" (Hulteng and Nelson, 1971). To them, these terms do not connote that they are extensions of government. Rather, they mean that newsworkers and news organizations act as gadflies to insure that government serves the people. This self-presentation was explicit in the aftermath of the Watergate conspiracy. The news media stated: Two enterprising and determined young reporters working for a newspaper insistent upon disseminating the facts, even in the face of intense public and governmental opposition, took on the most powerful men in the country. The media sought to restore integrity to the executive branch of government. The *New York Times*, the *Washington Post*, the *Boston Globe* and other involved newspapers presented their publication of *The Pentagon Papers* in a similar light. They revealed facts about American involvement in Vietnamese affairs and battled against the government's attempt to hide the truth by imposing unnecessary restraints upon the free press (Porter, 1976).[1]

Reporters identify newspapers' crusades against the dysfunctional consequences of either existing laws or governmental activities as their finest hour. The New York reporter who first wrote about the fiscal crisis took great pride in that accomplishment. The local news editor of the *Seaboard City Daily* was more than gratified by a series of stories attacking illegal practices in the state legislature. He spoke of such stories as what newsworkers live for—the justification for daily newswork, yielding great personal and professional satisfaction.

[1]Porter (1976) points out that, in their briefs against the government's restraining order, some of these papers recognized the right of the government to censor in the name of national security.

Newsworkers take similar pleasure in prompting the public to organize against wrongs, and in defending the "little guy." The assistant managing editor of *Seaboard City Daily* was enthusiastic about an investigative series on leaders of organized crime. He expressed his hope that the public would rally to combat the activities exposed, explaining "we can only carry the ball so far"—but added that the paper would carry it as far as possible. Newsworkers at NEWS were proud of a series of stories about an imprisoned soldier who had been reared in their viewing area. The army had accused him of war crimes (killing civilians), but the television staff felt he was being made into a scapegoat since his supposed crime was common in war. They saw their stories as standing up for the little guy who was being buffeted and beleaguered by forces beyond his control.

The Cultural Arm of the Industrial Order

Two recent studies provide some evidence linking the development of news with the development of today's social structure. They also provide some justification for viewing news crusades as legitimating the status quo. One, by Schudson (1978), is a sociological history of the emergence of objectivity in journalism. The other is Dahlgren's (1977) analysis of the close relationship between news and the contemporary state.

The Growth of Professionalism: Schudson argues that the American penny press was associated with the growth of a free-market economy.[2] Challenging the old partisan press, the penny papers rejected the structures and values of a mercantile elite and became the first press to be oriented toward a readership with which it had no face-to-face connections (Schudson, 1978: 18–30).[3] Competing among themselves for readers, the popular newspapers also abided by the rules of a free-market society by competing with each other and with

[2]Other histories of news (e.g., DeFleur, 1966) also point to new developments in print technology and increased rates of literacy.

[3]Habermas (1974) emphasizes that the lack of "face-to-face" connections helped to eliminate the eighteenth century's notion of a bourgeois public and to reconstitute citizens as a fragmented audience.

other media for advertisers. Additionally, the newspapers accepted ideas offered by the new capitalist elite to justify its replacement of the older mercantile order. Among these ideas were that all private individuals had the right to purchase public knowledge and that all individuals act in their own self-interest. Such views, Schudson demonstrates, brought a slow but radical redefinition of the public and private spheres of life. For instance, in the eighteenth century the lawyer was viewed as a public figure responsible to the community; during the nineteenth century he emerged as a professional responsible to a client, whether the client were an individual or a railroad. The penny papers fed such radical redefinitions by valuing political independence and stressing news, not opinion. Factual news attracted readers, and so affirmed the notion of popular democracy explicit in the capitalist challenge to the colonial mercantile society.

The emphasis upon news was an emphasis upon fact. Party newspapers that survived the challenge of the penny papers adopted aspects of the new journalism, including use of the wire services and dependence upon facts. But the term "fact" had a different meaning in 1848, when the first American wire service was founded, than it did in 1865, 1890, or 1925. For the early wire services, presenting facts connoted presenting information acceptable to the editorial policies of all newspapers subscribing to the service. During the Civil War, presenting facts meant conveying government accounts of battles without assessing their validity. In the 1890s Lincoln Steffens (quoted in Schudson, 1978: 80) wrote, "Reporters were to report the news as it happened, like machines, without prejudice, color and without style; all alike. Humor or any sign of personality in our reports was caught, rebuked and, in time, suppressed." Yet, while proud of their lack of "moralistic mush" (Dreiser, quoted in Schudson, 1978: 89), reporters sought to convey their assessments of situations by marshaling facts. (Frequently those assessments were adopted from their editors, learned through blue-penciling and apprenticeships.)[4] That purpose was explicit in the work of the muckrakers. It was also found among William Randolph Hearst's reporters. For instance, when attacked for misrepresentation in an article about an event in Havana, one of Hearst's reporters stressed the veracity of his account. Then he added in his own defense, "My

[4]For an account of contemporary practices, see Breed (1955) and Sigelman (1973).

only object in writing the article was to try and show the people in the United States how little protection they may expect on one of their own vessels, under their own flag, in the harbor of Havana, where there should have been an American man-of-war stationed for the last six months [quoted in Schudson, 1978: 89]." As Schudson points out, "For a contemporary journalist to make such a confession and still contend that he or she had been scrupulously faithful to the facts would be . . . a contradiction in terms [1978: 89]."

Although professionalism emerged among newsworkers in the 1890s, it was not until the 1920s that facticity connoted professional neutrality and objectivity, and that newsworkers demonstrated their impartiality by explicitly eschewing distortion and personal bias. Then, recognizing that reporters were necessarily personally subjective, newspapers introduced signed political columns. However, even as an "institutional acknowledgement that they . . . were only individually constructed interpretations [Schudson, 1978: 149]," those columns could not solve the problem of objectivity in daily journalism. And (as discussed in chapter 5 of this text) signed columns identified as news analyses insistently distinguish between their constructed interpretations and the facticity of general news. According to Schudson, early-twentieth-century understanding of science offered a solution to the dilemma. Rather than stress facts, journalists such as Walter Lippmann invoked the importance of the *methods* used to gather facts.

By stressing methods—gathering supplementary evidence, presenting conflicting truth-claims, imputing facts through familiarity with police procedures, and using quotation marks, to name some techniques analyzed earlier—newsworkers produced a full-blown version of the web of facticity. American society faced uncertainty after World War I, when the new industrial order accelerated the introduction of new modes of rationalizing labor and brought a recognizably interdependent world economy. The belief that mere facts could elicit democratic participation in government waned as public-relations skills honed by the war were extended to peacetime governance. By adopting the scientific rationale of ascertaining facts through professional methods, Schudson suggests, the news media carved a new role for themselves. Instead of simply representing a democratic ideal by making information available through competitive journalism, the media and newsworkers saw themselves as arbiters of social reality. Just as scientists discovered the facts about nature by using normatively established objective methods, so, too, the news media and the news professionals would use their methods to reveal social reality to the news consumer.

The task of the news media and newsworkers, conveying information, remained the same. But their interpretation of that task was now radically different: Not only must newsworkers be factual, but facts must also be fair. By balancing opinions of newsmakers and weighing evidence, newsworkers must strive to achieve a fair presentation of the facts in order both to inform the public and to maintain credibility. They may launch crusades, as did the journalists of the 1890s, but they must do so in a spirit of fairness that aims to protect the public from the excesses of government, and the government from the excesses of the people. Using professional methods, the news media now stand between the government and the people. This role was implied, for instance, in the remark of the *Seaboard City Daily* editor about the paper's stories on organized crime. The newspaper would "carry the ball" as far as it could in order to arouse public pressure for governmental action against the underworld leaders.

Public and Private in Contemporary Times

Dahlgren (1977) argues that the late nineteenth and early twentieth centuries, when the web of facticity fell into place, represent the period when the concentration, centralization, and conglomeration of capital became significant socioeconomic processes. They undercut the competitive marketplace and transformed governance, prodding the state to play an ever more active role in the economy.[5] Today the state employs one-third of the workers (one-third is employed by the monopoly sector and the remainder by the residual competitive businesses). More important, the state politically supports the growth of the monopoly sector, "the dynamic innovative agent in modern society . . . where the major share of profits is realized and where 'economic growth' (as measured by such statistics

[5]Dahlgren uses the term "state" instead of "government" because the latter, more conventional term implies a concern with the interrelationship of conflicting institutions and branches of government, as opposed to the desired emphasis on a three-sector economy composed of state, conglomerates, and residual free enterprise.

as GNP) is determined [Dahlgren, 1977: 17]. '' Both the other economic sectors and the major institutional structures of society, react to the monopoly sector.

Accordingly, the mid-nineteenth-century distinction between ''public and private'' became problematic because of state-supported measures to maintain the growth of corporate capital. The state may foster competition artificially, as, for example, through the Newspaper Preservation Act, designed to support economically marginal newspapers. It may feed some conglomerates and so limit competition, as is done by federal contracts to electronic and aerospace industries. It may enact measures to alleviate somewhat the impoverished condition of the permanent underclass created by the technology that spurred the growth of corporate capitalism. In all these instances, the government (the public sector) becomes so enmeshed with industry (the private sector) and with the welfare of private individuals that the distinctions between public and private, so painfully worked out in the nineteenth century, no longer hold.

Schudson (1978) points out that during the nineteenth century the term ''private'' became identified with self-interest and took on a strong economic component. To be sure, ''all types of societies are limited by economic factors. Nineteenth-century society alone was economic in a different and distinctive sense for it chose to base itself on a motive only rarely acknowledged as valid in the history of human societies, and certainly never before raised to the level of justification of action and behavior in everyday life, namely, gain [Polanyi, 1944: 46].'' In the nineteenth century newspapers for the first time were organized for economic gain.

Schudson's sociological history of nineteenth-century journalism leads one to expect the twentieth-century news media to participate in the redefinition of public and private activities much as the nineteenth-century newspapers did. Following Schudson, it is logical to assume that the twentieth-century media became involved in the new economic transformation—the processes of concentration, centralization, and conglomeration. And it is sensible to expect the media to justify the new social order, just as nineteenth-century newspapers supported the ideology of the early capitalists. But history is not that simple.

Dahlgren claims, as have others (Milliband, 1969; Enzensberger, 1974; Wolfe, 1977), that the increased involvement of the state in private (economic) affairs has created a crisis in legitimacy, since, through its economic intervention, the state explicitly violates previously held norms. Furthermore, those same authors argue, the state has a vested interest in the fragmentation of public knowledge, including understanding government's involvement with corporate interests. A radical analysis of government's intertwinement with the corporate sector could lead to a revolutionary challenge, especially from those lacking a vested interest in the contemporary social system. And, inasmuch as the most powerful of the news media are themselves corporations, conglomerations, and monopolies (Tuchman, 1974; Eversole, 1971), they, too, have a vested interest in maintaining the status quo, including the legitimacy of the state.[6]

However, in direct contrast to the nineteenth-century media, the twentieth-century media do not propound a new sensibility with which to define public and private. Instead, the mass media maintain that the previous distinctions describe the contemporary situation. They play down the heady involvement of the corporate sector and the government in one another's activities. As we have seen, following early twentieth-century practice, news about the corporate sector of the economy is called financial news and is segregated in a separate section of the news product. On network news shows, special visual slides, used nightly, also segregate financial or stock-market news from more general information. Of course, financial news is sometimes placed on general news pages, where it is treated with special care. This is done when government is openly intervening in major economic matters, such as developing an energy program or considering subsidizing Boeing's plan to build an SST. At such times, economic news becomes the basis of observable governmental actions falling within defined territorial news beats, and so is presented within the nonanalytic frame of the web of facticity.[7]

More generally, though, news organizations are more apt to re-

[6]It must be emphasized that not all television stations are part of conglomerates. Some are family businesses, though they are many steps removed from "mom and pop stores." Conglomerates are most likely to be found in the major markets. Consider New York City's seven VHF stations: three are owned by networks; two are owned by groups (corporations owning up to five television stations in addition to other holdings); one is owned by a newspaper; and one is a public broadcasting station.

[7]The principles applied to coverage of the women's movement also apply here.

port about public institutions than about powerful private ones. For instance, the New York City media freely criticize spending by the public City University, but not that of private Columbia University.[8] They report on spending at city hospitals, but not at Presbyterian Hospital or New York Medical Center. Yet the private universities and hospitals receive federal and state funds. The private hospitals are partially financed by Medicare and Medicaid monies. A portion of New York State's budget for higher education is earmarked for the so-called private institutions, and, in the mid-1970s, their share of public monies increased, while funding of City University decreased and tuition was imposed.

By maintaining an aritificial distinction between public and private, the news media mask the actual organization of significant services. They also allow "private institutions" not to make news, much as in an earlier day, when members of the upper class sought to keep their names *out* of the papers except for announcements of birth, marriage, and death. The power to keep an occurrence out of the news is power over the news.[9]

Similarly, references in the news to the corporate sector of the economy as "big business," rather than "corporate capitalism" or "monopoly capitalism," reinforce corporate power. As metaphor, "big business" invokes images of the competitive marketplace of an earlier era, not the contemporary economic situation. Linguistic practices such as these hamper an analytic understanding of societal issues. Like the web of facticity with which they are associated, such practices unintentionally create and control controversy by limiting possible analyses of the interrelationship between and among phenomena.

In 1968, I observed reporters attending a news conference of five anti–Vietnam war activists, including Dr. Benjamin Spock, who had been accused of conspiracy. The reporters were dismayed when one activist introduced the topic of an American ship, the *Pueblo*, seized by the North Koreans earlier that day. They insisted that the Vietnamese war and America's relationship to North Korea were not interrelated, and that the activist was spouting off. The American journalists' reaction resembled that of the British reporters who saw

[8]Fred Goldner (personal communication) reminded me of this phenomenon.

[9]Everett C. Hughes (personal communication) reminded me of this interpretation (see Molotch and Lester, 1975).

picket signs decrying inflation at an antiwar rally (as discussed in chapter 7). In the same vein, daily news reports associating fluctuations in the stock market with traders' views of the day's political events obscure the structure of our economic system even as they claim to elucidate it. In the case of the news conference, the event orientation of the reporters prevented them from recognizing the validity of drawing connections between international events. The connections drawn by the financial reporters represent "the logic of the concrete, a present time orientation and an emphasis on contingent events" rather than economic structure. In both cases, newsworkers impose their professional understandings upon occurrences to shape a reality that legitimates the status quo.

The brief history of news reporting I have sketched highlights the past associations between the media's self-conception and its legitimating function, and thus encourages another look at the contemporary situation.

Whose Freedom of Speech? Whose Right to Know?

Since the eighteenth century the media have identified their activities with freedom of speech as provided for in the First Amendment of the Bill of Rights. But some recent claims of the media to freedom of speech also blur the distinction between the public and private spheres. Additionally, the media have identified contemporary journalistic methods aiming for fairness with free speech.

Like the Constitution itself, the First Amendment is based on ideas prevalent during the Enlightenment. Drawing upon a rationalist notion of discourse and truth, the Enlightenment presupposed that when conflicting ideas and opinions compete freely with one another, the truth will emerge. This supposition builds two different and potentially antithetical rights into the First Amendment. The first, freedom of speech, provides that amendment with its popular name. The other and less frequently discussed provision is the right to know. According to the Enlightenment model of rational discourse, the public must be exposed to competing ideas if truth is to prevail. Unless the public can determine truth by assessing diverse opinions, it cannot wisely decided how it will be governed. To protect the public's right to know, the various branches of government must guarantee free speech.[10]

Ultimately, of course, freedom of speech and the right to know can interfere with governmental activities. Thomas Jefferson's views on the primacy of the First Amendment are particularly popular with the news media, for Jefferson insistently confirmed his faith in the Enlightenment model. In 1787 he wrote: "Were it left to me to decide whether we should have a government without newspapers or newspapers without a government, I should not hesitate to prefer the latter." In 1807, during his presidency, Jefferson reiterated his faith in the Enlightenment model despite the press' scurrilous attacks upon him. At least, his language continues to juxtapose "the press" and "truth." "It is a melancholy truth that suppression of the press could not more completely deprive the nation of its benefits, than is done by its abandoned prostitution to falsehood. Nothing can now be believed which is seen in a newspaper. Truth itself becomes suspicious by being put in that polluted vehicle." Finally, in 1823, he strongly reaffirmed, "The only security of all is in a free press." (All quotes are from Cater, 1959: 75.)

Several assumptions in this model are keys to understanding its applicability to contemporary conditions. First, in the eighteenth century the term "public" still connoted a general responsibility to the community and the community's assessment of its own interests. Second, those subscribing to the journals of opinion and, accordingly, those constituting the community and responsible for the assessment of truth were mostly the mercantile elite. Third, the rationalist model of determining truth was based upon the Enlightenment assumption that the methods of scientific discourse aimed at determining truth could be extended to social and political phenomena.

We have seen that the first two assumptions of the First Amendment were transformed during the nineteenth century. Economic self-interest and professionalism replaced public responsibility as pervasive motives for action. The penny press replaced the partisan press. These two changes enter into an assessment of the propriety of viewing science as a model for ascertaining social and political truth, for the model is heavily based upon the rationalists' own patterns of

[10]An interesting contrast of French and American interpretations of these ideas is found in Habermas (1973).

discourse through face-to-face social interaction. Gathering at salons in France, coffee shops in England, and clubs and taverns in New York, these men of ideas explored and debated philosophic issues concerning the conduct of inquiry and the laws of nature and of political systems.[11] For them, public discourse presupposed active personal interaction in which ideas were assessed and from which social organization proceeded. Agreeing to the identification of truth through informed and rational dialogue, the public could organize to implement social policy and bring about conceptually valid social change. Since "public" had a specific referent—the rationalists and the mercantile elite with whom the editors associated—public discourse as envisioned by the authors of the Bill of Rights was undermined by the introduction of the penny press. As noted, these journals were the first newspapers lacking face-to-face connections with their readers.

But even when one can locate a group that resembles a public in the eighteenth-century sense of that term, one finds that truth does not necessarily emerge from rational debate; nor is it necessarily cumulative. Consider the "community of discourse," to use Chaney's (1977) term, upon which the Enlightenment model is based: the community of science. The rationality of scientific argument (the assessment and revision of ideas accomplished through interactive exchange and empirical testing) supposedly establishes what is true of natural phenomena. And the eighteenth-century rationalists extended that tenet of natural science to social and political phenomena. Through what we now think of as their naive empiricism, eighteenth-century thinkers assumed a nonreflexive relationship between social thought and social phenomena. (Indeed, that assumption continued to hold sway in American social science well into the twentieth century.) Pointing out that contemporary philosophies insistently distinguish between social science and natural science, in part because of the role of reflexivity in social inquiry (Giddens, 1976; see chapter 10 of this volume), puts a dent in the Enlightenment model.[12] An even more important criticism is implicit in histories and sociologies of natural science.

[11] I stress New York, since it has historically served as the center of American journalism, where most new developments have been introduced.

[12] Reflexivity also plays an important role in the Heisenberg principle (as discussed in chapter 9 of this text).

Recent work on patterns of scientific thought (Kuhn, 1962) and publication (Mullins et al., 1977) demonstrates that the state of a natural science depends not only on its topic but also on the structure of interaction among scientists. What is identified as scientific truth is embedded in a complex of professional arrangements, including networks of associations (described as invisible colleges by Crane, 1972) and norms about publication of ideas and findings. For an idea to be influential, it must gain access to leading professional journals, and that access is associated with specific career patterns (Reskin, 1977). Noting such patterns as the young gradually taking power from older scientists and then imposing their own theories, Kuhn argues that scientific "advances" are not cumulative. The discontinuity in the progression of dominant scientific paradigms, he claims, necessarily suggests that the truth does not evolve through a straightforward linear progression of the assessment of ideas. Rather, an era's truths emerge from the social organization of science and scientists during a specific historical period.

Of course, using twentieth-century findings to debunk eighteenth-century ideas announces that in the long run, the Enlightenment model of the emergence of truth through conflict may well be true. Yet contemporary findings about the community of science remain pertinent because they alert us to the importance of *access* to the media in the determination of truth. Questions of access are embroiled in contemporary court cases involving the First Amendment. Those questions are particularly problematic because of legal distinctions between owning a newspaper and holding the license for an electronic medium.

Newspapers and the First Amendment: Because of the introduction of advertising, the pervasiveness of the wire services, the processes of centralization, concentration, and conglomeration of ownership, and the emergence of journalistic professionalism, newspapers no longer resemble the eighteenth-century press whose freedom Jefferson so strongly affirmed. Nonetheless, newspapers are identified as private property, and those who own newspapers have the right to publish what they will—within certain limitations pertaining to national security (see Porter, 1976). Newspapers are not legally required to grant access to their pages to anyone who wants it. And publishers are well within their rights to challenge the news professionals' claims to be the arbiters of what is newsworthy. That news-workers claim the right to determine what is news and how it will be covered is an indication of their claim to professional expertise. But ultimately, for newspapers, "Freedom of the press is guaranteed only to those who own one," as A. J. Liebling so perceptively re-marked. As Benét (1978) explains, although an owner may rarely in-terfere with news coverage, he or she has the last word on how an issue will be handled.

The Supreme Court affirmed the right of owners in a case in-volving the *Miami Herald*, a member of the Knight newspaper chain.[13] In 1972 a candidate for public office sued for access to the *Herald* in order to rebut its charges against him. Denying the right of access, one judge argued that the Constitution guaranteed a free press, not a fair press. Editors may edit according to their judgment. Newspaper owners may publish what they will. Yet the clear affirma-tion of the press' right to free speech contains problems.

First, as Barron (1973: 19) points out, government has inter-fered with the free press by passing the Newspaper Preservation Act of 1970. That legislation was designed to support economically fal-tering newspapers in order to increase the published viewpoints available to consumers. Barron argues, "If Congress has constitu-tional power to enact legislation to encourage diversity of viewpoints in the press, Congress . . . can enact legislation to give readers rights of access to the press." In other words, by interfering in the market-place of publishing, the private sphere, Congress has blurred the dis-tinction between private and public rights, and so opened the door to limiting the freedom of speech as the freedom of newspaper owners.

Second, the Newspaper Preservation Act assumes that news-papers compete only with one another. But most news consumers get their information from television and trust its credibility more than that of newspapers (Roper Organization, Inc., 1971). Newspapers have altered their format to maintain readership in the face of elec-tronic competition. And, in any one area, there are inevitably more television stations than newspapers. For instance, in Miami in 1972, the *Herald*, with a circulation of 396,797, competed directly with a weak afternoon paper, the *Miami News* of the Cox chain, with which it shared printing facilities and advertising staff. Miami also had

---

[13]This account and the next few pages draw heavily on Friendly (1976), although his interpretation is quite different from mine.

three UHF and six VHF television stations.[14] Does federal regulation of television interfere with competition between the two media? The question has not been raised in the courts, so far as I know. But it, too, points to the transformation of the meaning of open competition and the blurring of distinctions between the public and private spheres. And it raises the complex issue of the right to free speech in the electronic media.

Television and the First Amendment: Since 1928 the federal government has regulated access to the airwaves, for the number of frequencies available for broadcasting has been limited by the physical properties of the medium (until the advent of cable television), and the "airwaves belong to the people," as Herbert Hoover announced when he was Secretary of Commerce (quoted in Tuchman, 1974). The government directly regulates only television and radio stations, not the networks, since the networks are essentially suppliers of programs who rent time from their affiliates.[15] However, because each network owns five VHF stations, the Federal Communications Commission can influence the networks by pressuring their stations or by regulating affiliates who carry network programming. Legally, according to various communications acts, those who hold licenses for television and radio stations are not "owners." Although the buying and selling of stations are still only loosely regulated, the government recognizes the holders of the right to broadcast on a specific frequency as "licensees."[16] Legally, licensees hold a public trust; owners have private rights.

Needless to say, the broadcasting industry is displeased with the definition of broadcasting licenses as public trusts. License holders claim to be owners, and thus to have the same freedom of speech as those who own newspapers. When he was president of NBC News, Reuven Frank defended the broadcasters' rights to unfettered freedom of speech. He argued that government limitations suggest "that the First Amendment might become the first constitutional provision repealed by technological advance" [quoted in Friendly, 1976:

[14]One of the VHF stations also broadcast on UHF.

[15]Exempt from direct regulation by the FCC, the networks are nonetheless the largest suppliers of national news.

[16]The FCC must approve sales of licenses, but it does not get to choose the new owner from among those seeking to purchase the license from its present owner.

211].'' For some lawyers, though, such as Barron (1971–72: 106), ''It is one of the great public relation triumphs of the twentieth century over the eighteenth that broadcasters have managed to identify themselves so completely with the First Amendment.''

Broadcasters willing to accept a definition of their licenses as franchises do so in the name of twentieth-century understanding of the role of the news media. They present themselves as defenders of the people against the excesses of government, and so as the purveyors of truth. Like Lippmann and his colleagues of the 1920s, these media owners take a proprietory attitude toward the public. In the 1920s:

> The educated middle class no longer heard in ''public opinion'' its own voice, the voice of reason. The professional classes now took public opinion to be irrational and therefore something to study, direct, manipulate and control. The professions developed a proprietory attitude toward ''reason'' and a paternalistic attitude toward the public [Schudson, 1978: 146].

Consider the defense of licenses as franchises offered by Charles H. Crutchfield, president of a broadcast group:

> At no time has the government even remotely interfered with us or applied any pressure. . .as far as trying to limit what we say. _ . . . If we in the media spent half the time defending the rights of our people against the excesses of the federal government that we do in protesting the real and imagined assaults upon our own ''rights,'' not only the public, but we ourselves would be better served [quoted in Friendly, 1976: 211].

Not only does Crutchfield identify the media as the defenders of the people, but he also emphasizes that for all intents and purposes, his stations broadcast without government interference. Thus, he implies, the distinction between franchise and private ownership is moot.

For the government, though, the question of access is more than who will hold a license to operate a public medium. It also entails access to a station's airwaves, as set forth in the Fairness Doctrine. In its 1959 version, Section 315(a) of the Communications Act, the Fairness Doctrine states:

> Nothing in the [equal-time rule, a provision that all sides of an electoral issue must be presented] shall be construed as relieving broadcasters in the presentation of newcasts, news interviews, news docu-

mentaries and on-the-spot coverage of news events from the obligation imposed on them. . .to operate in the public interest and to afford reasonable opportunity for the discussion of conflicting views on issues of public importance [quoted in Friendly, 1976: 27].

A 1961 ruling of the Federal Communications Commission adds:

> A broadcast licensee has an affirmative obligation to broadcast programs devoted to discussion and consideration of public issues, and may engage in editorializing. However, the licensee also has an obligation to see that persons holding opposing viewpoints are afforded a reasonable opportunity for the presentation of their views. Where attacks of a highly personal nature have been made on local public officials, the licensee has an affirmative duty to take all appropriate steps to see to it that the persons attacked are afforded the fullest opportunity to respond [quoted in Friendly, 1976: 30].

At one time or another, the three commercial networks, the National Association of Broadcasters, the Radio–Television News Directors Association, assorted holders of radio and television licenses, Walter Cronkite, David Brinkley, and Harry Reasoner have all claimed that such regulations impinge on their freedom of speech. The networks and others who have licenses for stations base their objections on their self-definition as owners, not as holders of franchises. But they and the news professionals raise other arguments, too. Foremost among them is that government regulation interferes with their activities and so has a "chilling effect" upon them.[17] And, they claim, professional news practices guarantee a fair presentation, so regulation is unnecessary.

In testimony before the Senate Subcommittee on Constitutional Rights, Walter Cronkite argued that the fairness regulations constituted a chilling effect: "News and dissemination cannot be accomplished without fear of failure . . . and if the reporter or editor constantly must be looking over his shoulder for those who would have this product reflect their standard of right and wrong, of fairness and bias . . . [news dissemination] cannot be achieved [quoted in Friendly, 1976: 209]."

The Radio–Television News Directors Association took a similar tack in the Red Lion case, a Supreme Court case involving the application of the Fairness Doctrine to a fundamentalist radio station

---

[17]That is, the possibility of being taken to court makes them overly cautious in expressing and disseminating potentially controversial ideas.

in Red Lion, Pennsylvania. That case is particularly interesting because the RTNDA sought to dissociate itself from the ultraconservative radio station, as did the National Association of Broadcasters and two television networks that also filed briefs before the court.[18] Rather than defend the right of extremist views to be heard, RTNDA argued that the Fairness Doctrine interfered with the work of its members as responsible professionals. In the words of a subsequent opinion, filed several years later by Justice Warren E. Burger about another case:

> For better or for worse, editing is what editors are for and editing is the selection and choice of material. That editors—newspaper or broadcast—do abuse this power is beyond doubt . . . but there [is] no accepted remedy other than a spirit of moderation and a sense of responsibility—and civility—on the part of those who exercise the guaranteed freedoms of expression [quoted in Friendly, 1976: 136].

By refusing to uphold the right of an extremist view to be heard without the rebuttal mandated by the Fairness Doctrine, the RTNDA, National Association of Broadcasters, the networks, and the court seem to be affirming the "scientific model" of journalism. They are asserting that the media are to establish and present "the true account" to the public, including the views of all responsible parties to a dispute. The public is not to choose between conflicting opinions, each presented by a different newspaper or news source, as was thought proper in the eighteenth century. Instead, the methods of contemporary journalism guarantee a fair presentation and capture "a spirit of moderation . . . a sense of responsibility . . . and civility."

This view of news processing was not implied but explicitly invoked by NBC when the fairness of one of its documentaries was challenged before the FCC.[19] The documentary was "Pensions: The Broken Promise." Accuracy in Media, Incorporated, contended that NBC had presented a one-sided account that would leave viewers

[18]The RTNDA wanted the ruling to focus on its professional claims, and the claims of the radio station as those of a little guy being pushed around. It feared that network briefs would prompt a concern with the activities of major corporations and would thus contaminate the issue. The station lost the case. This account draws on Friendly (1976).

[19]Again I draw on Friendly (1976), the best source on recent Fairness Doctrine cases. His interpretation stresses, though, that you can't tell the "good guys" from the "bad guys" when it comes to First Amendment rights.

with the impression that all pension plans are inadequate. NBC replied that the program had included the appropriate disclaimers: The script pointed out that it was not possible to generalize from the flaws of some plans to make statements about all plans. It was true, NBC argued, that its staff had not balanced every criticism with a defense. But, acting in good faith, it had contacted each of the worst offenders mentioned in the program and invited them to appear before NBC's cameras. Through no fault of its own, the staff could not convince a representative to defend his or her company. NBC did obtain a general defense of pension plans through interviews with pension holders, employers, and industry spokespersons, including an executive of the National Association of Manufacturers. Finally, NBC cited Justice Burger's opinion that "editing is what editors are for." Taken together, NBC's arguments state that professional news practices ensure fairness and so guarantee the public's right to know.

In this formulation, the right to know is the right to know the facts established by NBC, not the right to know all possible opinions on the topic. For the practices cited by NBC, including offering time for rebuttal to the worst offenders, are core elements of the web of facticity. The notion that carefully assessed facts, including the fact that some people disagree, constitute freedom of speech is also contained in another of NBC's contentions. It claimed that its program was not controversial because it did not discuss specific legislative reforms. Rather, NBC felt, as David Brinkley wrote independently to the FCC: "To be found guilty of 'unfairness' for not expressing . . . the view that most people are not corrupt or that pensioners are not unhappy is to be judged by standards which simply have nothing to do with journalism [quoted in Friendly, 1976: 153]."

For NBC, then, fair speech is equated with free speech; governmental regulations interfering with newsworkers' professional activities inhibit free speech by interfering with newswork. That stations carrying NBC's documentaries are legally public franchises is irrelevant to this argument. NBC invoked professionalism, practices common to both ink and electronic journalism, not the rights of owners. Like news professionalism itself, the NBC argument blurs distinctions between what properly belongs to and in the public sphere and what belongs in the private sphere of life.

News professionalism claims independence of both ownership and management by claiming the right to judge what news is. As might be expected, the principle of professional dominance conflicts with the principle of control by owners and managers and can be a source of bitter dispute. Fred Friendly resigned from his position as head of CBS News when network officials refused to broadcast live the first Senate hearings on the Vietnam war (Friendly, 1967). Preferring to air profitable reruns of situation comedies, the network insisted that coverage on the evening news would suffice to tell the story; they rejected Friendly's news judgment. Similarly, according to the *New York Times* (1977: 15), the editors of two papers owned by the Pan-Ax newspaper chain were fired after they refused to run a story by Washington correspondent George Bernard, hired by the publisher, John P. McGoff. A former employee of the *National Enquirer*, which eschews the web of facticity, George Bernard wrote that President Carter condones promiscuity for his male staff and is grooming his wife for the vice-presidency. One complaint of the editors—that the correspondent's story took material out of context—is a professional affirmation of the web of facticity. Their refusal to run the disputed story is an affirmation of the claimed license (E.C. Hughes, 1964) of professionals: They should determine what is news.

It would, however, contradict available data to state that news professionals always fight to maintain their right to determine news. Both newspaper and television stations carry "must stories," items that the business office, advertising staff, or front office say "must be carried" to satisfy either advertisers or friends of well-placed executives in the news organization.[20] Newsworkers dislike this practice, found more commonly at newspapers than at television stations, but journalism textbooks adhere to organizational constraints. Thus Hohenberg (1962: 45) instructs students that the slug "must" can be used to label only such stories, since they "must" be run and are exempt from the competition for dissemination applied to other items uncovered by the news net. Using the "must" label to identify an optional story unearthed by the reporter would interfere with the editors' appropriate exercise of their own news judgment.

Additionally, television newsworkers follow organizational mandates by occasionally linking their news judgment to the pref-

[20]Additionally, executives may recommend interviews with their friends when the friends are experts on a topic in the news. However, such recommendations are very rare. I learned of only one example of this during my observations at NEWS.

erences of advertisers. For instance, if a bank and an airline company take turns sponsoring the evening news, sponsorship may influence the ordering of stories about bank robberies and plane crashes. When there was a newsworthy bank robbery on the day the bank sponsored the NEWS program, a newsworker would call both advertisers and arrange for the airline to run its commercials that evening. A similar procedure would be followed when an air crash occurred when the airline was scheduled to be the sponsor. When there were items about both a bank robbery and an air crash, the "touchy" item would not be run next to the related commercial, even if news judgment suggested that as the appropriate placement in the ranking of the day's news.

Newsworkers' adherence to organizational realities in these cases does not invalidate their claim to professionalism. It suggests that professional practices are encouraged so long as they uphold the interests of news organizations (see Molotch and Lester, 1975). And, once again, it affirms that the same practices and associated problems crop up in both media. To be sure, newspapers carry more "musts" than newscasts. But newspapers generally carry more items than newscasts, and so their "musts" are less conspicuous. Technological differences provide marginal distinctions in professionalism between the two media. The dissimilar technologies do not mean that the relationship of newspaper professionals to owners is intrinsically different from the relationship of their TV counterparts to holders of television licenses.

In practice, the distinction between private ownership and public ownership is blurred. In both spheres news professionalism claims to hold sway. In both spheres professionalism connotes the web of facticity and places itself between newsmakers and the public. And the television news narrative is a visual enactment of the web of facticity. In both spheres those responsible for management and finances may either resist or accede to professional dominance (see Freidson, 1971). In sum, the distinction between the free speech of the press and that of the electronic medium is empirically invalid and hence theoretically problematic. Furthermore, as we have seen, professional practices found in both media limit the access of radical views to news consumers, and so limit everyone's use of the media as a political and social resource. Those practices limit the right to know.

News as Ideology

The above discussion suggests that news limits access and transforms dissent. It legitimates the contemporary state by eschewing analysis through ahistoricity, the logic of the concrete, and an emphasis on the contingency of events rather than on structural necessity. According to theories recently introduced to social science, such practices are ideological. To understand the contemporary application of the term "ideology," we must examine how that concept has been used in the past.

Ideology and the Situational Determination of Knowledge: Since the publication of Karl Mannheim's treatise *Ideology and Utopia*, sociologists have held that all knowledge is situationally determined. What one knows is based on one's location in the social structure, including one's class position and class interests. When applied to news, that tenet implies that news presentations are inherently middle class. For instance, Gans (1966) points out that American newsworkers are middle class (as is professionalism itself, according to Schudson [1978]) and hence the attitudes implicit in the news are inevitably those of middle-class Americans.

Past sociological theories differentiate knowledge from ideology by saying that knowledge reveals the truth while ideology skews truth to move people to action. It follows that news may be said to express middle-class ideology to the extent that middle-class truths are distinct from objective truths. By implication, then, assessing the degree to which news is ideological involves investigating and determining truth, and then comparing that truth with the supposed ideology. This implication that ideology and knowledge may be distinguished by independently determining truth introduced severe analytic problems to social-science inquiry. If all knowledge is situationally determined, who can determine the truth?

Mannheim (1936) sought to get around this problem by claiming that the intelligentsia were structurally marginal to contemporary societies. Living by their own norms, eschewing the values of all social classes, and prizing knowledge above all else, they alone were qualified to distinguish between truth and ideology. Mannheim's

solution is flawed. First, the norms of the intelligentsia are not necessarily objective. They may be merely different. The very attachment
of the intelligentsia to some ideas may make them incapable of seeing that those ideas are invalid. Indeed, that is one implication of
Kuhn's (1962) finding that older scientists are not convinced to abandon their paradigms by contradictory findings. Second, today's academic intelligentsia has become part of the professional sector of the
middle class. The professionalization of the intelligentsia implies
that sociologists, like doctors, lawyers, and journalists, have a class
position and class interests, so their knowledge, too, is situationally
determined (Gouldner, 1970).

Dorothy E. Smith summarizes the problem of the situational determination of knowledge and the concomitant identification of
ideology this way:

> If the perspectives and concepts of the knower are determined not by
> the object of knowledge, but for example by his or her class position
> and . . . class interests, then it is argued that knowledge is irremediably
> ideological, and "knowledge" a term which must continually be re-
> solved back into "ideology" [1972: 1.].

If all knowledge is situationally determined, it is impossible for any
individual to identify his or her knowledge as objective, non-
ideological truth. To clarify her reasoning, Smith adds:

> It must be stressed that knowing is always a relation between knower
> and known. The knower cannot therefore be collapsed into the known.
> To know is always to know on some terms and the paradox of knowing
> is that we discover in its object the lineaments of what we already
> know. There is no other way to know than humanly and therefore the
> knower is situated historically and culturally. This is the fundamental
> human condition of knowing. The very concept of knowledge itself . . .
> is historically and culturally given. If to be situated as such entails
> ideology (indeed, if to be human entails ideology), then knowledge
> [and science as knowledge] is fundamentally ideological [1972: 2].

Newsworkers themselves have incorporated a version of Smith's
reasoning into their own professionalism. They argue that the critic
wishes to substitute his or her personal and inevitable biases for
those of professional newsworkers. The critics' accusation that
newsworkers are ideological is said to translate into the statement,
"My biases are preferable to yours." And newsworkers take com-

fort that, in the aggregate, their accounts of events are true by noting that those accounts were independently produced by newsworkers in a variety of organizations, and so do not represent personal bias. As for the problem of professional or class bias, they revert to identifying the methods they use to gather and assess news as guarantees of objectivity.[21]

An Alternative View of Ideology: Recent social-science theories offer an interesting solution to both the problem of the situational determination of knowledge and the newsworkers' claim to knowledge gathered through objective methods. Smith proposes to distinguish analytically between knowledge and ideology by examining what is *not* said or done rather than what is articulated or accomplished. She proposes to examine how methods of knowing obscure truth instead of revealing it: "Ideology as contrasted with knowledge identifies . . . the interested procedures which people use as a *means not to know* [1972: 3]." By "interested" Smith means based in class position or class interest. Expanding her distinction between knowledge and ideology, Smith draws on an idea common to interpretive theories: Concepts specify what is already known in an amorphous way, what is already taken for granted. Accordingly, she explains:

> Ideology can be viewed as a procedure for sorting out and arranging conceptually the living actual world of people so that it can be seen to be as we know it ideologically. This is a characteristic of any ideological practice in thinking, regardless of its place in the political spectrum of ideas. It is a practice which has the effect of making the fundamental features of our own society mysterious because it prevents us from recognizing them as problematic. The concept becomes a substitute for reality. It becomes a boundary, or a terminus through which inquiry cannot proceed. What ought to be explained is treated as fact or as assumption [1972: 12].

Viewing ideology as "interested procedures people use as a means not to know" connotes that ideology prevents knowledge by limiting inquiry—by closing off the possibilities of an analytic examination of social life.

Several of the practices Smith identifies are characteristic of the procedures of news professionals and news organizations:

---

[21]Newsworkers thus address the issue of personal bias, not class bias.

Ideology makes the structure of society mysterious by substituting concepts for reality: News presents the terms "public" and "private" as though they described the contemporary corporate state, thus hiding the socioeconomic structure of contemporary society.

What ought to be explained is treated as fact or assumption: News stories eschew analysis, preferring instead an emphasis on the concrete and the contingency of events as well as a present-time orientation. They avoid structural linkages between events.

Ideological procedures are a means not to know: The temporal and spatial anchoring of the news net, as well as professionalism, prevent some strips of occurrences from being defined and disseminated as news events. Professional practices, as frames, dismiss some analyses of social conditions as soft-news novelties and transform others into ameliorative tinkerings with the status quo.

Following the reasoning Smith offers, one may then suggest that news, like knowledge, imposes a frame for defining and constructing social reality. But, as ideology, news blocks inquiry by preventing an analytic understanding through which social actors can work to understand their own fate. Ultimately, news as ideology prevents the realization of the Enlightenment model of free speech and public governance by preventing the ascertainment of truths about contemporary society, by limiting access to ideas.

This treatment of news as ideology draws heavily on Smith's work. But her analysis is not idiosyncratic. Lazarsfeld and Merton (in Merton, 1968; see also Gitlin, 1977) speak of the emphasis on unanalyzed facts as "technological propaganda," a notion implying ideology. Following Habermas (1971), Schudson (1978), Dahlgren (1977), and the Glasgow Media Group (1976) write of the naive empiricism of newswork as the "technocratic strategy" of legitimation and social control. Yet, merely to accept Smith's argument and the concepts of these other authors as proof of the ideological nature of newswork is to engage in the naive empiricism of the news professional. Mere acceptance appeals to the testimony of legitimated experts—academic social scientists—to validate a truth-claim. Accordingly, in the concluding chapters I will examine theories about the social construction of knowledge to reconsider how newswork shapes news. Chapter 9 explicates the theoretical concepts that are central to my ethnographic discussions of newswork and that also inform Smith's treatment of ideology. Chapter 10 uses those concepts to reconsider news as ideology.

CHAPTER NINE
News as a Constructed Reality

Sociologies maintain a stance toward people as social actors. More traditional sociologies than those used in the preceding descriptions of newswork characterize the activities of men and women as products of their socialization to norms derived from objective characteristics of the social structure. Tersely put, they argue that society creates consciousness. In contrast, recent interpretive sociologies, whose concepts underlie the preceeding chapters, hold that the social world provides norms that actors invoke as resources or constraints as they actively work to accomplish their projects.[1] Through this work, actors shape the social world and its institutions as shared and constructed phenomena. Two processes occur simultaneously: On the one hand, society helps to shape consciousness. On the other, through their intentional apprehension of phenomena in the shared social world—through their active work—men and women collectively construct and constitute social phenomena.

[1] "Projects" is a technical term. Schutz (1962: 48–85) views action as a project (or projection) of present concerns and past experiences into the future, and stresses that social actors work to bring them about. He also suggests that the basis of actions in the past and present means that action takes place in the future perfect tense; one bases action on what one expects will have been the case.

Each of these two views of social actors implies a different theoretical approach to news. Taking the first and more traditional view, one might logically argue, much as Roshco (1975) does, that any society's definition of news is dependent upon its social structure. The social structure produces norms, including attitudes that define aspects of social life which are of either interest or importance to citizens. News supposedly concerns those recognizable items. Socialized to those societal attitudes and to professional norms, newsworkers cover, select, and disseminate stories about items identified as either interesting or important. By newsworkers' fulfillment of this function, news reflects society: News presents to a society a mirror of its concerns and interests. For a society's definition of news to change, it follows logically, the structure of society and its institutions must first change. As Roshco explains, news may play a role in social change by reporting "interesting" deviant acts in the form of soft news, as in the prototypical example of man bites dog. If a sufficient number of people adopt those forms of deviance, the social structure may be modified and its definition of news may be altered. But, in this view, definitions of news remain dependent upon the social structure, not on the activities of newsworkers and news organizations.

The studies reviewed in chapter 8 discredit this traditional view of news and social change. Modern conceptions of news developed together with America's social structure. The popular press drew on the existence of both the new capitalists and changing definitions of democracy, but it was also inextricably linked to those phenomena. It gave life to a then-radical distinction between public and private morality, for it embodied the notion of public information distributed for private (corporate) profit. It also severed the face-to-face relationship between the producers and consumers of communication, a transformation crucial to subsequent forms of parasocial interaction and role segmentation in advanced industrial societies.

The interpretive approach to news (as discussed in terms of the window-frame metaphor in chapter 1) is more active. It emphasizes the activities of newsworkers and news organizations, rather than social norms, as it does not presuppose that the social structure produces clearly delineated norms defining what is newsworthy. Instead, it argues, as newsworkers simultaneously invoke and apply norms, they define them. That is, notions of newsworthiness receive their definitions from moment to moment, as, for instance, newspaper editors negotiate which items are to be carried on page one. Similarly, this approach argues, news does not mirror society. It helps to constitute it as a shared social phenomenon, for in the process of describing an event, news defines and shapes that event, much as news stories construed and constructed the early period of the modern women's movement as the activities of ridiculous bra burners.

By emphasizing the activities of newsworkers, the interpretive approach also delineates a different treatment of social change. Like the more traditional view, it accepts the idea that stories about deviants bear some relationship to the social structure, but it uses a different verb to describe that relationship. Instead of saying that stories about deviants may "modify" the social structure, interpretive sociologies argue that these stories actively define both what is deviant and what is normative. Conversely, stories about positively sanctioned social acts and social actors are resources for the definition of both conformity and deviance. Each type of story implies or affirms the presence or absence of the other type, for each type of story is embedded in the processes that newsworkers use to reduce the glut of occurrences as the raw material of news (as discussed in chapter 3). Stories about deviant social groups, such as the women's movement, are, for instance, transformed into soft news (as discussed in chapter 7), or, when carried as hard news, they are described as people gathered in inappropriate places at inappropriate times for inappropriate purposes (Molotch and Lester, 1975), as threats to social stability. By imposing such meanings, news is perpetually defining and redefining, constituting and reconstituting social phenomena.

In previous chapters I used an interpretive approach to the study of news to demonstrate how newswork transforms everyday occurrences into news events. Sometimes explicitly, sometimes implicitly, those descriptions of newswork used the concepts "reflexivity" and "indexicality," proposed by the ethnomethodologists (particularly Garfinkel, 1967); "frame" and "strip," offered by Goffman (1974); and "the social construction of reality," developed by Berger and Luckmann (1967). All of these concepts stress that men and women actively construct social meanings. All ultimately derive from readings of the work of Alfred Schutz (1962, 1964, 1966, 1967), a philosopher of social science whose ideas also influenced Smith's (1972) formulation of ideology. Schutz' own writings derive from his study of Edmund Husserl's phenomenology, the work of Henri Bergson and the American pragmatists, and the sociology of Max Weber.

Alfred Schutz and the Study of the Everyday World

One essay by Schutz, incorporating the ideas of William James, has had a particularly powerful impact on recently developed schools of interpretive sociology.[2] In "On Multiple Realities," Schutz (1962) outlines the basic phenomenological properties of the shared social world.[3] First, Schutz accepts James' notion that we experience many subuniverses, including the world of the senses or of physical things, the world of science, the world of dreams, and the world of madness. Then Schutz distinguishes the everyday world of the senses and of other people from other multiple realities. He asks, how do we experience these multiple realities? How, for instance, does our experience of the world of dreams differ from our grasp of the everyday world? Schutz is particularly interested in the everyday world because, like James, he identifies it as the paramount reality.

Of particular importance are two ideas that Schutz draws from Husserl. In developing his philosophy, Husserl (1960, 1967) emphasized the relationship between the knower and that which is known. He stressed consciousness as an intentional phenomenon.[4] Additionally, Husserl proposed that the philosopher may apprehend the essence of phenomena by adopting a specific attitude, which he referred to as either bracketing or the phenomenological reduction. The philosopher adopting this attitude casts the existence of an ob-

[2]Schutz' uses of James underscores how knowledge evolves through patterns of exchanges. Schutz' work is addressed to the work of Husserl, who was greatly influenced by Brentano. James was also influenced by Brentano.

[3]Heap and Roth (1973) offer a useful discussion of the relationship between Schutz' work and subsequent phenomenological sociologies. They stress and explicate the notion of intersubjectivity.

[4]See Heap and Roth (1973) for a discussion of intentionality and intersubjectivity.

jective phenomenon into doubt in order to examine its essence, as opposed to its material embodiment in the social world. For instance, the philosopher might doubt the existence of news in order to discover its idealistic essence, as opposed to its past, present, or possible future forms in the social world.

Husserl's (1967) explanation of the phenomenological reduction is complex and has been analyzed by others (e.g., Farber, 1966). It is important here only inasmuch as Schutz inverts Husserl's idea of bracketing. Husserl proposed bracketing as the distinctive attitude of the phenomenological philosopher; Schutz explains that the everyday world is distinguished by its very lack of bracketing. Rather than adopt an attitude of doubt toward phenomena in the social world, actors in the social world accept phenomena as given. For instance, although a newspaper reader might challenge the veracity of a specific news story, he or she does not challenge the very existence of news as a social phenomenon. The reader may attack the slant of a specific story or of a specific newspaper or newscast, but newspapers, newscasts, and news itself appear as objective givens. Schutz calls the cognitive style that accepts the objective existence of social phenomena the "natural attitude." That term contains the implication that we all take the existence of social phenomena for granted, that we view them as givens, as being "naturally" there. But Schutz never claims that those givens are themselves "natural." In "On Multiple Realities" he is not concerned with phenomena in the world, but rather with the attitude with which social actors approach the world.[5]

By using the term "natural attitude," Schutz claims that whatever the specific cultural, structural, and personal contents of an individual's life, all competent individuals experience similar cognitive styles when dealing with social reality. That is, a Samoan, a Ukranian, and an American would, despite their differences in background, experience similar cognitive styles. Individuals accept their world (whatever its contents may be) as "natural," as the way things are. Imagine two people reading the same newspaper story. One is politically middle-of-the-road; the other is a revolutionary. The revolutionary may doubt that the occurrence reported in the paper happened in the way the story claims it did. But he or she does not doubt

[5] This use of "attitude" is very different from its common sociological usage. It does not refer to mood (as in a "positive attitude"), nor to opinions and ideas (as in the "middle-class attitude toward sexuality"). Again, see Heap and Roth (1973).

the existence of the occurrence itself. Indeed, in trying, for instance, to predict the effect of the story on news consumers or to grasp how the story may influence his or her attempt to set forth a new political program, the revolutionary may pay even more attention to the story than does the person who is politically conservative.[6] In Schutz' writing, the concept of the everyday world is almost tautological: The everyday world is constituted in its very taken-for-grantedness. Casting doubt thrusts one into another of the mulitple realities or subuniverses. For instance, casting doubt, one might enter the world of science in which individuals doubt (bracket) the existence of phenomena in order to study them.

But Schutz does not define the natural attitude in a tautological manner. Rather, he proposes six "classic characteristics that constitute the specific cognitive style" of the everyday world and differentiate it from other "finite provinces of meaning" (other multiple realities).[7] For my purposes, two interesting strains run through Schutz' list. First, he emphasizes the taken-for-grantedness of basic elements of social life, such as time and intersubjectivity (taking the role of the other), as socially given. Second, Schutz stresses that, in the natural attitude, social actors actively "work" in the sense that they take an active "wide awake" stance toward the world through which they apprehend and create meanings. Thus, for instance, reading a newspaper, an actor takes for granted that news exists and that the stories are "today's news." He or she apprehends the stories in a clearly delineated time frame that is socially defined in terms of the

[6]A distinction must be made between "paying attention" to something and "attending" to it. Acting within the natural attitude, both readers are "attending" to the story; they are apprehending it. In Schutz' framework, apprehension is not a continuum; "paying attention" is a matter that can be measured in more traditional social science.

[7]These are, according to Schutz (1962: 230, 231):

1. A specific tension of consciousness, namely wide-awakedness, originating in full attention to life.
2. A specific epoché, namely suspension of doubt.
3. A prevalent form of spontaneity, namely working (a meaningful spontaneity based upon a project and characterized by the intention of bringng about the projected state of affairs by bodily movements gearing into the outer world).
4. A specific form of experiencing one's self (the working self as the total self);
5. A specific form of sociality (the common intersubjective world of communication and social action).
6. A specific time-perspective (the standard time originating in an intersection between *durée* and cosmic time as the universal temporal structure of the intersubjective world).

intersection of human experience with the movement of the moon and the planets. In the world of dreams, time is collapsed, expanded, or suspended; it loses its social referent.

News readers also work to find meaning in the inked squibbles on the page. They perceive words and sentences, facts and interpretations. They actively apprehend and attribute meaning to those squibbles, much as they actively apprehend articulated noises as utterances and language. Similarly (as discussed in chapter 2), reporters work to apprehend and attribute meaning when they identify some items, but not others, as news. Through this work, according to Schutz, social actors create both meaning and a collectively shared sense of social order. Social order is dependent upon shared meanings.

Schutz' notion of the natural attitude has served as the point of departure for several interpretive sociologists, all stressing how men and women work to create social meanings. Theories derived from Schutz' approach apply to newswork and news as social phenomena, just as they apply to the apprehension of articulated noise as meaningful utterance. Consider the concepts of "reflexivity" and "indexicality" developed by the ethnomethodologists.

News as a Reflexive and Indexical Enterprise

Led by Garfinkel (1967) and Cicourel (1964, 1973), ethnomethodologists examine how people make sense of the everyday world as they operate within the natural attitude.[8] ("Ethnomethodology," a term coined by one of Garfinkel's students, means the study of the methods of the people.) They are not interested in the categories people employ to make sense of the world; for instance, they do not consider the stereotypes that one group may apply to another. Instead, they study the daily work of making categories (or, to use their term, "doing" categories); for example, how stereotypic meanings come to be attributed to the acts of other people, as in the stereotyping of early members of the women's movement (as discussed in chapter 7), the identification of some members of social movements as "responsible leaders" (as discussed in chapter 5), or the rejection of the stereotype of all presidents as crooks (also discussed in chapter 5).

[8]Mehan and Wood (1975) present a valuable explication of ethnomethodology.

Specifically, ethnomethodologists propose: Just as the natural attitude exists in all societies and cultures, so, too, there are invariant features or methods of the natural attitude that people use to make sense of the everyday world. Those features are not content specific, but rather may be invoked to make sense of a variety of contents. Those features of the natural attitude identified by the ethnomethodologists specify how people work in a state of wide-awakedness to apprehend and create meanings.

"Reflexivity" and "indexicality" are two invariant features delineated by ethnomethodologists. Twin concepts (indexicality implies reflexivity and vice versa), they may be used to describe how people make sense of one another's utterances in shared conversations; how people make sense of news reports as accounts of the everyday world; how reporters make sense of occurrences; or how people extrapolate from any particular item to a characterization of the everyday world.

Both reflexivity and indexicality refer to the contextual embeddedness of phenomena. Reflexivity specifies that accounts are embedded in the very reality that they characterize, record, or structure. Indexicality specifies that in using accounts (terms, utterances, or stories), social actors may attribute meanings to them apart from the context in which those accounts are produced and processed. For instance, a person attributes meaning to a statement made in a conversation in which he or she is involved by considering the statement's context. (Without a context, the utterance "uh" is meaningless.) Pulling that statement out of the context of its production and repeating it in a second conversation, he or she may be engaging in the indexical attribution of meaning. Consider the hypothetical conversation between the professor and her husband (discussed in chapter 1). Negotiating the news of the day, they conversed about Joe's behavior at a department meeting. In the future the couple might refer to that day as "the day that Joe said x. Severing the characterization "the day that Joe said x" from the process of its production, they transform that characterization into an indexical particular.

Both reflexivity and indexicality are integral components of the transformation of occurrences into news events. They are components of both the public character of news and of newswork itself.

The Public Character of News: News simultaneously records and is a product of social reality, because it provides news consumers with a selective abstraction designed to be coherent despite its neglect of some details. When news consumers read or view news, they add details—but not necessarily those deleted in the processing of the story. Selective abstraction and representation of information and the reflexive attribution of meaning to events-as-news are natural features of everyday life.

Consider both the My Lai massacre and the Watergate break-in. Although hundreds were slaughtered at My Lai, their deaths had no public existence for Americans until the eventual dissemination of selective accounts of the massacre. Without news accounts, the occurrence was a personal trouble for involved soldiers and survivors. Similarly, the break-in at Democratic National Headquarters in the Watergate Office Building was a public issue for the arrested burglars but a personal trouble for a few men eventually identified as conspirators—as long as no one else knew of the conspirators' involvement. The public dissemination of information was necessary for judicial and congressional processes to be initiated and for Richard Nixon ultimately to be forced to resign the presidency. In both of these cases, news accounts indicated what was happening or had happened in the everyday world; in both cases, news reports were clearly active participants in the sociopolitical processes. The military tried to bury the story of My Lai; the president's associates tried to bury the stories about Watergate. The media were part and parcel of the drama of structuring and releasing information that would become the basis for the shaping of knowledge.

News stories not only lend occurrences their existence as public events, but also impart character to them, for news reports help to shape the public definition of happenings by selectively attributing to them specific details or "particulars." They make these selected details accessible to news consumers. Take the case of a riot. In disseminating such particulars as the number of participants, the number wounded or killed, the amount of property damaged, and the sequence of activities (that is, a man was arrested and then a mob of citizens congregated at the police station), news reports transform *a* riot as an amorphous happening into *the* riot (this particular riot) as a public event and public concern. The news reports also shape notions of the general characteristics of *all* riots. Kapsis et al. (1970) note that riots go through phases of milling about, when "nothing much" appears to be happening, just as battles have "lulls." News reports commonly ignore such phases, collapsing the course of riots into continuous intensive activity. Through their reports of specific riots, news reports help to shape a public definition of what a riot is, and that public definition exists without reference to the processes that shaped the riot-as-occurrence into riots-as-news-events. Indeed, ultimately, social scientists may use the newspaper account as though it were a veridical depiction of the occurrence, as though the news story were the event itself (see Danzger, 1975, 1976; Tuchman, 1976). For instance, at one and the same time, some historians and traditional sociologists use news reports as data revealing both the nature of events and the changing foci of public concerns. By using news as data without reference to the context of its production, these sociologists draw upon the indexical character of news.

News and Newswork: Just as the public character of news is both indexical and reflexive, so, too, newswork is contextually embedded. Throughout the discussions in previous chapters, we have seen how news is enmeshed in the social organization of newswork. It is embedded in conflicting modes of territorial, institutional, and topical chains of responsibility (described in chapter 2 as the news net) requiring ongoing negotiation; in temporally grounded typifications rooted in the rhythm of work (as discussed in chapter 3); and in the mutual constitution of fact and source accomplished by both the anchoring of the news net in legitimated insitutions and negotiations among competitor-colleagues (as discussed in chapter 4).

According to Garfinkel (1967; see also Cicourel, 1968), workers draw on their understandings of an institution's processes to produce records of aspects of those processes. In Garfinkel's example, intake interviewers use their understandings of a clinic's work processes to produce records of intake interviews. Those records are then objectified as factual accounts of a patient's medical and life history. In the process of producing these records, Garfinkel tells us, workers reproduce and objectify the social arrangements of the clinic. Molotch and Lester (1975) alert us that one can view news as the reproduction of newsworkers' understandings of both news processes and political processes, and thus as the reproduction of those processes. For instance, when a reporter or editor identifies an occurrence as hard news, the newsworker is drawing on a personal understanding of the processing of hard news. When the municipal government is identified as "the city," the reporter is drawing on understandings of both political and news processes that transform politicians into representatives of the city and so into significations of the city. When Betty Friedan was identified as a "responsible spokesperson" or leader of the women's movement, newsworkers drew upon their methods of determining responsible leadership (as discussed in chapters 5 and 7). In all of these instances, newswork is reflexively embedded in the context of its production and presentation. It both draws on and reproduces the political structure, just as it draws on and reproduces the organization of newswork.

Despite the reflexive production of news, stories are frequently presented indexically—divorced from the context of their production. This aspect of news is captured in the objectification of facts. A reporter may quote a source without indicating how a certain question prompted the source's answer (see page 96). A reporter may identify a fact without explaining how that fact was produced as a nonproblematic detail or "particular" (as in the news story quoted on page 88). And the indexicality of news is contained in both its ahistoricity and its logic of the concrete, the newsworkers' insistent refusal to present stories in their ongoing situational context—to analyze the relationship among yesterday, today, and tomorrow.

News as Frame

Goffman (1974) clearly draws upon an ethnomethodological interpretation of Schutz for two concepts central to his work on frame analysis.[9] A "frame" is "the principles of organization which govern events—at least social ones—and our subjective involvement in them." Frames organize strips of the everyday world (or any other of the multiple realities). Goffman defines a "strip" as "an arbitrary slice or cut from the stream of ongoing activity [1974: 10–11]." Like Schutz, Goffman assumes that the experiencing of reality imposes order on reality. Like the ethnomethodologists, he ignores the possibility that order is an intrinsic characteristic of the everyday world. Thus frames turn nonrecognizable happenings or amorphous talk into a discernible event. Without the frame, they would be mere happenings of mere talk, incomprehensible sounds. Consider the following exchange presented as a strip:

[9]But Goffman credits Bateson (1955) for those terms and applies Bateson's usage.

"How was it?"
"Not much."
"Six graphs?"
"Okay."

In and of itself, this exchange is meaningless. However, by providing a frame in the form of additional information, the strip is transformed:

> A reporter returns to the city room from the scene of a fire. He approaches the city editor, who looks up from his work and asks the reporter, "How was it?" Referring to the fire, the reporter replies, "Not much." The editor asks, "Six graphs?" (Will six paragraphs be a sufficient amount of space to tell the story of the fire?) The reporter replies, "Okay," and goes to his desk, where he writes six paragraphs about the fire.

Framed, the strip becomes recognizable as a conversation concerning an occurrence. It can be seen as the negotiation about the newsworthiness of that occurrence as a news event. And it imparts a character to that occurrence. The fire that the reporter observed is not any fire; it is a minor fire, a specific fire that is worth six paragraphs of news coverage.

Throughout this book, editors and reporters have been shown searching for frames. Van Gelder sought a frame that would enable her to get her story about the women's demonstration at the Atlantic City Miss America Contest into her newspaper (p. 138). *Seaboard City Daily* editors sought a frame that would enable them to state that there was no heat in a tenement owned by a slum landlord (p. 95). Television news film uses specific camera shots as frames lending social meanings to spatial relationships (as discussed in chapter 6). And sequences of those shots are then themselves framed (or placed in conventional juxtapositions) to create additional relationships among the components of a story. In all of these cases, two processes occur simultaneously: An occurrence is transformed into an event, and an event is transformed into a news story. The news frame organizes everyday reality and the news frame is part and parcel of everyday reality, for, as we have seen, the public character of news is an essential feature of news.

Goffman's notion of frame analysis recognizes the simultaneous existence of news in two realities. Unlike Schutz and the ethnomethodologists, Goffman does not assume that the everyday world is the paramount reality. He is interested in other multiple realities, such as the theatre and the world of purposive deception (as enacted by con men and marks, spies and double agents). He offers his concepts of frame and strip to ask: By what constitutive rules of everyday behavior do people organize their experience in one world (multiple reality) so that it can be translated into another? For instance, by what rules is everyday reality transformed into fiction? And he notes that fiction, in the form of movies, novels, or deceit, is a component of the everyday world. For Goffman, frames themselves are negotiated phenomena.

Perhaps Goffman's long-standing interest in deception leads him, but not the ethnomethodologists, to stress the vulnerability of experience to framing. For the ethnomethodologists, "documentary" is a method of illustration, as in the "documentary method of interpretation," one of the invariant features of the natural attitude. The "documentary method of interpretation" is a way of making sense out of phenomena by associating them with a general principle, notion, or concept.[10] For Goffman, the term "documentary" refers to transformation, not association, and reveals the vulnerability of streams of experience (strips) to framing devices. Speaking of news and filmed documentaries, he points out (1974: 448, 450) that documentary framing "must turn upon a limitation of information regarding . . . the interconnectedness of literal events in the real world. . . . Paradoxically, . . . what we have come to call documentary . . . is exactly what should be suspect relative to standards of documentation." By imposing order, by limiting the information about a strip that is included in and disseminated by the documentary frame, that documentary frame necessarily creates meaning. It creates both the reporter at the scene of a story as reporter-standing-outside-and-commenting-on-events, the "objective reporter," and the occurrence as public event.

Yet, paradoxically, precisely because Goffman is interested in the vulnerability of experience and the social organization of experience, he explicitly rejects a concern for social organization per se. He

[10]For instance, Zimmerman and Pollner (1970) accuse symbolic interactionists of using the documentary method of interpretation by reorganizing the folk knowledge of their informants instead of analyzing how that knowledge is an intersubjective accomplishment (see Wilson, 1970). Their theoretical critique also involves an epistemological argument about the social scientist's production of data.

is interested in the moods and gestures that "key" a phenomenon from one frame to another, but not in the institutional mechanisms that accomplish transformation. Indeed, he refuses to identify organizational and professional resources that may be drawn upon to organize experience even as he acknowledges their role in organizing experience. Some of those resources, though, are explicitly discussed in the work of Peter Berger and Thomas Luckmann, also students of Schutz' work.

News and the Construction of Reality

Berger and Luckmann (1967) fuse the ideas of Alfred Schutz with traditional sociological concerns about the contents of the reality encountered in the natural attitude. Like Schutz and James, they recognize the everyday world as the paramount reality. Like Schutz' topical essays (1964), their writing explores the impact of social institutions and social processes, as they unfold historically, upon the generation and definition of social facts. Included in the study of social facts are the categories into which groups sort their collective experiencing of reality and the processes through which those categories emerge. Thus Berger and Luckmann speak of the world into which we are born as given, handed down to us by the world of our predecessors (and shared by our contemporaries, including our consociates; see Schutz, 1962: 15ff.), and as a world that we shape in our organization of daily interactions and our invocations of relevance. We create, for instance, the relevance of our collective past to our present and future actions by invoking elements of the past to justify present actions. For example, the newsworker invokes past "what-a-stories" to process "what-a-stories" at hand.

Berger and Luckmann also stress how institutions objectify social meanings. They suggest that social meanings, constituted in social interactions, are transformed into institutional and organizational rules and procedures that may be invoked as resources to justify actions. ("We can include this comment in your news story, if you get me more quotes.") In their invocation, meanings may be modified, much as the meanings of words are transformed when they are applied to emerging situations. They may also be codified apart from the contexts in which they were originally developed. Removed from the context in which it was proposed, a procedure may become "the way to do things"; that is, it may be handed down to the world of our successors as an objective historical given. For instance, Americans take as given that news is ahistorical, atheoretic accounts of daily happenings in specific institutions, and that it employs the logic of the concrete. We take for granted the daily production of news as a consumer commodity without noting its historic association with the development of advertising by the penny press. We take for granted the embeddedness of the news net in legitimated institutions and the existence of centralized news gathering, as handed down to us from the nineteenth century. And we fail to realize how that embeddedness militates against the emergence of new forms of news. For so long as hard news continues to be associated with the activities of legitimated institutions and the spatial and temporal organization of newswork remains embedded in their activities, news reproduces itself as a historical given. It not only defines and redefines, constitutes and reconstitutes social meanings; it also defines and redefines, constitutes and reconstitutes ways of doing things—existing processes in existing institutions.

Ideology as Objectified Procedures

In her treatment of ideology, Smith (1972) argues that the embeddedness of procedures in legitimated institutions—their indexicality and reflexivity (Garfinkel, 1967), their objectification (Berger and Luckmann, 1967), their simultaneous framing of and participation in the everyday world (Goffman, 1974), and their structuring of vulnerable experience (Goffman, 1974)—identifies them as *means not to know*. In her terms they become "interested procedures," methods of not knowing that are embedded in the legitimated institutions that they reproduce. At one and the same time, they present social actors with materials for producing social structures and they truncate actors' abilities to transform institutions and structures.

Smith's identification of ideology as a means of not knowing goes beyond the stance that ideology adumbrates the possible projects of social actors working in the wide-awakedness of the natural attitude. Based on interpretive sociologies, it includes a critique of how "interested procedures" are blind to their own self-fulfilling prophecies. That critique applies to newswork, as well as to social science.

CHAPTER TEN
News as Knowledge

Many of the ideas I have reviewed in chapter 9 derive from recent critiques of sociology. Schutz' work is an attempt to devise a philosophy of social science (see especially Schutz, 1962, 1966, 1967). Garfinkel and other ethnomethodologists offer searing criticisms of sociology in their programmatic essays. For instance, they claim it is codified folk knowledge. Smith's (1972) distinction between knowledge and ideology, based partially on the work of ethnomethodologists and of Marx, is intended as an indictment of sociology. She contends that its supposedly scientific methods are a means not to know, because those methods "make the structure of society mysterious by substituting concepts for reality."

To varying degrees, all these writers stress how sociological reasoning both draws on everyday life and contributes to it. Sociology codifies attitudes and opinions and births and deaths through its manipulation of data. According to such critics as Smith, Garfinkel, and Cicourel, its theories are based on the pretheoretic formulations of social actors making sense of everyday life. At the same time, sociology serves as a social resource for gleaning understandings of structural phenomena, and so as a resource for social action. Like news, according to these sociological critics, sociology is indexical and reflexive, both a description of society and an actor in society.

To assess news as ideology and as knowledge, this concluding chapter reviews their critique and recent philosophies of science.

Social Science versus Natural Science

For well over a century, philosphers and theorists have been trying to clarify whether the methods of natural science apply to social science. Two related problems are of particular interest here. First, are laws of social science equivalent to laws of natural science? Second, of what significance is it that the subject of social science, people and human societies, is itself a subjective phenomenon? For twentieth-century positivists the answers are relatively straightforward: The subjectivity of human life does not hamper our ability to generalize and test laws about human conduct. Some positivists even specify that since the proper topic of sociology is social structures and institutions, the problem of subjectivity does not obtain, for unlike people, institutions and structures do not have consciousness. For interpretive sociologists, myself included, the answers are neither so simple nor so immediate. Consider some of the problems critics of positivism locate.

First, human intervention in nature does not invalidate natural laws. It is possible to change the boiling point of water by altering the air pressure to which the water is subjected. Altering the boiling point of water is therefore a confirmation of the law, not a contravention of it. However, the use of sociological ideas to intervene in society is frequently said to invalidate those ideas. For instance, Marx held that the contradictions inherent in capitalism and its institutions give rise to socialism. Accordingly, he expected the first socialist revolution to occur in either England or Germany, the most advanced capitalist nations of his day. Instead, the revolution occurred in Russia, where an organized group managed to seize power and impose its version of Marxism on the people. The emergence of governments based on interpretations of Marx' ideas in China and other agrarian nations of Asia, such as Vietnam and Cambodia, can be said to be based on conflicts with advanced capitalist societies. But they do not arise out of industrial conditions in those nations themselves. Rather than confirming Marx' theory and his laws of the dialectic of history, the emergence of these governments requires re-fining and amending Marxist theory.

Of course, to protect social-science laws from human interven-tion, one could try to make them inaccessible to laypersons (and the heady jargon of the social scientist does seem designed to obfuscate rather than to reveal). However, such a solution robs social science of its vitality by isolating it from other fields of inquiry. It also trans-forms social science into a parasite: Members of the society are to present themselves as objects of research without the right to choose among the alternatives derived from inquiries focused on them as subjects. Social scientists would then feed off society, but other social actors could not use social science. By implication, the social scientists would also be autocrats: They could claim the license to im-pose policies derived from their expert knowledge without a previous review by laypersons.

Second, the methods used by natural scientists have a different sort of impact on findings than do those of social scientists. Through the Heisenberg Principle, natural science recognizes that its discover-ies are based on techniques devised by scientists and are therefore de-pendent on human creativity and ingenuity. As Heisenberg pointed out, viewed through humanly devised equipment, such as an electron microscope, a phenomenon appears different than it does when viewed with the naked eye. Viewed through an oscilloscope, it may have radically different properties. And some more recently dis-covered phenomena, such as quarks, are accessible to study only through sophisticated equipment of, obviously, human design. Hu-man limitations and abilities thus guide and determine scientific findings.

The methods and techniques of the social scientists are also de-rived for and by human actors, and so they, too, guide researchers to answers. For answers, and theories drawn from and tested by these methods and techniques, are obviously limited by the technical means used to pose questions. But natural phenomena cannot self-consciously alter their own properties in response to scientists' ac-tions. The objects of social-scientific study—people—obviously can. They may tell lies; they may hide their feelings and opinions; they may concretely alter their behavior. Coping with these abilities is not simply a matter of designing research protocols and statistical techniques capable of catching informants in contradictory statements or other obfuscations.

In order to hide the truth, an informant must first have interpreted the researcher's question. He or she must have developed a pretheoretic notion of what is being asked. Similarly, an informant who responds truthfully must also have a pretheoretic understanding of the researcher's question. For the research format is analogous to everyday conversation inasmuch as interactants always base their responses on their understandings of one another's utterances. The research protocol uses the same wording and ordering of questions for every interview, but it cannot prevent informants from formulating pretheoretic understandings of the questions. Indeed, it requires that they do so. Therefore, social scientists must deal with informants' answers and behaviors as their pretheoretic formulations. They must recognize the embeddedness of answers in such methods of understanding the everyday world as reflexivity and indexicality. To do otherwise—simply to design better research protocols and more sophisticated statistical techniques—is, Garfinkel (1967) writes, to tear down the walls of the house in order to find out what holds the roof up.

Ethnomethodologists have applied this critique to statistical studies (Cicourel, 1964), including sociological classics. To take an example, Durkheim's *Suicide* develops some rather elegant distinctions among sorts of suicide and sorts of society. But to apply the distinctions in order to test his theory, Durkheim had to rely on official statistics. Those who gathered the statistics did not have Durkheim's definition of suicide in mind when they categorized deaths. Accordingly, his findings do not test his theory. More important, Durkheim's tests necessarily incorporate the pretheoretic formulations of those who officially define deaths, such as coroners. Similarly, Cicourel (1968) and Emerson (1969) have shown, sociologists' data on juvenile delinquency are the product of the everyday reasoning of those who process delinquents. Sociological studies using those data are thus necessarily basing their work on the pretheoretic formulations of social actors.

This critique—that sociological studies are based on the pretheoretic formulations of members of a society—is not limited to statistical studies. Wilson (1970) discusses this problem in the work of symbolic interactionists. Zimmerman and Pollner (1970) analyze it in ethnographies. Giddens (1976) finds it to be a general flaw of dominant sociologies, including the work of Durkheim and Marx. According to Giddens:

> Sociology, unlike natural science, stands in a subject–subject relation to its "field of study," not a subject–object relation; it deals with a pre-interpreted world, in which the meanings developed by active subjects actually enter into the actual constitution or production of that world [1976: 146].

Therefore, Giddens (1976: 146) argues, "the construction of social theory thus involves a *double hermeneutic* that has no parallel elsewhere" (emphasis added). Loosely, "hermeneutic" means interpretation, and Giddens is pointing toward the reflexivity of social life.

Giddens' use of the term "reflexivity" is slightly different from the meaning used by ethnomethodologists (discussed in chapter 9). The ethnomethodologists identify reflexivity as a feature of the process of making sense of the world found within the natural attitude. Giddens draws upon reflexivity as a more general interpretive practice, connoting the interaction and exchange always present in the interpretation of phenomena and the attribution of meaning. For Giddens, reflexivity connotes both the sociologist's use of informants' pretheoretic formulations and lay use of social science to glean understandings of self and others. But the ethnomethodologists emphasize, as Giddens does, that sociology "stands in a subject–subject relation to its field of study."

Giddens (1976: 148) compares social science to the arts in this respect. In both, "portrayals of human life are bound to the reflexive capacity of human beings to imaginatively reconstruct, and develop an emotional relation toward, experiences that are not their own; and thereby to further their understandings of themselves." Both art and sociology "draw upon the resources of mutual knowledge in order to develop a dialogue whereby the self-understanding of the reader may be furthered through new understandings of others." Art, of course, is permitted to depart from "veridical" descriptions of social reality; by definition, social science is not. Thus, "Social-scientific analyses are rarely likely to yield the dramatic impact that is possible to attain through imaginative literature or poetic symbolism. But the significance of this [difference] should not be exaggerated" (Giddens, 1976: 149). As Giddens points out in the same passage, "Goffman's analyses of staged performances . . . draw from, and appeal to, mutual knowledge; and by comparing all sorts of activities, from the most elevated to the most humble, to such performances [Goffman] is able to achieve the sort of deflationary effect which comes from turning an existing order of things upside down." That sort of inversion is a common theme in comedy and farce.

To be sure, some positivists may object that Goffman's work is not scientific and may charge that comparison between art and Goffman is, therefore, a comparison of art to art, not art to social science. But even in the dryness of statistical treatises, one may find dramatic impact. One thinks, for instance, of the way the lay public gobbles up sociological studies of the social organization of sex, research about the impact of television on children, and work on busing children to achieve integration. Some of those studies debunk popular belief; others alarm or titillate. All contain the potential ability to alter social understandings dramatically.

The lack of compelling drama in most social science does not invalidate Giddens' notion that sociology must contend with a double hermeneutic. Nor does it prevent one from asking whether the same problem of a subject–subject relationship is characteristic of news as a veridical account of social life. Indeed, the notion of dramatic impact debunking or reaffirming everyday understandings compels one to ask about the subject–subject relationship in news inquiry.

First, news can have a dramatic impact, particularly through its manipulation of symbols. One thinks of the news photograph of John-John Kennedy saluting his father's casket as it was carried past him by pallbearers from the Washington Cathedral. One thinks of photographs of street celebrations at the news that World War II had ended. And one recalls the newsworkers' own care with stories about ghetto riots: In the 1960's, the Seaboard City daily newspapers had a mutual agreement to run any items about riots elsewhere in a relatively inconspicuous part of the front page, lest a prominent display of "riot stories" encourage imitative behavior in their own metropolis.

Second (as discussed in chapter 8), news professionalism draws upon common understandings of scientific inquiry. There is some irony to this. News professionalism's invocation of science dates to the 1920s, the period when the Heisenberg Principle of Indeterminacy, dealing with the impact of scientists upon inquiries in physics, was being formulated. There has, of course, been some contemporary adjustment of journalistic philosphy to take a version of the Heisenberg Principle into account. The "new journalism" symbolized by Tom Wolfe's (1968) work uses the personal pronoun and introduces the reporter's feelings. He writes "I saw" and "I felt" rather than "a recent visitor found" something to be true. But the "new journalism" (also called "first-person journalism") is largely confined to magazines and signed work by recognized columnists.

Finally, news itself may be described as a theoretic activity, drawing on the pretheoretic formulations of news sources. Take the newsworkers' rule that some members of a committee are in a better position than others to know the facts. This rule prompted one reporter at NEWS to use the following practice in his coverage of a continuing story about school integration. He informally asked the chairperson of the school committee how events would unfold and then based his plans for future coverage on her predictions. Furthermore, news stories engage in theorizing by juxtaposing facts gleaned from sources. Juxtaposition is a form of categorizing, since it encourages the understanding that these facts have something to do with one another. It both claims and creates a theoretic relationship between and among the phenomena presented as facts.

The Glascow Media Group offers a fresh example, taped and transcribed from a British newscast:

> The week had its share of unrest. Trouble in Glascow with striking dustmen and ambulance controllers, short time [cutting the length of the workday to save money] in the car industry, no Sunday *Mirror* or Sunday *People* today, a fair amount of general trouble in Fleet Street, and a continuing rumbling over the matter of two builders' pickets jailed for conspiracy [1976: 355].

"In this piece of news talk," these authors point out, "the category 'unrest' is used simultaneously to gloss such diverse phenomena as different strikes, shortened work hours, and a conspiracy case." The preferred interpretation "is clearly that we see (since we are talking of television) all of these as merely cases of 'unrest.'" That is, the category "unrest" is presented as applying to "striking dustmen" in just the same way as it applies to the absence of the Sunday newspaper or the jailing of two men. The common category implies that each event is governed by rules or norms pertaining to disorder or social conflict: The act of categorizing is an act of theorizing.

A comparison to social science helps to clarify categorizing as theorizing. When a sociologist introduces the variable "social class" into a research design, he or she theorizes that social class must contribute to an explanation or model of the phenomenon being studied. If social class were not held to be pertinent, there would be no reason to notice it or include it as a variable in the study. As a variable, "social class" varies; that is, there are different social classes. Here I hypothetically call them "landowners," "capitalists," "professionals," and "workers." By introducing these names, I have theorized that all "landowners" have an element in common different from the common element shared by "capitalists" or "professionals" or "workers." Of course, I could have labeled the social classes as groups 1, 2, 3, and 4. But to classify individuals into these groups, I would have to identify a series of criteria that sort out the individuals and discriminate between and among the groups. I would have to theorize that those criteria are pertinent to the identification of social class, that two individuals in group 1 have more in common with each other (at least in terms of class) than either has with an individual in group 3. That is, I demand that all members of group 1 are to be seen as having something in common, much as the news talk of "unrest" demands that all members of that category be seen as sharing common elements.

Whether every example of "unrest" is governed by the same rules by being a member of the category is irrelevant for my purposes. Rather, I wish to stress that news is a theoretic activity. To assess the sociological significance of newswork as a theoretic activity, I now turn to sociological theories that try to cope with the double hermeneutic of social science. Those theories help analyze news as a dramatic, theorizing activity legitimating the status quo.

Everyday Understandings as Social Resources

All sociologists accept the notion that ideas, as well as material conditions, have an impact on institutions and, therefore, on social structure. In the dominant model, though, ideas and culture are treated as properties of individuals internalized through socialization. That is, contemporary American theories presuppose that institutions and social classes generate norms. Through agencies of socialization, such as the family, schools, and professions, individuals master these norms and incorporate them into their identities. Through the process of socialization, then, individuals conform to the dictates of their society.

Unfortunately, as has frequently been pointed out, the opposition of individual and society expressed in this model cannot explain social change. Individuals' participation in social movements aimed at altering social institutions, nonconformity, and crime is attributed to inadequate socialization rather than being viewed as active response to social phenomena. For, in this model, the research task is necessarily defined either as "What makes these individuals different from all other individuals who accept the norms of the society?" or "What makes the groups to which these individuals belong different from groups whose members accept the norms of the society?" In the first case one might ask: What is there about these youths that made them oppose the war in Vietnam when others supported the war? In the second, one might ask: Why do lower-class adolescents and young men destroy property and steal more than do middle-class adolescents and young men? How does social class contribute to or cause attitudes about property?

Even the introduction of conflict as a force for social change does not alter this model significantly. According to the model, conflicting groups have internalized different norms, derived their identities from different social institutions, or conformed to rules governing conflict as the expression of contradictions inherent in any era's social institutions. In sum, this model objectifies individuals as members of groups and robs them of the power to create new meanings subjectively. All meanings seemingly derive from institutional phenomena, not from creative and subjective actions.

An alternative and phenomenologically oriented model (reviewed in chapter 8) argues that institutions cast forth norms. Through socialization, people learn to use these norms or rules as a resource for the construction of meaning. The use of rules is a creative, subjective, interpretive, and pretheoretic activity, not a mechanical response to their internalization. Further, inasmuch as social life is based in structured social interaction (see Wilson, 1970), social meanings are collective constructions that reproduce social structures from moment to moment. As Zimmerman and Pollner explain, institutions and norms present themselves to individuals as taken-for-granted objective phenomena contained within social settings:

> The features of a setting attended to by its participants include, among other things, its historical continuity, its structure of rules and the relationship of activities within it to those rules, and the statuses . . . of its participants. Under the attitude of everyday life, these features are "normal, natural facts of life" . . . objective conditions of action that, although participants have had a hand in bringing about and sustaining them, are essentially independent of any one's or anyone's doing [1970: 94].

The "attitude of everyday life" cited by Zimmerman and Pollner is the "natural attitude" defined by Schutz (discussed in chapter 9). Its acceptance of the "normal, natural facts of life" as objective conditions is a pretheoretic activity, for it makes sense of everyday life as a field of action. The natural attitude also constitutes the social world as a field of action, for the facts of life taken for granted by members of a society exist as resources to be invoked for the accomplishment of action. They also serve as resources for the reproduction of social structures. For example, accepting that news is a veridical account of the interesting and important events of the day reaffirms and reproduces the role of news as a social institution disseminating veridical accounts. Similarly, the attempt of social movements to use the news to disseminate information affirms and reproduces the news media's role as a legitimating institution.

An extended example clarifies how the "facts of life" established under the natural attitude are resources for the accomplishment of action and the reproduction of social structure. Speakers draw on their un-self-conscious knowledge of language to produce new utterances and to understand them. Even without the ability to explain the appropriate grammatical rules, they are capable of making and comprehending utterances they have never heard. By creating and comprehending new utterances, people not only use language but also constitute language as a collective phenomenon—an intersubjective accomplishment. Furthermore, utterances may themselves constitute social activity. To use a famous example from British language philosophy, uttering the words "I do" in a marriage ceremony is not a mere use of language as a description of feelings or a state of affairs. In and of itself, that utterance is an event—an action. Under the appropriate conditions, in a setting collectively defined as a marriage ceremony, "I do" is the act of getting married. So, too, when members of a society identify aspects of culture and structure as objective phenomena (the normal, natural, taken-for granted facts of life), they are affirming the facticity of the world as given by the natural attitude. They are also using those facts to generate and constitute social activity. And they are reproducing those facts of life as structured rules (and relationships among rules) that guide action. Inasmuch as those rules constitute social activity, they also constitute social structures. As Giddens (1976: 127) puts it, "systems of generative rules and resources" on which social interaction and society are based "only exist as the reproduced conduct of situated actors with definite intentions and interests."

Furthermore, "situated actors" have at their disposal different resources, intentions, and interests. Associated with competing institutions and social classes, individuals have access to different generative rules and resources, much as members of social classes have variants of the same language accessible to them. Rules and resources, such as power, are socially distributed. Power is also unequally distributed. When the intentions and interests of situated actors conflict, some have at their disposal more resources than others do, including power, to impose their definitions of the situation. Some social actors thus have a greater ability to create, impose, and reproduce social meanings—to construct social reality. Newsworkers are one group with more power than most to construct social reality.

What are the implications of this review of sociological theories? It pertains to both sociology and news as ideologies. The reflexive view of societal action implicit in the discussion assumes that there is a subject–subject relationship between social science and its topic of investigation. It seeks to look at social actors as coparticipants in the construction of social reality, and it pays specific attention to the distribution of power in social conflicts and other aspects of human life. The review tries to transform sociology from an ideological practice—from a codification of everyday and pretheoretic knowledge, a means not to know, as Smith (1972) puts it—into a humanistic social science. For this theory seeks to demystify the structure of society, to avoid substituting concepts for reality. The technical concepts presented are complex, but they are aimed at revealing how people experience the everyday world. Additionally, although the discussion makes the philosophic assumption that people experience the world in the natural attitude, it seeks to separate facts from assumptions. That is, rather than identify social phenomena as pregiven and objective, it seeks to study them as social constructions and perpetual human accomplishments. It remains to be firmly established that news processing abjures a recognition of phenomena as humanly structured accomplishments. But by affirming that news, like sociology, is indexical and reflexive, the theoretic review explodes the news professionals' claim to produce veridical accounts of social life. It questions whether those accounts are necessarily and inevitably fair, for news professionalism is based on established methods of gathering and processing information and does not reflect on those methods as collective human enterprises.

News as the Reproduction of the Status Quo: A Summary

Let me review once more the constituent features of the news frame, stressing that frames both produce and limit meaning. To return to the analogy of news as a window frame, characteristics of the window, its size and composition, limit what may be seen. So does its placement, that is, what aspect of the unfolding scene it makes accessible. Furthermore, simultaneously, news draws on social and cultural resources to present accounts, and is itself a social and cultural resource for social actors.

Definitions of news are historically derived and embedded. At any one moment, defining what is newsworthy entails drawing on contemporary understandings of the significance of events as rules for human behavior, institutional behavior, and motives. Members of society and participants in its institutions, newsworkers have rules available to them as social resources. Among those rules as resources are some that newsworkers use to define the relationship between news and other forms of knowledge, between newsworkers and other workers, and between news organizations and other social institutions. For instance, in the 1920s, when newsworkers defined themselves as professionals and news as a veridical representation of events, they drew on two cultural resources. One was popular notions of science current in the 1920s. The second was the professionals' distrust of the "reasonableness" of public opinion, because public opinion was no longer identified as the articulation of reason. The claims to both professionalism and veridical representation served, with other factors, as resources for an additional assertion. News articulated itself as the embodiment of provisions of the First Amendment (a historical resource) and as the protector of the people (a class interest).

Needless to say, all social actors did not have to accept this definition of the role of news. But although news professionalism conflicted with the rights of owners and managers to freedom of speech as an attribute of private property ("Freedom of the press is guaranteed only to those who own one"), news professionalism also served the owner's articulation of other interests. For professionalism ignored the impact of the socioeconomic processes of concentration, centralization, and conglomeration on the applicability of existing ideas to economic and political life. News organizations simultaneously participated in these processes—inventing wire services, newspaper chains, news syndicates, and radio and television networks—and sought to define conglomerates and corporations as private enterprise. By invoking eighteenth-century concepts (such as its model of free speech) and applying nineteenth-century distinctions (such as public and private rights) to twentieth-century phenomena, news limits knowledge. News obfuscates social reality instead of revealing it. It confirms the legitimacy of the state by hiding the state's intimate involvement with, and support of, corporate capitalism.

Additionally, news both draws upon and reproduces institutional structures. Through its arrangement of time and space as intertwined social phenomena, the news organization disperses a news net. By identifying centralized sources of information as legitimated social institutions, news organizations and newsworkers wed themselves to specific beats and bureaus. Those sites are then objectified as the appropriate sites at which information should be gathered. Additionally, those sites of news gathering are objectified as the legitimate and legitimating sources of both information and governance. Through naive empiricism, that information is transformed into objective facts—facts as a normal, natural, taken-for-granted description and constitution of a state of affairs. And through the sources identified with facts, newsworkers create and control controversy; they contain dissent.

The dispersion of reporters to glean facts generates its own organizational structure replete with assigned responsibilities and priorities. These are the territorial, institutional, and topical chains of command. Distinctions between and among these three spheres, which necessarily overlap one another, require ongoing negotiations of responsibility and newsworthiness. At least in part, newsworthiness is a product of these negotiations intended to sort out strips of everyday occurrences as news. These negotiations also legitimate the status quo. Each day the editors reproduce their living compromise —the hierarchy among the editors. They also reestablish the supremacy of the territorial chain of command, which incorporates political beats and bureaus but excludes topical specialties such as women's news and sports. These sorts of news are thus rendered institutionally uninteresting. In contrast, the topics of the territorial chain of command—stories about legitimated institutions—receive attention and so substantiate the power of those institutions.

Social actors also produce the rhythm of daily life, which they base in societal institutions. In newswork that rhythm is embedded in the intersection of news organizations and legitimated institutions. Faced with a glut of information by the dispersion of the news net, newsworkers and news organizations battle to impose a uniform rhythm of processing upon occurrences. They impose deadlines on defined stages of processing, and so objectify a news rhythm. They draw on the way occurrences are thought to happen, in order to reproduce a state of affairs conducive to news processing. Using past experiences as guides for the present, they typify occurrences as news events. The application of a typification to an event is subject to revision, redefinition, and reformulation, as are the typifications themselves. For typifications are based in present understandings of past situations, and such understandings of the past are continually revised. For instance, the events associated with Watergate were successively cast as a break-in (spot news), a conspiracy uncovered by news investigation (soft news), a scandal prompting comment by officials (spot news), legislative and judicial investigations (continuing news), and a presidential resignation contravening historical precedent (what-a-story). Associated with taken-for-granted assumptions about institutional processes and practices, typification may generate newsworthiness.

When an occurrence does not unfold as professionals had predicted it would, the newsworkers revise the typifications applied to it. President Johnson's speech announcing that he would not run for another term of office is one example of typification and retypification, replete with a call to historical precedent—Calvin Coolidge's statement, "I will not run." That example is interesting theoretically because newsworkers had previously invoked their objectified (taken-for-granted) knowledge to predict that Johnson would turn back Senator Eugene McCarthy's campaign for the Democratic presidential nomination. They then interpreted the error as an affirmation that Johnson's announcement was particularly newsworthy. In this case, too, the invocation of professional knowledge generates newsworthiness. Furthermore, the appeal to history and the immediate redispersion of the news net to gather reaction stories about politicians' responses to the announcement also reaffirm the status quo.

News processing is itself routinized according to the way occurrences at legitimated institutions are thought to unfold; predicting the course of continuing stories at legitimated institutions enables editors to plan which reporters will be available for spot-news coverage on any one day. The news net is based in legitimated institutions. So, too, the redispersion of the news net to gather reaction stories invokes legitimated authority by seeking out governors, mayors, presidential aspirants, senators, other legislators, and quasi-legitimated leaders. It evenhandedly gathers comments from Republicans and Democrats as the embodiment of political processes and so affirms the legitimacy of those processes. The symbolic "man [or woman] on the street" contributes his or her opinion as a representation of others, not as a representative of others. Representativeness is thought to rest in either legitimated institutions or amassed quantities of supporters.

Although typifications limit the idiosyncrasy of occurrences as the raw material of news, they still enable great flexibility. Newsworkers' activities are relatively unsupervised, and the lack of direct supervision provides room for newsworkers to claim professionalism and to both modify and ignore organizational rules. Sharing and hoarding, working together at the scene of stories, reading one another's work, socializing together, newsworkers produce professional understandings of how work is to be done. These understandings are subject to negotiation and reformulation: Editors and bureau chiefs negotiate who will cover a story and how it will be covered. Reporters negotiate their intricate relationships with one another and with sources, including the kind and amount of sharing appropriate to situations. Through this ongoing interaction, they identify the sorts of people who will serve as good sources of information about occurrences at legitimated institutions. Again invoking past experience, they extend those ideas and practices to social movements as well, creating quasi-legitimated leaders as they do so. They also blur distinctions between public and private, for they objectify political representatives and bureaucrats as "the city," "the state," or "the country." They identify the population as "the public." Simultaneously, then, politicians and bureaucrats are said to be representatives and are divorced from the population they are said to represent. Newsworkers and the news itself are left to adjudicate between "the city" (or country) and "the public." The newsworkers legitimate the role they have claimed for themselves and they legitimate politicians and bureaucrats as embodiments of political units.

Additionally, through their interaction with sources and with one another, newsworkers develop ways of identifying facts. Facts and the need for facts, sources and methods of reporting are mutually self-constituting phenomena. I do not mean to imply either that one person's fact is another's bias or that facticity is relative and unobjective. Rather, I mean that methods of identifying facts, including methods of identifying appropriate sources, objectify social life and, at times, *reify* social phenomena.

Berger and Luckmann explain:

> Reification can be described as an extreme step in the process of objectification, whereby the objectivated world loses its comprehensibility as a human enterprise and becomes fixated as a non-human, non-humanizable inert facticity. . . . Man [sic], the producer of the world, is apprehended as its product, and human activity as an epiphenomenon of non-human processes [1967: 89].

As we have seen, news sometimes uses symbols as the representation of reality and presents them as the product of forces outside human control. That is the typical presentation of economic activity and civil disorders, such as riots. These facets of social life are presented as alien, reified forces, akin to fluctuations in the weather, a natural phenomenon. Indeed, television's visual representation of the web of facticity frames riots and tornadoes in a similar manner and insistently distinguishes them from interviews with talking heads.

The reification of economic activity and civil disorders also reaffirms the status quo. First, reification affirms that the individual is powerless to battle either the forces of nature or the forces of the economy. The individual as symbol is presented as a representation of a common plight. The news consumer is encouraged to sympathize or to rejoice, but not to organize politically. Writing of radio, Lazarsfeld and Merton describe the news consumer's reaction as a narcotizing dysfunction:

> The individual takes his secondary [media] contact with the world of political reality . . . as a vicarious performance. He comes to mistake *knowing* about problems of the day for *doing* something about them. His social conscience remains spotlessly clean. He is concerned. He is informed. . . . But, after he has gotten through his dinner and listened to his favorite radio programs and after he has read his second newspaper of the day, it is time for bed [1948, reprinted 1964: 464].

That dysfunction is partially based on the news consumers' relationship to the media: Walter Cronkite of CBS or James Reston of the *New York Times* may enter their homes, but neither Cronkite nor Reston interacts directly with the consumer. They do not mutually negotiate definitions of reality.

Second, news presentations soothe the news consumers even as they reify social forces. To present the facts, newsworkers go to centralized sources responsible for handling the problems created by reified forces. Accordingly, a governor and a high-ranking officer in the National Guard may be quoted to describe a riot or a flood area. They may also be quoted about what they are doing to solve the crisis. Similarly, the president's economic advisors may describe a problem and the solution they propose. If they fail, it is because they contend with reified "natural forces." If they succeed, success symbolizes the legitimacy of their activities. If experts look into a "freak accident," it is to ensure that a similar disaster could never happen again. By implication, news consumers have decided correctly by watching television, reading the newspaper, and going to bed. They are ill equipped to deal with reified forces, and legitimated experts and authorities are doing everything they can.

In addition to reifying some phenomena, the mutual constitution of facts and sources imposes sequences of questions and answers on news events. By their very availability as resources, these professionally validated sequences encourage a trained incapacity to grasp the significance of new ideas. Instead, new ideas and emerging social issues—innovations—are framed by past experience and are typified as soft news. Lacking the appropriate questions and answers, blind to the possibility that there are questions and answers they do not know, reporters may not "be able to get a handle" on innovation. To make it a suitable topic of news, they may dismiss it, mock it, or otherwise transform it. The news professionals have many justifications they can invoke to explain their inability to deal with innovation. All are their own organizational and professional objectifications of experiences as constraints or resources. Among the constraints are the press of work, the omnipresence of deadlines, and the struggle to present factual accounts of events. Collectively derived typifications serve as constraint and resource: They are intended to facilitate news processing. But if an occurrence does not readily present itself as news easily packaged in a known narrative form, that occurrence is either soft news (requiring more reportorial time and editorial attention) or nonnews. It is dismissed by the limits inherent in the news frame.

To do otherwise, news professionals would have to question the very premises of the news net and their own routine practices. They would have to see the ways their affirmation of professionalism serves to legitimate both news as an account and social institutions as the source of news. They would have to recognize the inherent limitations of the narrative forms associated with the web of facticity. And they would have to come to terms with news as an indexical and reflexive phenomenon—a resource for social action in their own lives, in the lives of news consumers, and in the lives of the socially, politically, and economically powerful.

It seems trite to observe that knowledge is power. Yet that rationalist dictum is both a tenet of our society and a ruling premise of newswork. For power may be realized through the dissemination of some knowledge and the suppression of other ideas. And it may be reinforced by the way knowledge is framed as a resource for social action. News, I have argued, is a social resource whose construction limits an analytic understanding of contemporary life. Through its dispersion of the news net, its typifications, the claimed professionalism of newsworkers, the mutual constitution of fact and source, the representational forms of the news narrative, the claim to First Amendment rights of both private property and professionalism—through all these phenomena, objectified as constraints or as resources—news legitimates the status quo.

I do not mean to accuse newsworkers of bias. The news professionals rightfully insist that those who shout "bias" be able to define objective truth in a definitive manner. I do not claim that ability. But I do claim that it is valuable to identify news as an artful accomplishment attuned to specific understandings of social reality. Those understandings, constituted in specific work processes and practices, legitimate the status quo. Furthermore, I claim that the theories developed here might fruitfully be applied to the social construction of other sorts of knowledge and other ideologies.

Telling Stories

In chapter 1, I stated that this book is a study in the sociology of knowledge as well as in the sociology of occupations and professions. Some might then have viewed my decision to use Goffman's (1974) notion of frame as an organizing principle for the analysis of newswork as a contradiction in terms. Although Goffman states that news reveals the vulnerability of experience to framings, he also explicitly warns that his work concerns the social organization of experience, not the organization of social structure. Goffman notes that the organization of experience is ineluctably tied to the production of meaning. I have tried to take Goffman's work to its logical conclusion: The production of meaning is intricately embedded in the activities of men and women—in the institutions, organizations, and professions associated with their activities and that they produce and reproduce, create and recreate.

By implication, various kinds of knowledge, including that taught in universities, can be viewed as products of the knowledge industry, replete with objectification, reification, and affirmation of the status quo. Consider, for instance, the education industry's division of knowledge into self-contained units: Universities are constituted by departments of self-interested professionals. They frame knowledge into discrete and seemingly self-perpetuating courses, arranged in catalogues. Courses, like news, claim to encapsulate a defined topic, to tell a story. By setting these boundaries on knowledge, courses objectify and, on occasion, reify knowledge. Their very subject matter becomes a self-perpetuating topic that must be contended with, as though it were a phenomenon in and of itself, not the creation of professionals. Hiring and firing may be done on the basis of courses that need to be taught to satisfy the listings in the catalogue. Or it may be done in terms of organizationally and professionally objectified criteria that attribute intellectual promise and professional standing to university personnel. Such practices encapsulate knowledge and constitute it as a bounded phenomenon.

Similarly, as Gusfield (1976) has begun to show, the professionally objectified form of writing scientific articles tells a story. It contains its own inherent logic, its web of facticity and associated narrative form, and so structures what can and will be reported as science. It bounds what can be said and will be said. Much the same can be applied to movies, television shows, and other encapsulated narratives—frames that are organizationally and professionally produced and bounded.

Some may view this comparison of news and university-based activities as a peroration against academe, for such self-indulgence is always tempting. I hope my comments are not taken that way, for I mean them to reaffirm that knowledge is always socially constructed. It always organizes experience, and it always shapes meaning. Ultimately, I mean to insist that knowledge as a means to know (humanistic endeavors and science) or as a means not to know (ideology) is socially embedded, and it is invoked in the interrelationships created by men and women. Those mutually constituting relationships necessarily include human creativity. They also necessarily include power. For men and women produce and reproduce the institutions that distribute power, even as they produce and reproduce the institutions that distribute knowledge as a social resource.

Telling stories of social life, news is a social resource. A source of knowledge, a source of power, news is a window on the world.

References

ADLER, RUTH
1971   *A Day in the Life of the "New York Times."* New York: Lippincott.

ALTHEIDE, DAVID
1976   *Creating Reality.* Beverly Hills, Calif.: Sage Publications.

BARNOUW, ERIC
1966   *A History of Broadcasting in the United States. Volume I: A Tower in Babel: To 1933.*
1968   *Volume II: The Golden Web: 1933 to 1953.*
1970   *Volume III: The Image Empire: From 1950.* [All volumes are New York: Oxford University Press.]

BARRON, JEROME A.
1971-72   *Testimony before Senate Subcommittee on Constitutional Rights.* Washington, D.C.: Government Printing Office.

_____
1973   *Freedom of the Press for Whom?* Bloomington, Ind.: Indiana University Press.

BATESON, GREGORY
1955 (rpt. 1972)   "A Theory of Play and Phantasy." Pp. 177-93 in his *Steps to an Ecology of Mind.* New York: Ballantine Books.

BENÉT, JAMES
1978   "Conclusion." Pp. 266-71 in Gaye Tuchman, Arlene Kaplan Daniels, and James Benét, eds., *Hearth and Home: Images of Women in the Mass Media.* New York: Oxford University Press.

References   219

BENSMAN, JOSEPH, AND ROBERT LILIENFELD
1973   *Craft and Consciousness.* New York: Wiley.

BERGER, PETER, AND THOMAS LUCKMANN
1967   *The Social Construction of Reality.* Garden City, N. Y.: Doubleday-Anchor.

BERNARD, JESSIE
1973   "My Four Revolutions: An Autobiographical History of the ASA." *American Journal of Sociology* 78: 773–91.

BERNSTEIN, CARL, AND ROBERT WOODWARD
1974   *All the President's Men.* New York: Simon and Schuster.

BREED, WARREN
1955   "Social Control in the Newsroom: A Functional Analysis." *Social Forces* 33 (May): 326–35.

CANTOR, MURIEL
1978   "Where Are the Women in Public Television?" Pp. 78–89 in Gaye Tuchman, Arlene Kaplan Daniels, and James Benét, eds., *Hearth and Home: Images of Women in the Mass Media.* New York: Oxford University Press.

CARDEN, MAREN LOCKWOOD
1973   *The New Feminist Movement.* New York: Russell Sage.

CATER, DOUGLASS
1959   *The Fourth Branch of Government.* Boston: Houghton Mifflin.

CHANEY, DAVID
1977   "Communication and Community." *Working Papers in Sociology No. 12.* University of Durham, Great Britain.

CICOUREL, AARON V.
1964   *Method and Measurement in Sociology.* New York: Free Press.

———
1968   *The Social Organization of Juvenile Justice.* New York: Wiley.

———
1973   *Cognitive Sociology.* Baltimore, Md.: Penguin Books.

COX, CLINTON
1977   "Meanwhile in Bedford-Stuyvesant . . . Why Whites Die on Page One." *Civil Rights Digest* 9 (2): 39–44.

CRANE, DIANA
1972   *Invisible Colleges: Diffusion of Knowledge in Scientific Communities.* Chicago: University of Chicago Press.

CROUSE, TIMOTHY
1972   *The Boys on the Bus.* New York: Random House.

DAHLGREN, PETER
1977   "Network TV News and the Corporate State: The Subordinate Con-

sciousness of the Citizen-Viewer.'' Ph.D. dissertation. The Graduate Center, City University of New York.

DANIELS, ARLENE KAPLAN
1975 "Feminist perspectives in social research." Pp. 340-80 in Marcia Millman and Rosabeth Moss Kantor, eds., *Another Voice: Feminist Perspectives on Social Life and Social Science.* Garden City, N.Y.: Doubleday-Anchor.

DANZGER, M. HERBERT
1975 "Validating Conflict Data." *American Sociological Review* 40: 570-84.

———
1976 "Reply to Tuchman." *American Sociological Review* 41 (December): 1067-71.

DARNTON, ROBERT
1975 "Writing News and Telling Stories." *Daedalus* (Spring): 175-94.

DEFLEUR, MELVIN
1966 *Theories of Mass Communication.* New York: David McKay.

EMERSON, ROBERT M.
1969 *Judging Delinquents: Context and Process in Juvenile Court.* Chicago: Aldine.

———, AND SHELDON MESSINGER
1977 "The Micro-Politics of Trouble." *Social Problems* 25: 121-34.

ENGWALL, LARS
1976 *Travels in Newspaper Country.* Manuscript. University of Uppsala, Department of Business Administration.

ENZENSBERGER, HANS MAGNUS
1974 *The Consciousness Industry.* New York: Seabury Press.

EPSTEIN, CYNTHIA FUCHS
1978 "The Women's Movement and the Women's Pages: Separate, Unequal and Unspectacular." Pp. 216-21 in Gaye Tuchman, Arlene Kaplan Daniels, and James Benét, eds., *Hearth and Home: Images of Women in the Mass Media.* New York: Oxford University Press.

EPSTEIN, EDWARD JAY
1973 *News from Nowhere: Television and the News.* New York: Random House.

EVERSOLE, PAM TATE
1971 "Concentration of Ownership in the Communications Industry." *Journalism Quarterly* 48: 251-60, 268.

FARBER, MARVIN
1966 *The Aims of Phenomenology: the Motives, Methods and Impact of Husserl's Thought.* New York: Harper & Row.

FISHMAN, MARK
1977 "Manufacturing the News: the Social Organization of Media News Production." Ph.D. dissertation. University of California, Santa Barbara.

FISHMAN, PAM M.
1978 "Interaction: The Work Women Do." *Social Problems* 25:397–406.

FREEMAN, JO
1975 *The Politics of Women's Liberation*. New York: David McKay.

FREIDSON, ELIOT
1971 *Profession of Medicine: A Study in the Sociology of Applied Knowledge*. New York: Dodd, Mead.

FRIEDAN, BETTY
1963 *The Feminine Mystique*. New York: Dell.

FRIENDLY, FRED
1967 *Due to Circumstances Beyond Our Control* . . . New York: Random House.

_____
1976 *The Good Guys, the Bad Guys and the First Amendment: Free Speech vs. Fairness in Broadcasting*. New York: Random House.

GANS, HERBERT J.
1966 "Broadcaster and Audience Values in the Mass Media: The Image of Man in American Television News." *Transactions of the Sixth World Congress of Sociology (Evian, 4–11 September 1966)* 4: 3–14.

_____
1972 "The Famine in Mass Media Research: Comments on Hirsch, Tuchman and Gecas." *American Journal of Sociology* 77 (January): 697–705.

GARFINKEL, HAROLD
1967 *Studies in Ethnomethodology*. Englewood Cliffs, N.J.: Prentice-Hall.

GERBNER, GEORGE
1972 "Mass Media and Human Communication Theory." Pp. 35–58 in Denis McQuail, ed., *Sociology of Mass Communications*. London: Penguin.

GIDDENS, ANTHONY
1976 *New Rules of Sociological Method*. New York: Basic Books.

GIEBER, WALTER
1956 "Across the Desk: A Study of 16 Telegraph Editors." *Journalism Quarterly* 33 (Fall): 423–32.

_____, AND WALTER JOHNSON
1961 "The City Hall 'Beat': A Study of Reporter and Source Roles." *Journalism Quarterly* 38: 289–97.

GILBRETH, FRANK B., JR., AND ERNESTINE GILBRETH CAREY.
1963   *Cheaper by the Dozen*. New York: Crowell.

GITLIN, TODD
1977   "Spotlight and Shadows: Television and the Culture of Politics."
College English 38 (8): 789–801.

GLASCOW UNIVERSITY MEDIA GROUP
1976   "Bad News." *Theory and Society* 3 (Fall): 339–63.

_____
forthcoming   *Bad News, Vol. II*. London: Routledge-Kegan Paul.

GOFFMAN, ERVING
1974   *Frame Analysis*. Philadelphia: University of Pennsylvania Press.

GOLDENBERG, EDIE
1975   *Making the Papers*. Lexington, Mass.: D.C. Heath.

GOMBRICH, ERNST
1971   *Art and Illusion*. New York: Pantheon.

GOULDNER, ALVIN
1970   *The Coming Crisis in Western Sociology*. New York: Basic Books.

GRAMLING, OLIVER
1940   *AP: The Story of the News*. New York: Farrar and Rinehart.

GREENBERG, BRADLEY
1972   "Children's Reactions to TV Blacks." *Journalism Quarterly* 49:
5–14.

GROSS, LARRY, AND SUZANNE JEFFRIES-FOX
1978   "What Do You Want to be When You Grow Up, Little Girl? Approaches to the Study of Media Effects." Pp. 240–65 in Gaye Tuchman, Arlene Kaplan Daniels, and James Benét, eds., *Hearth and Home: Images of Women in the Mass Media*. New York: Oxford University Press.

GUENIN, ZENA B.
1975   "Women's Pages in Contemporary Newspapers: Missing Out on Contemporary Content." *Journalism Quarterly* 52 (Spring): 66–69, 75.

GUSFIELD, JOSEPH
1976   "The Literary Rhetoric of Science: Comedy and Pathos in Drinking Driver Research." *American Sociological Review* 41: 16–34.

HABERMAS, JÜRGEN
1971   *Knowledge and Human Interests*. Boston: Beacon Press.

_____
1973   *Theory and Practice*. Boston: Beacon Press.

_____
1974 (rpt.)   "The Public Sphere: An Encyclopedia Article (1964)." *New German Critique* 3 (Fall): 49–55.

HAGE, JERALD, AND MICHAEL AIKEN
1969 "Routine Technology, Social Structure and Organizational Goals."
Administrative Science Quarterly 14 (3): 366–78.

HALL, EDWARD
1966 *The Hidden Dimension.* Garden City, N.Y.: Doubleday.

HALLORAN, JAMES D., PHILIP ELLIOTT, AND GRAHAM MURDOCK
1970 *Demonstrations and Communication: A Case Study.* London:
Penguin.

HEAP, JAMES L., AND PILLIP A. ROTH
1973 "On Phenomenological Sociology." *American Sociological Review*
38 (3): 354–66.

HEILMAN, SAMUEL
1976 *Synagogue Life.* Chicago: University of Chicago Press.

HOCHSCHILD, ARLIE
1974 "Marginality and Obstacles to Minority Consciousness." Pp.
194–99 in Ruth B. Kundsin, ed., *Women and Success.* New York: Morrow.

HOHENBERG, JOHN
1962 *The Professional Journalist.* New York: Holt, Rinehart.

HOLE, JUDITH, AND ELLEN LEVINE
1971 *Rebirth of Feminism.* New York: Quadrangle.

HUGHES, EVERETT C.
1964 *Men and Their Work.* New York: Free Press.

HUGHES, HELEN MACGILL
1940 *News and the Human Interest Story.* Chicago: University of Chicago
Press.

HULTENG, JOHN L., AND ROY PAUL NELSON
1971 *The Fourth Estate: An Informal Appraisal of the News and Opinion
Media.* New York: Harper & Row.

HUSSERL, EDMUND
1960 *Cartesian Meditations: An Introduction to Phenomenology.* The
Hague: M. Nijhoff.

———
1967 *Ideas: General Introduction to Pure Phenomenology.* New York:
Humanities Press.

JENKINS, CRAIG
1975 "Farm Workers and the Powers: Insurgency and Political Conflict
(1946–1972). Ph.D dissertation. State University of New York, Stony
Brook.

KAPSIS, ROBERT, BRUCE SAUNDERS, JIM SMITH, PAUL TAKAGI, AND OSCAR
WILLIAMS

1970   *The Reconstruction of a Riot: A Case Study of Community Tensions
and Civil Disorder.* Waltham, Mass.: Brandeis University Lemberg Center for the Study of Violence.

KIMBALL, PENN

1967   "Journalism: Art, Craft or Profession?" Pp. 242–60 in Kenneth S.
Lynn and the editors of *Daedalus*, eds., *The Professions in America.* Boston: Beacon Press.

KLAPPER, JOSEPH T.

1960   *The Effects of Mass Communication.* New York: Free Press.

KUHN, THOMAS

1962   *The Structure of Scientific Revolutions.* Chicago: University of Chicago Press.

LANG, KURT, AND GLADYS ENGEL LANG

1953 (rpt. 1960)   "The Unique Perspective of Television and Its Effects: A
Pilot Study." 544–60 in Wilbur Schramm, ed., *Mass Communications.*
Urbana: University of Illinois Press.

LARSEN, OTTO N.

1964   "Social Effects of Mass Communication." In Robert E. L. Faris,
ed., *Handbook of Modern Sociology.* Chicago: Rand McNally.

LASSWELL, HAROLD

1948   "The Structure and Function of Communication in Society."
Pp. 37–51 in Lyman Bryson, ed., *The Communication of Ideas.* New
York: Institute for Religious and Social Studies.

LAZARSFELD, PAUL, AND ROBERT K. MERTON

1948 (rpt. 1964)   "Mass Communication, Popular Taste and Social Action." Pp. 457–73 in Bernard Rosenberg and David Manning White
(eds.), *Mass Culture: the Popular Arts in America.* New York: Free
Press.

LESTER, MARILYN

1975   "News as a Practical Accomplishment: A Conceptual and Empirical
Analysis of Newswork." Ph.D. dissertation. State University of New
York, Stony Brook.

LOVE, RUTH LEEDS

1965   "The Business of Television and the Black Weekend." Pp. 73-86 in
Bradley S. Greenberg and Edwin Parker, eds., *The Kennedy Assassination and the American Public.* Stanford: University of California Press.

MANN, THOMAS

1946   *The Magic Mountain.* New York: Knopf.

MANNHEIM, KARL
1936 (rpt. 1968) *Ideology and Utopia: An Introduction to the Sociology of Knowledge*, trans. Louis Wirth and Edward Shils. New York: Harcourt, Brace.

MARCH, JAMES, AND HERBERT SIMON
1958 *Organizations*. New York: Wiley.

MCCOMBS, MAXWELL E., AND DONALD L. SHAW·
1972 "The Agenda-Setting Function of Mass Media." *Public Opinion Quarterly* 36: 176–87.

MCKINNEY, JOHN C.
1970 "Sociological Theory and the Process of Typification." In John C. McKinney and Edward Tiryakian, eds., *Theoretical Sociology*. New York: Appleton-Century-Crofts.

_____, AND LINDA BOURQUE
1972 "Further Comments on 'the Changing South': A Response to Sly and Weller." *American Sociological Review* 37 (April): 230–36.

MCLUHAN, MARSHALL
1964 *Understanding Media: The Extensions of Man*. New York: McGraw-Hill.

MEHAN, HUGH, AND HOUSTON WOOD
1975 *The Reality of Ethnomethodology*. New York: Wiley.

MERRITT, SHARYNE, AND HARRIET GROSS
1978 "Women's Page/Lifestyle Editors: Does Sex Make a Difference?" *Journalism Quarterly*.

MERTON, ROBERT K.
1968 *Social Theory and Social Structure*. New York: Free Press.

_____
1973 "The Matthew Effect in Science." Pp. 439–59 in *The Sociology of Science: Theoretical and Empirical Investigations*. Chicago: University of Chicago Press.

MILLET, KATE
1974 *Flying*. New York: Ballantine Books.

MILLIBAND, RALPH
1969 *The State in Captialist Society: An Analysis of the Western System of Power*. New York: Basic Books.

MOLOTCH, HARVEY L.
1978 "The News of Women and the Work of Men." Pp. 176–85 in Gaye Tuchman, Arlene Kaplan Daniels, and James Benét, eds., *Hearth and Home: Images of Women in the Mass Media*. New York: Oxford University Press.

———, AND MARILYN LESTER
1974 "News as Purposive Behavior." *American Sociological Review* 39: 101–12.

———
1975 "Accidental News: The Great Oil Spill." *American Journal of Sociology* 81: 235–60.

MORRIS, MONICA B.
1973 "Newspapers and the New Feminists: Black Out as Social Control?" *Journalism Quarterly* 50: 37–42.

———
1974 "The Public Definition of a Social Movement: Women's Liberation." *Sociology and Social Research* 57: 526–43.

———
1975 "Excuses, Justifications and Evasions: How Newspaper Editors Account for the Coverage of a Social Movement." Paper delivered at the annual meetings of the American Sociological Association, San Francisco, August.

MOTT, FRANK LUTHER
1952 *The News in America.* Cambridge, Mass.: Harvard University Press.

MULLINS, NICHOLAS C., LOWELL L. HARGENS, PAMELA K. HECHT, AND EDWARD L. KICK
1977 "The Group Structure of Cocitation Clusters: A Comparative Study." *American Sociological Review* 42(4): 552–62.

NATIONAL ADVISORY COMMISSION ON CIVIL DISORDERS
1968 *Report.* New York: Bantam Books.

NEWSWEEK
1977 "Letters to the Editor." October 10: 10–16.

NEW YORK TIMES
1977 "2 Editors Dismissed in Articles Dispute. Michigan Papers Refused Orders to Publish Reports Concerning Carter's Wife and Staff." June 26, p. 15.

NEW YORKER
1976 "Talk of the Town." March 1: 23–24.

OBERSCHALL, ANTHONY
1973 *Social Conflicts and Social Movements.* Englewood Cliffs, N.J.: Prentice-Hall.

PARK, ROBERT, AND ERNEST BURGESS
1967 *The City.* Chicago: University of Chicago Press.

PERROW, CHARLES
1967 "A Framework of the Comparative Analysis of Organizations." *American Sociological Review* 32 (April): 194–208.

PHILLIPS, E. BARBARA
1976 "What is News? Novelty without Change?" *Journal of Communication* 26 (4): 87–92.

POLANYI, KARL
1944 *The Great Transformation*. Boston: Beacon Press.

PORTER, WILLIAM E.
1976 *Assault on the Media: The Nixon Years*. Ann Arbor: University of Michigan Press.

RATHER, DAN
1977 *The Camera Never Blinks: Adventures of a TV Journalist*. New York: William Morrow.

RESKIN, BARBARA F.
1977 "Scientific Productivity and the Reward Structure of Science." *American Sociological Review* 42 (3): 491–504.

ROBINSON, JOHN P., PHILIP CONVERSE, AND ALEXANDER SZALAI
1972 "Everyday Life in Twelve Countries." Pp. 113–44 in Alexander Szalai, ed., *The Use of Time*. The Hague: Mouton.

ROBINSON, MICHAEL J., AND CLIFFORD ZUKIN
1976 "Television and the Wallace Vote," *Journal of Communication* 26(2): 79–83.

ROPER ORGANIZATION, INC.
1971 "An Extended View of Public Attitudes toward Television and Other Mass Media 1959–71." New York: Television Information Office.

ROSENBLUM, BARBARA
1978 *Photographers and Their Photographs*. New York: Holmes/Meier.

ROSHCO, BERNARD
1975 *Newsmaking*. Chicago: University of Chicago Press.

ROTH, JULIUS
1963 *Timetables: Structuring the Passage of Time in Hospital Treatment and Other Careers*. New York: Bobbs-Merrill.

RYAN, MARY P.
1975 *Womanhood in America*. New York: Franklin Watts.

SCHUDSON, MICHAEL
1978 *Discovering the News: A Social History of American Newspapers*. New York: Basic Books.

SCHUTZ, ALFRED
1962 *Collected Papers, Volume I: The Problem of Social Reality*. The Hague: M. Nijhoff.

———
1964 *Collected Papers, Volume II: Studies in Social Theory*. The Hague: M. Nijhoff.

1966 *Collected Papers, Volume III: Studies in Phenomenological Philosophy.* The Hague: M. Nijhoff.

1967 *The Phenomenology of the Social World.* Evanston, Ill.: Northwestern University Press.

SHIBUTANI, TAMOTSU
1966 *Improvised News: A Sociological Study of Rumor.* Indianapolis: Bobbs-Merrill.

SIGAL, LEON V.
1973 *Reporters and Officials: The Organization and Politics of Newsmaking.* Lexington, Mass: D. C. Heath.

SIGELMAN, LEE
1973 "Reporting the News: An Organizational Analysis." *American Journal of Sociology* 79 (1): 132–51.

SMITH, DOROTHY E.
1972 "The Ideological Practice of Sociology." Manuscript excerpted as "Theorizing as Ideology." Pp. 41–44 in Roy Turner, ed., *Ethnomethodology.* Baltimore, Md.: Penguin Books, 1974.

1973 "Women's Perspective as a Radical Critique of Sociology." *Sociological Inquiry* 44 (1): 7–13.

1975 "An Analysis of Ideological Structures and How Women Are Excluded." *Canadian Review of Sociology and Anthropology* 12 (4): 353–69.

SMITH, HEDRICK
1976 *The Russians.* New York: Ballantine Books.

SNYDER, DAVID, AND WILLIAM R. KELLY
1977 "Conflict Intensity, Media Sensitivity and the Validity of Newspaper Data." *American Sociological Review* 42 (1): 105–23.

SOROKIN, PITRIM A., AND ROBERT K. MERTON
1937 "Social Time: A Methodological and Functional Analysis." *American Journal of Sociology* 42 (5): 615–29.

STARK, RODNEY
1962 "Policy and the Pros: An Organizational Analysis of a Metropolitan Newspaper." *Berkeley Journal of Sociology* 7 (Spring): 11–31.

STELLING, JOAN, AND RUE BUCHER
1973 "Vocabularies of Realism in Professional Socialization." *Social Science and Medicine* 7: 661–73.

References   229

STINCHCOMBE, ARTHUR
1959 "Bureaucratic and Craft Administration of Production: A Comparative Study." *Administrative Science Quarterly* 4: 168–87.

SUDNOW, DAVID
1967 *Passing On: The Social Organization of Death and Dying.* Englewood Cliffs, N.J.: Prentice-Hall.

TALESE, GAY
1966 *The Power and the Kingdom.* New York: World.

THOMPSON, JAMES
1967 *Organizations in Action.* New York: McGraw-Hill.

THORNE, BARRIE
1970 "Resisting the Draft: An Ethnography of the Draft Resistance Movement." Ph.D. dissertation. Brandeis University.

TUCHMAN, GAYE
1969 "News, the Newsman's Reality." Ph.D. dissertation. Brandeis University.

_____
1972 "Objectivity as Strategic Ritual." *American Journal of Sociology* 77 (January): 660–79.

_____(ed.)
1974 *The TV Establishment: Programming for Power and Profit.* Englewood Cliffs, N.J.: Prentice-Hall.

_____
1976 "The News' Manufacture of Sociological Data: A Comment on Danzger." *American Sociological Review* 41 (December): 1065–67.

TUNSTALL, JEREMY
1971 *Journalists at Work: Specialist Correspondents, their News Organizations, News Sources, and Competitor-Colleagues.* London: Constable Books.

TURNER, RALPH, AND LEWIS KILLIAN
1957 *Collective Behavior.* Englewood Cliffs, N.J.: Prentice-Hall.

TURNER, ROY
1974 "Words, Utterances and Activities." Pp. 197–215 in Roy Turner, ed., *Ethnomethodology.* Baltimore, Md.: Penguin Books.

VAN GELDER, LINDSY
1974 "Women's Pages: You Can't Make News Out of a Silk Purse." *Ms*, November: 112–16.

VIDMAR, NEIL, AND MILTON ROKEACH
1974 "Archie Bunker's Bigotry: A Study in Selective Perception and Exposure." *Journal of Communication* 24 (1): 36–47.

WEST, CANDACE, AND DON H. ZIMMERMAN
1977 "Women's Place in Everyday Talk: Reflections on Parent-Child Interaction." *Social Problems* 24 (5): 521-29.

WICKER ,TOM
1965 "That Day in Dallas." Pp. 29-36 in Bradley S. Greenberg and Edwin B. Parker, eds., *The Kennedy Assassination and the American Public.* Stanford, Calif.: Stanford University Press.

WILSON, THOMAS P.
1970 "Normative and Interpretive Paradigms in Sociology." Pp. 57-79 in Jack D. Douglas, ed., *Understanding Everyday Life.* Chicago: Aldine.

WISE, DAVID
1973 *The Politics of Lying: Government Deception, Secrecy and Power.* New York: Random House/Vintage.

WOLFE, ALAN
1977 *The Limits of Legitimacy.* New York: Free Press.

WOLFE, TOM
1968 *The Pump House Gang.* New York: Farrar, Straus, and Giroux.

WORTH, SOL
1978 "Man Is Not a Bird." *Semiotica: The International Journal of Semiotics* 23 (1/2): 5-28.

———, AND JOHN ADAIR
1970 "Navajo Film-Makers." *American Anthropologist* 72: 9-34.

ZERUBAVEL, EVIATAR
1977 "The French Revolutionary Calendar: A Case Study in the Sociology of Time." Paper presented at the meetings of the Eastern Sociological Society, New York City, March.

ZIMMERMAN, DON H.
1970 "Record-keeping and the Intake Process in a Public Welfare Organization." Pp. 319-54 in Stanton Wheeler, ed., *On Record: Files and Dossiers in American Life.* New York: Russell Sage.

———, AND MELVIN POLLNER
1970 "The Everyday World as a Phenomenon." Pp. 80-103 in Jack D. Douglas, ed., *Understanding Everyday Life.* Chicago: Aldine.

Index

231